Teaching Climate Change to Adole

The scientists and engineers have done their work, providing a timely warning on climate change and producing the technologies like solar panels that would help take it on. It's the rest of us that have so far failed, and it's largely a failure of . . . imagination, precisely the reason that we have English class. This book will help many teachers understand their craft in light of the planet's great crisis.

Bill McKibben, Editor, *American Earth: Environmental Writing Since Thoreau*

I'm always looking for topical and innovative subjects to discuss with my high school students. This book can be used both as a good resource to justify the teaching of climate change in my curriculum and to help me teach it as well.

Cara Arver, English Teacher/English Department Chair, Centreville High School, USA

This book is fantastic! It is beautifully written, thorough in its approach to content, and powerfully presented. We need this book! It provides a thorough and thoughtful analysis of the crises we are facing and how English language arts teachers can begin to address those problems with their students today. Students will be awakened to an important critical analysis as well as what they can and should do to respond in their own communities. I applaud Beach, Share, and Webb!

Rebecca A. Martusewizc, Eastern Michigan University, USA

Teaching Climate Change to Adolescents is THE essential resource for middle- and high-school English language arts teachers to help their students understand and address the urgent issues and challenges facing life on Earth today. Classroom activities written and used by teachers show students posing questions, engaging in argumentative reading and writing and critical analysis, interpreting portrayals of climate change in literature and media, and adopting advocacy stances to promote change. The book illustrates climate change fitting into existing courses using already available materials and gives teachers tools and teaching ideas to support building this into their own classrooms. A variety of teacher and student voices makes for an appealing, fast-paced, and inspiring read. Visit the website for this book http://climatechangeela.pbworks.com for additional information and links.

All royalties from the sale of this book are donated to Alliance for Climate Education https://acespace.org.

Richard Beach is Professor Emeritus of English Education at the University of Minnesota, Twin Cities, USA.

Jeff Share is Teacher Education Faculty Advisor, University of California, Los Angeles, USA.

Allen Webb is Professor of English Education and Postcolonial Studies at Western Michigan University, USA.

Teaching Climate Change to Adolescents

Reading, Writing, and Making a Difference

Richard Beach
Jeff Share
Allen Webb

Co-published by Routledge and
the National Council of Teachers of English

Routledge
Taylor & Francis Group

NEW YORK AND LONDON

NCTE
National Council of
Teachers of English

First published 2017
by Routledge
711 Third Avenue, New York, NY 10017

and by Routledge
2 Park Square, Milton Park, Abingdon, Oxon, OX14 4RN

Routledge is an imprint of the Taylor & Francis Group, an informa business

Library of Congress Cataloguing-in-Publication Data
A catalog record for this book has been requested

ISBN: 978-1-138-24524-2 (hbk)
ISBN: 978-1-138-24525-9 (pbk)
ISBN: 978-1-315-27630-4 (ebk)

NCTE stock number: 45259

Typeset in Minion Pro and Helvetica Neue
by Florence Production Ltd, Stoodleigh, Devon, UK

Contents

Preface

As we were working on this book in 2015 and 2016, the world experienced all-time record temperatures with devastating results including heat waves, droughts, fires, super storms, floods, warming and acidifying oceans, and rapid Arctic and Antarctic melting. Worldwide, hundreds of thousands of people are dying every year from climate-change-related causes. Many more become climate migrants. In North America, there have been, and continue to be, severe droughts, fires, and flooding. Because of human activity, the Earth is warming faster than ever before in its history, and we all must act quickly to avert even more dire consequences.

While the topic of climate change is typically taught in Earth Science classes, we believe that climate change should be addressed in many subjects, especially English language arts. English language arts teachers, the primary audience for this book, can play an essential role in the struggle against climate change because they understand the power of literacy to critique multiple sources of information, to comprehend various perspectives, to create alternative discourses, and to generate possibilities for hope and activism. English teachers know about the human imagination and its capacity to understand the experiences of others, comprehend complex problems in human terms, and create alternative visions of the future. *Literacy and the imagination are critical tools for comprehending and addressing climate change.* In contrast, by not teaching about climate change, we are allowing our silence to normalize unsustainable systems and ideologies with disastrous consequences for everyone and everything.

When we recognize our interconnectedness with the natural world and understand our current ecological state, we know that we must do something. The chapters that follow explore many opportunities we have as English teachers to empower students to experience our interconnected relationship with nature, to understand the significance of climate change, and to be inspired by the numerous possibilities for taking action. *Teaching Climate Change to Adolescents* is brimming with the voices of English language arts teachers and students offering and responding to innovative methods for critically and creatively teaching about climate change. This book shows how to reimagine and reshape the future through reading fictional portrayals and poetry, watching movies and social media, listening to songs and spoken word, and creating texts in multiple formats to explore the issues and make change.

We hope to inspire students to challenge the dominant ideologies that are limiting transformational action to reduce CO_2 and other greenhouse gas emissions and end fossil fuel extraction. Students can play an influential role in this struggle by writing essays and creating digital media about humans' impact on the environment, engaging in drama and games enacting future worlds coping with a warming planet, working in solidarity with other students and teachers across subject matter to execute interdisciplinary curriculum on climate change, and participating in collective action to change the status quo.

English language arts teachers can foster critical inquiry about problems and issues through reading, writing, speaking/listening, and digital media production, and that includes addressing ethical and moral questions portrayed in fiction and nonfiction. Students can inquire into the unequal roles of humans in adversely shaping the Earth in the Anthropocene Age that began in the nineteenth century. Who causes global warming and who suffers first and most? Is climate change addressed by individuals or governments? Our students need to grapple with these moral dilemmas in order to recognize the importance of transforming unsustainable status quo systems, to reduce dependency on fossil fuel, and to restructure current agricultural practices.

In 2017, the roll-back of American environmental regulations by the Republican administration reflects a denial of the reality of climate change as a serious threat to life on Earth. More than ever, teachers and students need to become knowledgeable about climate change, educate their communities, and foster laws and actions essential to reducing greenhouse gases.

In this book, we describe the climate change crisis, explain why it should be addressed in English classrooms; examine practical questions of standards, textbooks, and "controversy"; and consider the ethical, moral, and values dimensions of the climate change story, as well as how to address it (Chapter 1). We set forward first steps English teachers can take initially to start teaching about climate change in almost any class and how to do so using inquiry that draws on students' questions and emotions (Chapter 2). Then we describe frameworks, inquiry questions, and specific resources/teaching ideas for thinking about climate change curriculum in four areas: indigenous and postcolonial perspectives; capitalism and consumerism; environmental literature and ecocritical approaches; and social systems including energy production, military/conflict, housing/community development, and agriculture (Chapter 3). We draw on the "cli-fi" imagination to provide new climate-change-informed approaches to literature currently in the curriculum and also describe instruction resources for adding picture books, poetry, and "cli-fi" short stories, film, young adult and adult novels, and testimonials (Chapter 4). We focus on students' place-based, creative, and persuasive writing to understand and take action on climate change (Chapter 5). We describe developing critical media literacy; the commercial media's depiction of climate change; advertising and the consumer economy; and critically analyzing and creating images, video, audio texts, podcasts, songs, television, and video games (Chapter 6). We examine the use of drama, including creating scenes and plays, using the alternative theater techniques of Augusto Boal, role play and online role play, and gaming activities for mitigating, coping, developing policy, and understanding local effects of climate change (Chapter 7). We explore connections between English language arts and different disciplines for applying biological, geographical, economic, urban planning, historical, sociological, psychological, and mathematical perspectives to teaching about climate change in English through interdisciplinary literacies (Chapter 8). In the final chapter, we explain how to motivate students to make a difference, imagine sustainable futures, take action at local levels, change the way we eat, and develop civic and democratic projects (Chapter 9). Every chapter describes language arts teaching that addresses climate change, sharing ideas from English teachers across the United States.

Accompanying this book is a wiki website http://climatechangeela.pbworks.com with additional resources, classroom activities, and further readings linked to each of these chapters. Because this is a wiki, readers are invited to contribute their own material by requesting editing privileges on the wiki itself or from Richard at rbeach@umn.edu. We also have a blog, ETCCC (English Teachers Concerned about Climate Change) http://etcccsite.com, for posting additional opinions and ideas on addressing climate change in ELA classrooms; comments by readers are welcomed.

Acknowledgments

We acknowledge with great appreciation the persistent support of Naomi Silverman at Routledge and Kurt Austin at the National Council of Teachers of English. We thank all of the teachers and Allen Webb's students for their contributions documenting English language arts teachers and students actively addressing climate change.

Chapter 1
Why Teach about Climate Change in English Language Arts?

> We don't have a problem with economies, technology, and public policy; we have a problem with perception because not enough people really get it yet. I believe we have an opportunity right now. We are nearing the edge of a crisis but we still have an opportunity to face the greatest challenge of our generation, indeed of our century.
>
> James Balog (Orlowski, 2012)

> The debate about climate change is not about greenhouse gases and climate models alone. It is about the competing worldviews and cultural beliefs of people who must accept the science, even when it challenges those beliefs.
>
> Andrew Hoffman (2015, p. 88–89)

With every sunrise and rotation of the Earth, humans are more interdependent on reading and writing. We are using more tools for communicating than ever before, creating increasing opportunities for people across the globe to share, organize, and solve all kinds of problems from attacks on democracy to a warming planet. These changes have moved the role of the English teacher to center stage. Humans have always been storytellers, and it has long been known that those who tell the stories control the future. It is by critically understanding the messages and stories engulfing them, and learning the skills to take action, that our students can create alternative discourses to change the present and shape the future. As English teachers, we have the potential to excite, inspire, and empower students to recognize this potential and become involved in the issue of our age, climate change and environmental justice.

Our planet has already irrevocably changed as a result of human-made emissions of carbon dioxide, methane, and other gases. Today, in line with predictions made for decades, we are seeing increasing temperatures, dramatic weather swings, devastating droughts, wildfires, huge storms, flooding, sea-level rise, warming and acidic oceans, enormous animal and plant extinctions, and more (Mann & Kump, 2015; Romm, 2015). Our planet has warmed one degree Celsius more rapidly than any time in Earth's history, with 2016, the year we wrote this book, the hottest year in recorded history.

Recent research indicates that global temperatures may increase by 4 degrees Celsius as early as the 2070s and perhaps even sooner (Intergovernmental Panel on Climate Change, 2016). A rise of 4 degrees Celsius would permanently devastate US food production, not to mention food production in other countries. The Antarctic and Greenland ice sheets have already begun to melt and break apart. No matter what humans do now, sea levels are going to rise, and rise substantially. Much of Florida and the East Coast of the United States will first be subjected to storm surges, and then inundated, as will many of the largest cities in the world (http://tinyurl.com/zbhldg5).

There is no going back. Each gallon of gasoline burned represents 100 tons of ancient plants (Dukes, 2003) and the carbon they captured being returned to the atmosphere. When carbon dioxide is released into the air it continues to affect climate for hundreds, even thousands of years. We are currently on the trajectory to 4 degrees and more. It is imperative to change what we are doing and limit temperature rise to 2 degrees. It is not certain that even with focused world attention on greenhouse gas reduction, that 2 degrees is still possible. For the sake of the human race and life on Earth, we must, nonetheless, do all within our power to limit global warming as much as possible and as soon as possible. As one of the world's most influential climate scientists puts it, "the difference between two and four degrees is human civilization" (Marshall, 2015, p. 241).

Whatever happens, climate change will be the defining feature of the world our students inhabit. Addressing climate change is everyone's responsibility, and that includes English teachers. As this book will show, there is much we can be doing.

We and our students can and must make a difference. We have the opportunity and obligation to educate our students about climate change; fire their imaginations, their talents, and their energies; inform our local and larger communities; and, join with others across the globe to demand and participate in one of the largest and most urgent transitions in human history.

THE CRISIS AND THE URGENCY OF CHANGE

In a simple model, humans impact the climate by releasing gases which accumulate in the atmosphere and bounce solar energy back to the Earth, as in a greenhouse, making the Earth grow continually warmer. Indeed, our planet is absorbing a lot of heat, warming all ecological systems. Scientists have calculated that in recent years Earth has been gaining as much heat every day as would be released by 400,000 Hiroshima atom bombs (Romm, 2013). Human emissions cause the increased warming, and natural feedback loops speed it up even faster. Ice and snow reflect 70 percent of solar energy while the open ocean absorbs 95 percent. So as polar ice caps melt and expose more ocean, a great deal more heat is absorbed and global warming is accelerated "naturally." Warming by human emissions releases methane, a greenhouse gas, from tundra and ocean beds, again accelerating warming (see Figure 1.1). As McCaffrey (2014) notes

> The interconnectedness of Earth's systems means that a significant change in any one component of the climate system can influence the equilibrium of the entire Earth system. Positive feedback loops can amplify these effects and trigger abrupt changes in the climate system. These complex interactions may result in climate change that is more rapid and on a larger scale than projected by current climate models.
>
> McCaffrey (2014, p. 136)

Global warming will have devastating impact in every country. Current understanding indicates that a catastrophic world of mass starvation, mass flooding, mass migration, and mass death of hundreds of millions, perhaps billions, of people may happen much sooner than most expect, particularly in developing countries. An entire lake in Bolivia, the size of Los Angeles, is now bone dry, resulting in residents having to flee. The largest city in the western hemisphere with 20 million residents, São Paulo, Brazil, is close to running out of water. Due to rising sea levels, many of the Marshall Islands and coastal regions of Bangladesh are under water or soon will be.

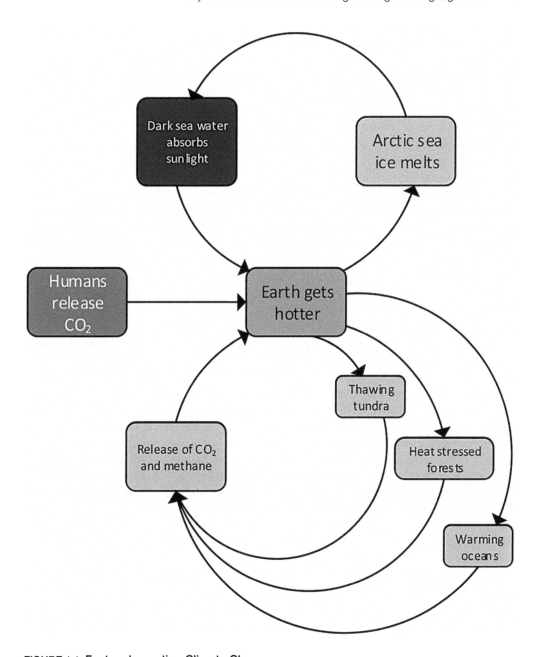

FIGURE 1.1 Factors Impacting Climate Change

Some of the first to suffer and endure the worst effects are the poorest countries, nations that have the least responsibility for the pollution that causes climate change. Poorer countries and poorer people have fewer resources to defend themselves, so the impacts of climate change will be unfair and unbalanced. The US Military considers climate change a threat multiplier that will cause hunger and disease, increase instability, undermine governments, and intensify conflicts and terrorism. It is already doing so in the Middle East and Africa. While climate change will be disastrous for the poorest regions of the world, it will also have horrific consequences for wealthy countries, the United States included.

We know about Hurricane Andrew in Florida, Hurricane Katrina in New Orleans, flooding in Baton Rouge, Superstorm Sandy in New York, the Texas drought of 2010–2014, the California drought of 2012–2016, and so on. In 2012, drought in the Great Plains and Prairies (the American "breadbasket") led to loss of half of American food crops. The northern jet stream that meandered south during winters in 2013–2015, caused by relatively warm Arctic temperatures that weakened the polar vortex and created frigid winters in the Midwest and Northeast punctured by surprising heat, resulted in 75 degrees on Christmas Eve in New York in 2015. And we are only at one degree Celsius above average so far.

Across the world, all social systems will be stressed and adversely affected by climate change. Just one example: health. People will experience adverse health effects from high temperatures, water and food shortages, toxic algae in drinking water, increases in stress and mental health issues, particularly for populations who will need to leave their regions due to high temperatures, drought, or sea-level rises. Thousands, especially older people and children in cities, will succumb to heat waves. Mosquitoes and ticks will proliferate and likely cause disease migration including increasing outbreaks of dengue fever and malaria, some of the world's most deadly diseases. Extreme weather events result in water source contamination and increased instances of waterborne diseases including cholera (Intergovernmental Panel on Climate Change, 2016). These adverse health effects will lead to increased health care costs for governments and individuals, expenses that need to be considered when weighing the costs of investing in clean energy options to limit emissions. As Professor Richard Gammon once said, "If you think mitigated climate change is expensive, try unmitigated climate change."

These terrifying scenarios have already begun. They will become far more common unless major changes to address global warming are rapidly undertaken across the globe. The current amount of greenhouse gases in the atmosphere as a result of human activity has already raised the Earth's temperature by one degree Celsius. The "carbon budget" is how much more carbon (from oil, coal, natural gas) can be emitted and still have a likelihood of keeping global warming at 2 degrees Celsius. Some of the carbon humans emit is removed by carbon "sinks"—oceans (becoming more acidic) and forests (disappearing due to clear cutting, fires, and pests)—the rest goes into the atmosphere. The most recent research indicates that if we are to hold global warming to 2 degrees, *80 percent of known carbon reserves must not come out of the ground* (McKibben, 2012; Clark, 2015).

The next two decades are absolutely critical to the future of the Earth hence the immediate need to reduce greenhouse gas emissions. Unfortunately, the general public, particularly in the United States, which leads the world in per capita emissions, still does not perceive climate change as a crisis. While public concern is growing about the need to address global warming, a Pew Research Center survey conducted in January, 2016 indicated that only 38 percent of the American people perceive climate change to be a priority issue needing to be addressed by Congress, ranking sixteenth in importance against all other issues (Pew Research Center, 2016). While 55 percent of Democrats ranked it as a priority, only 14 percent of Republicans listed climate change as a priority. Younger people are more concerned about climate change than the older people, with 52 percent of young adults indicating that climate change is a very serious problem compared to 38 percent of people 50 years and older.

Even though 97 percent of scientists confirm that climate change is caused by humans and predict with certainty that catastrophic consequences will occur if carbon emissions are not reduced immediately, a small number of powerful people, organizations, and corporations, who have much to lose from a change to alternative energy, have managed to dominate the public discourse and frame climate change as "debatable" and "controversial" (Oreskes & Conway, 2011). These few vested interests have been highly successful at influencing mainstream US media to spin the facts about climate change and create a false narrative. In a culture of immediate media spectacle, when the primary news providers are owned by transnational corporations, journalism becomes entertainment and profit, trumping social responsibility and full reporting of the facts (Sperry, Flerlage, & Papouchis, 2010).

Being able to critically question and understand the stories of our time is an important goal for all literacy teachers and the objective of this book. Throughout these pages we unpack the facts and stories about climate change with practical examples of how English teachers have fostered their students' imagination and engaged them in powerful literacy lessons.

RECOGNIZING THE NEW REALITIES

There was a sense of urgency for the 196 nations attending the 2015 United Nations Climate Change Conference in Paris as scientists confirmed only 25–30 years are left to dramatically lower emissions to keep global warming to no more than 2 degrees Celsius. With the cooperation of President Obama and Chinese President Xi Jinping an important and historic agreement to limit greenhouse gases and address global warming was reached.

Unfortunately, in many ways the Paris agreement is not enough. The agreement does not call for leaving carbon in the ground, which is essential. It did not establish a global carbon tax, though individual nations can impose one. All the pledges made in Paris were strictly "voluntary." The richest countries, which have benefited the most from industrialization and put the most carbon in the air, provided only a pittance to address climate change in the poor countries. India, with 25 percent of its 1.3 billion people living in extreme poverty, is understandably reluctant to lessen energy production associated with economic growth. China, with its 1.4 billion people is in a similar situation, though both countries did make commitments. Even under the most optimistic assumptions, the pledges at best still set the world on a path to increasing global temperatures beyond 2 degrees.

So in the aftermath of the Paris agreement, and before the next climate summit in 2020, there remains a tremendous need for people the world over to understand the new realities and participate in the radical transitions necessary to avert the impending danger of climate change. Change is required in more than consumption habits. In our roles as workers and citizens we will need to transform energy, economics, transportation, agriculture, housing, media, health care, and community life. These are huge tasks that require creative actions by countless numbers committed to the cause. Who better to people this movement than students who see their future on the line. And who better to prepare these students than English teachers who understand the power of imagination to grasp big ideas and use literacy to change the world.

Indeed, climate change can be overwhelming. It involves thinking beyond what we already know and it goes against our natural tendency toward safety and normality. Global warming is incorrectly viewed as a topic for the distant future, not an urgent issue in the here and now. Being presented with the science of climate change does not mean everyone will accept its reality or start to do something about it. As students learn about climate change they may experience concern, doubt, anxiety, or ambivalence. Yet, their emotional responses can be starting points for developing hopeful and active engagement.

Our experience and that of the other English teachers we have been working with is that while students may come to the subject of climate change with doubts and questions, when they are able to inquire into the topic they become engaged, eager to educate others and address the problem.

Global warming is a topic that should and does matter to young people. A survey by the Yale Climate Change Communication Project found that the vast majority of parents (77 percent) support teaching climate change in schools (Adler, 2016). Yet, the education students do receive is limited. While 57 percent of teens understand that climate change is caused by human activities, only 27 percent say they have learned "a lot" about global warming in school (Leiserowitz, Smith, & Marlon, 2011). If, in the public sphere, informed and reasoned discussion about climate change does not always take place, in our classrooms we and our students can openly inquire into new realities, engage in civilized discussion, imagine and begin to enact change. Students can script and rehearse conversations with family or friends who may be less knowledgeable. As young people work to inform others, new understandings and behavior can come about quickly through social and new media, and through our students' modeling of behavior and enthusiasm.

ADDRESSING CLIMATE CHANGE IN ENGLISH LANGUAGE ARTS

English language arts students are transported across the globe, back in time or into the future as they engage with the imaginations of poets, playwrights, novelists, journalists, advertisers, filmmakers, lyricists, and the best storytellers the world has encountered. English classrooms are spaces of discovery, possibility, and participation where students learn to empathize with experiences of people like and unlike themselves. They are places of moral and ethical reflection about new ideas and complicated human realities. In English language arts classes, students can read about the devastating effects of global warming, comprehend its human-made causes, and understand the creative ways people in all corners of the globe are responding to this challenge. And it is also in this space of possibility, where students can learn to write with many tools to express their ideas, voice their concerns, and contribute to the environmental justice movement.

Learning to critically read their world, English language arts students can draw on informational texts and documentaries to understand climate change and examine portrayals of the effects of climate change in literary, nonfiction, and media texts. They can critically examine the influence of human economic, political, agriculture, transportation, and housing systems impacting ecological systems. ELA students can explore creative utopias and dystopias, climate fiction and film to imagine different futures and a safe, healthy, just, and environmentally sustainable world. Students need to be critical of the claims that deny the science, skeptical of the people who assert nothing can be done, and empowered to act with the kind of courage we have seen in the past when humans have risen together against overwhelming odds (Klein, 2015).

David Kangas, who teaches at Memorial High School, in Wayne, Michigan, believes that English language arts students need to better understand the world they live in, and that means critically thinking about how climate change is presented to us and how we respond. He wants his students to examine how the carbon-based social systems both hinder understandings and create openings for critical thinking. He invites his students to use their literacy skills to express their concerns and create alternative media messages. Kangas explains,

> Climate change is in my view primarily a human problem and therefore worth exploring in the ELA classroom. Many catastrophic images of weather are the ways people frame climate change. What is harder to detail are the systems people inhabit that contribute to making climate change a difficult problem to understand. I am thinking here about post-carbon humanities. I think it is important to understand the ecological principles

behind climate change but also to understand the media ecologies we inhabit as well and how these two systems might actually be interdependent. We need to help our students critically consume texts so that they can create texts of what they are observing in their own schools' neighborhoods or cities when it comes to how the climate—both physical and textual—influence[s] their understanding of the social worlds they inhabit.

David gets that students are surrounded by media and that the media are not doing an adequate job educating us about climate change. He sees an important place for the humanities in the transition to a post-carbon world.

Our relationship to the land and to the animals and plants that live on it was called by Aldo Leopold, the "Land Ethic." This ethic rejects a strictly human-centered view of the environment and focuses on the preservation of healthy, self-renewing ecosystems. The Land Ethic raises questions about our relationship to the natural world, to other animals, and to plants. These ethical and environmental questions are appropriate to English language arts. lisa eddy, an English teacher from Adrian, Michigan explains:

The Land Ethic teaches us that we should consider our actions in light of their impact on the living, breathing community that is the land, and that we should select the alternative available that does the least violence, or impact, to that community. We are at a crisis point in human existence. Because of our ignorance of and/or resistance to the idea of Land Ethic, we have brought our planet to a place where things are out of balance: our energy, food, and transportation systems must be drastically changed to slow carbon output and slow Earth's temperature rise. When it comes down to it, we are one people who live on one planet, and we can teach in such a way as to focus on our local landscape in a global context.

We believe that a purely science-oriented approach to climate change can miss the social, historical, ethical, and human realities that are critical to the problem. Climate change is an accelerator that exacerbates economic, racial, and social inequality. English language arts involves understanding and creating relationships with and between people and characters mediated through language, texts, and media. This knowledge is necessary to understand and address climate change. Pieter Maeseele (2015) explains that framing climate change primarily in the discourse of science limits consideration of the politics of how humans understand and relate to the environment and to each other, and how and whose voices are heard.

Fostering civic engagement can also shift the overall focus of English from positioning students as autonomous individuals or consumers set apart from the world to students as social participants whose ways of being and acting directly affect the local and global ecology (Yagelski, 2011). This shift involves redefining academic success based less on individual achievement and test scores and more on one's social and collaborative relationships with others and how our actions can contribute to sustainability and environmental justice.

As teachers of English, in this book we set forward a perspective and a set of values for teaching about climate change. Our approach emerges from an understanding of the Anthropocene era in which we now live, when environmental, geological, and ecological systems are profoundly altered by human activity. Our beliefs are based in world citizenship, the rights and well-being of all, and the recognition of connections between the diverse members of the world family. Adopting this climate change perspective involves:

1. Foregrounding climate change as the most important issue facing life on Earth.
2. Understanding the causes and effects of climate change locally and globally, as well as the efforts to deny them.

3. Overcoming individualism and nationalism, and adopting a systems-based, global perspective.
4. Creating solidarity with the oppressed and exploited, addressing the unequal impacts of climate change, and striving for social justice.
5. Envisioning and enacting transformational changes through individual and collective action, in which everyone is accountable for their actions and inactions.

The rest of this chapter examines key issues about climate change necessary to consider and frame the teaching of climate change in English language arts.

STANDARDS, TEXTBOOKS, "CONTROVERSY," AND OTHER COMPLEXITIES OF TEACHING ENGLISH

There are plenty of pressures on secondary English teachers that make it challenging to develop and implement new ideas and new curriculum. This book includes examples of English teachers describing their efforts to meaningfully address climate change in their classrooms—it is important to ask: how were they able to do it?

In the United States, most states have adopted the English language arts Common Core State Standards (CCSS), and teachers are increasingly told that they need to address those standards. For the most part, the CCSS are not content based, but skills based. That is they do not require specific curriculum, specific literary works, specific topics, or specific themes. As their Introduction states, "A great deal is left to the discretion of teachers" (Common Core State Standards, 2010, p. 6). Part of the very idea of the CCSS is to free teachers and curriculum developers to identify meaningful, engaging content that will raise academic and intellectual expectations. Climate change can provide this kind of content.

Instruction about climate change relates to a number of the CCSS anchor standards. CCSS encourage bringing more "informational texts" into English classes. Quoting the CCSS Introduction, "They [the standards] actively seek the wide, deep, and thoughtful engagement with high-quality literary and informational texts that builds knowledge, enlarges experience, and broadens worldviews" (p. 3). The standards emphasize close and careful reading, persuasive writing, and developing arguments. The standards expect students to "demonstrate the cogent reasoning and the use of evidence that is essential to both private deliberation and responsible citizenship in a democratic republic" (p. 3). In English language arts, the standards explicitly foster an integrated model of literacy, using research, developing technology and media skills, and understanding other cultures and perspectives. The standards encourage an understanding of literacy across disciplines and, when appropriate, it makes sense to build bridges between content areas—climate change offers many opportunities for this type of interdisciplinary teaching.

Another challenge that English teachers confront is obtaining the texts they need to do the teaching they believe in. This book provides classroom tested examples of a wide variety of new materials, including climate fiction short stories and novels, "informational texts," young adult fiction, film, documentaries, websites, and so on. We share stories about entire English language arts courses devoted to climate change as well as significant units on the subject. At the same time we remain conscious of the challenges many teachers face in changing the curriculum, finding time for new approaches, and obtaining new materials.

Throughout this book we tell stories about English classes that address climate change in ways that worked in their context. We describe teachers who use shorter works, stories, poetry, essays, novellas, movies, that fit easily into crowded curricula and help develop important climate change teaching. We draw on new approaches in climate fiction that can be brought to almost any literary work in your curriculum and allow you to address climate change in your class with the works you are currently teaching. We talk about instructional strategies that are effective in working with limited resources including choice reading, literature circles, and jigsaw approaches. We point to a variety of information from essays, images, videos, and websites that are available free, online. The wiki we have created to accompany this book http://climatechangeela.pbworks.com has many more suggestions and links; because it is a wiki, teachers can post and continue sharing ideas on this wiki.

Sometimes teachers or administrators are reluctant to address "controversial" topics. As we have learned there is, in fact, no legitimate controversy in the scientific community that climate change is happening, is caused by humans, and poses a frightening challenge to life on Earth. The "controversy" is in fact bogus, a sham created by climate change deniers often funded by carbon companies that stand to lose money in the short run if necessary actions are taken to protect the planet. English teachers have never let Holocaust deniers stop us from teaching about the Holocaust. Climate change deniers are not denying something in the past; they are denying something in the future that we can now act to prevent or ameliorate, thus saving millions of lives. Not so long ago we were told that tobacco was good for you and doctors were seen on television promoting their favorite brands of cigarettes. However, the general public has since learned what the tobacco companies knew for years: tobacco is devastating to human health. Some of the same public relations firms and pseudo-scientific experts that distorted the truth about smoking are now at work spinning public discourse to doubt the science of climate change (Oreskes & Conway, 2011). In the case of climate change we are talking about human health, and much more. If our society fails to address climate change it will insure the destruction of a liveable world for all of us. The stakes could not be higher.

Our approach is to engage students as co-learners by tapping into their concerns, questions, and interests. We have found that rather than taking away time and energy, teaching about climate change inspires and empowers students to use literacy as a meaningful tool for change. While writing this book in the spring of 2016, Allen was teaching his first literature course for college students at Western Michigan University entirely focused on climate change. He began with the first chapter of Bill McKibben's (2010) book, *Eaarth: Making Life on a Tough New Planet*. His students wrote passionate blog posts you can still read http://OurPlaceInNature3110.blogspot. com. One of his students, Lauren Koch, explained:

> Most of us are okay remaining ignorant and in the happy routine of our lives. We need to wake up. We need to become completely aware of what is going on around us, and the effect that we have on it. Earth has already changed, and it is going to continue to. That is exactly what Bill McKibben is doing through the first chapter of *Eaarth*. Through all of the crazy statistics and future scenarios, he's preparing us for what has already been happening. He's making us aware.

Another of Allen's students, Maddie Reeves wrote:

> The chapter made me think long and hard about my individual choices. We may all feel like drops in the ocean, but added up, each of our choices, ranging from what car we drive and how much we drive it to whether we throw that plastic Coke bottle in the trash or the recycling bin, make a huge impact on the planet and its future.

Allen reports that the first class meetings were full of passionate and intense discussion. At the beginning of the second week he asked his students how many of them had talked to someone else outside the class about what they were learning. In a moment, every student in the class had a hand in the air.

CLIMATE CHANGE IS A STORY

In every discourse whether that be of science, the mass media, or literary, or cultural artifacts, climate change is a story, and the plot, the characters, and how that story has different variations (Gaard, 2014). The way a story is told makes a difference in how we understand it and respond to it.

A common version of the climate change story is that transportation and energy production are the main characters and the plot develops around the need to transition to solar, wind power, and batteries. A different version emphasizes animal agriculture, asserting that worldwide production of beef, chicken, and pork emits more greenhouse gases than transportation or industry—and the importance of eating far less meat. Another version features large corporations as the primary actors, the need for regulating carbon consumption and methane leaks, and the challenge of addressing corporate lobbying and misinformation.

The global warming story is also told contrasting first world versus developing countries' consumption and lifestyles, and raises questions about climate justice: who benefits from causing climate change and who suffers? Poor countries ask to have the carbon pollution that they did not create removed from their skies, and the rich countries who developed by burning carbon pay for the consequences in the poor countries and accept the climate change migrants forced to flee their homes (People's Agreement of Cochabamba, 2010). Related retellings of the story emphasize the inequality of the rich and the poor both between and within countries and questions of responsibility and consequences, or the differential impacts of climate change on people of color and women.

Another way to tell the climate change story is to focus on the impact on natural systems, plants and animals, species extinction, and the role of humans. This story has versions about deforestation or agriculture or the oceans. The story can be about changing our approach to nature from extraction to sustainability, from insensitivity to respect, even reverence.

These different and yet interrelated stories of climate change explain natural phenomena, as have stories since ancient times in all societies. The different climate change stories engage alternative values, beliefs, and discourses, from science as truth to religious stewardship of nature, from free-market economics to government regulation and international cooperation, from multicultural understanding to basic ideas about justice and equal rights. Which versions of the story do we hear and which do we not hear? Whose experience is visible and whose is invisible? Whose voices are heard and not heard?

The stories of climate change may not be the stories that English teachers have traditionally wrestled with, but they are the stories that will increasingly dominate the news and shape our existence. As this book shows, they are increasingly the stories of literary works and nonfiction. English teachers are experts at helping students examine relevant, complex, and connected stories, and look for meaning and truths in and behind the words. We foster our students comparing, contrasting, and evaluating stories and making large and small life choices based on what they learn.

CLIMATE CHANGE AS AN ETHICAL AND MORAL ISSUE

Students are motivated to care about climate change because of deeply held ethical concerns for the human race (Weber, 2016). Complex and uncertain comparisons of costs of climate change mitigation versus costs of adaptation to climate change have their place but students are more likely to adopt a climate change perspective because of a moral sense of responsibility

(Schmidtz & Willott, 2011; Broome, 2012). One analysis of college students' propensity toward pro-environmental behaviors found that their attitudes and values had a stronger effect on adopting behaviors than their knowledge, suggesting the need to combine knowledge, attitudes, and values (Arnon, Orion, & Carmi, 2015). It is telling that Pope Francis' 2015 Encyclical Letter "On Care for Our Common Home" "reframes climate change and other ecological challenges from economic and technological issues to one of the moral stewardship of public goods" (Weber, 2016, p. 131).

Contemporary writers who address the moral questions of climate change often talk about the extent to which current generations are willing to invest so as to not devastate future generations. They talk about how humans are morally obligated to not:

> hand over a planet Earth that has less worth or in a more miserable condition than the planet we ourselves have had the good fortune to live on. Fewer fish in the sea. Less drinking water. Less food. Less rainforest. Less coral reef. Fewer species of plants and animals.
>
> Gardner (2015)

These writers miss the point when it comes to teaching the current generation of middle-school or high-school students. As far as our students are concerned, that handing over has already taken place.

Future climate projections used by the international scientific and political communities generally go only as far as the year 2100. The average life expectancy of American and European children today is about 90 years. A child born in 2005 is likely to live into the 2090s. Our students are the first generation whose whole lives will be lived as the enormous impacts of climate change are playing out. Although those climate change projections that do go beyond 2100 are terrifying indeed, as far as our students are concerned, we are not talking about their children or their grandchildren; we are talking about them, their world, the direct moral and ethical questions they face.

While students, given their geographic locale, may not directly experience the worst impacts of climate change right now, they can vicariously begin to imagine and understand the effects of climate change on real people as portrayed through traditional media, social media, testimonials, documentaries, images, art, essays, film, and literature. This kind of textually based human perspective teaching is at the heart of English language arts instruction. Examining multiple perspectives raises important questions:

– Who is suffering from climate change? What is their experience like? How have prior history and current social conditions shaped their options?
– What would it be like to be a climate change victim or refugee? What responsibility do we have to victims and refugees? How can we help them? What is our role in the global community?
– Who is responsible for climate change? How does inequality shape the causes and impacts of climate change? What is our responsibility in the present for events that will occur in the future?
– What responsibilities do humans have to animals, plants, and the natural world?
– What would a just and fair approach to addressing climate change look like? What values are important when addressing climate change?
– Will the market alone address climate change? What is the role of local, national, and world governments? How does climate change impact political choices and thinking?
– What is climate justice and how do we help create it?

In responding to literature or media, or in writing about their daily experiences, students reflect on characters' or people's actions as measured by ethical and moral beliefs (Martusewicz, Edmundson & Lupinacci, 2014; Turner, 2015). A climate change perspective calls for overcoming individualism or nationalism, and adopting a systems-based, global view. As Naomi Klein (2015) notes in her book, *This Changes Everything: Capitalism vs. the Climate* (for study guide lessons for this book: http://tinyw.in/4z4C.

> Fundamentally, the task is to articulate not just an alternative set of policy proposals but an alternative worldview to rival the one at the heart of the ecological crisis—embedded in interdependence rather than hyper-individualism, reciprocity rather than dominance, and cooperation rather than hierarchy.
>
> Klein (2015, p. 462)

Great literature and English language arts have always been places for thinking about the moral and ethical dimensions of human behavior and society. As the Anthropocene era encourages us to rethink the relationship between humans and the natural world, English language arts classrooms are now a crucial space for addressing climate change.

MOVING BEYOND INDIVIDUALISTIC VALUES

English language arts is also a place for considering values. Young people are making important decisions about their values, about what will, for them, define success in life. Is success accumulating material goods? What other dimensions of success are there? How does relationship with the environment factor into what we consider a good and successful life? As they learn about climate change, students can develop and refine their conception of a successful person based on harmonious rather than adversarial relationships with ecosystems. As Richard Kerridge (2013) describes, this entails a shift of emphasis in the way we imagine the self, from the self as an atomized individual with hard boundaries to a self always already in the process of producing the world and being produced by it; a self through which the world flows; a self that is as conceptually inseparable as it is materially inseparable from the larger ecosystem that sustains its physical body. Ecological perception dissolves unifying notions of selfhood and strong dualistic separations between culture and nature, subject and object, or human and non-human (p. 353).

Adopting an "individualist" stance may also reflect students' economic status. The fact that higher income people have assumed rights to personal car use as opposed to employing mass transit, high energy use for heating or cooling their homes, or ready access to food and services often not available for lower income people raises questions about inequality related to all people's rights to inhabit a healthy planet (Newell et al., 2015).

Research on people ages 18–34 and their levels of concern about climate change finds that those with "individualist" or "hierarchical" values are more skeptical about climate change (Corner et al., 2015). In contrast, young people who adopted "self-transcendent" values were more likely to be concerned about climate change and the need to address it (Corner et al., 2015). Clearly, addressing climate change involves going beyond an egocentric, individualistic perspective. As Timothy Clark (2011) notes:

> Deep ecologists urge a drastic change in human self-understanding: one should see oneself not as an atomistic individual engaged in the world as a resource for consumption and self-assertion, but as part of a greater living identity. All human actions should be guided by a sense of what is good for the biosphere as a whole. Such a biocentrism

would affirm the intrinsic value of all natural life and displace the current preference of even the most trivial human demands over the needs of other species or integrity of place.

Clark (2011, p.4)

Young people are bombarded with advertising selling not only products but values, and a lifestyle of consumption. This book provides examples of classrooms where these values are analyzed in relation to climate change and sustainability.

ENVISIONING AND ENACTING CHANGE

Students need to learn about what they can do as individuals, families, and community members to decrease their own emissions and lower their "carbon footprint." This is a crucial dimension of climate change education particularly for Americans, especially middle class and above, who use the most greenhouse gases www.nature.org/greenliving/carboncalculator. Equally, and perhaps more important, English students can and should consider the larger social and political dimensions of addressing climate change.

In thinking about using literary texts to address climate change, Lidström and Garrard (2014) emphasize responding to literature in ways that examine collective, institutional forces influencing climate change and engagement to make a difference. Previously cited English teacher David Kangas talks about how he used the film *The Hunger Games* to focus his high-school students on moral issues and making a difference:

> My experience in teaching climate change began when I taught ethics and *The Hunger Games*. Popular culture is a rich source for teachers and students to explore the ethical dimensions of climate change. We viewed the film as a class, taking note of where characters faced moral dilemmas using contemporary ethical theories to interpret Katniss' actions and to ask whether the film favored one ethical view over another. This popular film provides a means for students to understand these philosophical theories by giving them necessary background to begin reading informational argumentative texts about how climate change challenges our traditional ethical views. Students engaged in researching why dystopian texts appear to be so popular and what this might mean in a context of climate change action. What would Katniss do, became a question students used to inform different climate change contexts from large scale climate talks to personal actions like the consumption of meat.

As English teachers, we believe that the collaborative envisioning component which draws on discussion, writing, and the imagination offers many creative and valuable starting points. In this sense, the classroom can foster the practice of freedom (Freire, 2000) and promote the kinds of understanding necessary for the world in which our students will live. In Chapter 9, and throughout this book, we relate stories and examples of teachers and students taking action, enacting change as they develop their own projects and join with and participate in organizations addressing climate change (for a list of these organizations, visit the book's website http://tinyw.in/qUpp).

Given their engagement in addressing climate change, students can create texts—reports, blog posts, websites, videos, drama productions, and so on, designed to challenge problematic media messages and influence their peers and other audiences to think critically about sustainability and environmental justice. Doing so requires that they employ effective rhetorical strategies using appropriate language, narrative, and images/videos to clearly communicate scientific knowledge and information about climate change, as well as consider how to engage their audiences' beliefs and attitudes (Pearce, Brown, Nerlich & Koteyko, 2015). These activities meet numerous Common Core Standards. When the Standards are applied and practiced through meaningful projects such as those addressing climate change, they are far more likely to be deeply understood and internalized.

In 2015, a group of children began a lawsuit to pressure then President Obama to fight climate change (Light, 2015). Students can engage in activities promoting sustainability, such as encouraging restaurants to purchase food from organic farms, supporting farmers' markets, pressuring businesses that waste energy, and praising companies that have switched to clean energy options or are improving their sustainability practices.

Literature has been written for students of all ages with examples of collective acts of consciousness raising and actions that have successfully challenged overwhelming odds. Students can benefit from learning about places and times when people have come together to challenge injustice, from Gandhi's resistance to British colonialism in India to the Civil Rights Movement in the United States, and from the indigenous resistance to the privatization of water in Bolivia to Wangari Maathai's Green Belt Movement against deforestation in Africa. Much can be learned from studying environmental actions like Greenpeace's media campaigns, protests at climate change conferences, and indigenous resistance to protect the Arctic from drilling, and the efforts of student-founded groups such as 350.org in stopping the tar sands project in Canada.

TOO LARGE TO BE COMPREHENDED?

The award winning poet Jane Hirshfield has a short poem called "Global Warming:"[1]

> When his ship first came to Australia,
> Cook wrote, the natives
> continued fishing, without looking up.
> Unable, it seems, to fear the too large to be comprehended.

Indeed, there is nothing small about the problem of global warming. The Australian natives Captain Cook describes couldn't know what the arrival of the Europeans meant for their world, and there was probably little that they could have done had they known more.

Our situation with climate change is different in the sense that we know what is coming and there are things we can do, and must do, to minimize global warming's impacts. At the time of writing this book most scientists agree that there are emission pathways that can likely keep warming at or near 2 degrees Celsius. There is a growing global movement to demand an end to fossil fuel extraction and create a more just and sustainable world. The price of wind and solar have been dramatically falling . . .

The English language arts classroom is an empowering space to read and write, critique and create written stories, multimedia narratives, and public discourse about our changing climate. Our classrooms are a space to use the imagination to understand climate change not only as science, but in its human meaning and social complexity. They are a space to imagine alternative futures, futures where climate change runs wild, and futures where global warming is substantially mitigated. English teachers and students need to be part of the effort to educate and mobilize citizens to provide the groundswell of public support needed for governments to take action.

Change happens when many people make decisions to go in the same direction. The next chapter sets forward first steps you and your students can take.

For additional resources, activities, and readings related to this chapter, go to http://tinyw.in/qsli on the book's website.

NOTE

1   "Seventeen Pebbles: Global Warming" from AFTER: POEMS by JANE HIRSHFIELD. Copyright 2006 by Jane Hirshfield. Reprinted by permission of HarperCollins Publishers (U.S.A. & its Dependencies, Canada, The Philippines) and by Jane Hirshfield.

REFERENCES

Adler, S. (2016, August 23). School's starting: A majority of Americans say global warming should be taught in the classroom [Web log post]. Retrieved from http://climatecommunication.yale.edu/?p=7927.

Arnon, S., Orion, N., & Carmi, N. (2015). Environmental literacy components and their promotion by institutions of higher education: An Israeli case study. *Environmental Education Research*, 21(7), 1029–1055.

Broome, J. (2012). *Climate matters: Ethics in a warming world*. New York: W. W. Norton.

Clark, D. (2015). How much of the world's fossil fuel can we burn. *The Guardian*.

Clark, T. (2011). Introduction. In T. Clark (Ed.), *The Cambridge introduction to literature and the environment* (pp. 1–14). New York: Cambridge University Press.

Common Core State Standards (2010). *English language arts Common Core State Standards*. Washington, DC: National Governors Association and Council of Chief State School Officers.

Corner, A., Roberts, O., Chiari, S., Völler, S., Mayrhuber, E. S., Mandl, S., & Monson, K. (2015). How do young people engage with climate change? The role of knowledge, values, message framing, and trusted communicators. *Wiley Interdisciplinary Reviews: Climate Change*, 6, 523–534.

Dukes, J. S. (2003). Burning buried sunshine: Human consumption of ancient solar energy. *Climatic Change*, 61(1–2): 31–44.

Gaard, G. (2014). What's the story? Competing narratives of climate change and climate justice. *Forum for World Literature Studies*, 6(2), 272–288.

Gardner, G. (2015). Mounting losses of agricultural resources. In Worldwatch Institute (Ed.), *State of the world 2015: Confronting hidden threats to sustainability*. Washington, DC: Worldwatch Institute.

Hoffman, A. J. (2015). *How culture shapes the climate change debate*. Palo Alto: Stanford University Press.

Intergovernmental Panel on Climate Change (IPCC). (2016). *Fifth assessment report*. New York: Cambridge University Press. Retrieved from http://ipcc.ch.

Kerridge, R. (2013). Ecocriticism. *The Year's Work in Critical and Cultural Theory*, 21(1), 345–374.

Klein, N. (2015). *This changes everything: Capitalism vs. the climate*. New York: Simon & Schuster.

Leiserowitz, A., Smith. A., & Marion, J. R. (2011). *American teens' knowledge of climate change*. New Haven, CT: Yale University

Light, J. (2015). 21 kids and a climate scientist are suing to force Obama to fight climate change. Bill Moyers & Company. Retrieved from http://goo.gl/p6eQy0.

Maeseele, P. (2015). The risk conflicts perspective: Mediating environmental change we can believe in. *Bulletin of Science, Technology & Society*, 35(1–2), 44–53.

Mann, M. E., & Kump, L. R. (2015). *Dire predictions: Understanding climate change*. New York: Penguin/Random House.

Marshall, G. (2015). *Don't even think about it: Why our brains are wired to ignore climate change*. New York: Bloomsbury.

Martusewicz, R., Edmundson, J., & Lupinacci, J. (2014). *EcoJustice education: Toward diverse, democratic, and sustainable communities*. New York: Routledge.

McCaffrey, M. S. (2014). *Climate smart & energy wise: Advancing science literacy, knowledge, and know-how*. Los Angeles: Corwin Press.

McKibben, B. (2010). *Eaarth: Making a life on a tough new planet*. Boston: St. Martin's Griffin.

McKibben, B. (2012). Global warming's terrifying new math. *Rolling Stone*. July 19.

Newell, P., Bulkeley, H., Turner, K., Shaw, C., Caney, S., Shove, C., & Pidgeon, N. (2015). Governance traps in climate change politics: Re-framing the debate in terms of responsibilities and rights. *Wiley Interdisciplinary Reviews: Climate Change*, 6, 535–540.

Oreskes, N., & Conway, E. M. (2011). *Merchants of doubt: How a handful of scientists obscured the truth on issues from tobacco smoke to global warming.* New York: Bloomsbury Books.

Orlowski, J. (Director). (2012). *Chasing ice* [Motion picture]. United States: Submarine Deluxe.

Pearce, W., Brown, B., Nerlich, B., & Koteyko, N. (2015). Communicating climate change: Conduits, content, and consensus. *Wiley Interdisciplinary Reviews: Climate Change, 6*(6), 613–626.

People's Agreement of Cochabamba. (2010). World People's Conference on Climate Change and the Rights of Mother Earth [Web log post]. Retrieved from http://tinyurl.com/n86pohf.

Pew Research Center (2016). *Budget deficit slips as public priority.* Washington, DC: Author. Retrieved from http://tinyw.in/SuPR.

Romm, J. (2013). Earth's rate of global warming is 400,000 Hiroshima bombs a day. *Think Progress,* December 22, 2013. Retrieved from: http://preview.tinyurl.com/j8gnecv.

Romm, J. (2015). *Climate change: What everyone needs to know.* New York: Oxford University Press.

Schmidtz, D., & Willott, E. (2011). *Environmental ethics: What really matters, what really works,* 2nd Ed. New York: Oxford University Press.

Sperry, C., Flerlage, D., & Papouchis, A. (2010). *Media construction of global warming.* Ithaca, NY: Project Look Sharp.

Turner, R. (2015). *Teaching for ecojustice: Curriculum and lessons for secondary and college classrooms.* New York: Routledge.

Weber, E. U. (2016). What shapes perceptions of climate change? New research since 2010. *Wiley Interdisciplinary Reviews: Climate Change, 7*(1), 125–134.

Yagelski, R. P. (2011). *Writing as a way of being: Writing instruction, nonduality, and the crisis of sustainability.* Cresskill, NJ: Hampton Press.

Chapter 2
Getting Started in Teaching about Climate Change

The Earth is not our creation. It has no respect for us. It has no use for us. And its vengeance is not the fire in the cities but the fire in the sky.

Ta-Nehisi Coates (2015, p. 150)

We might soon find that we were building a different sort of society, one emphasizing quality of life before raw statistics of economic growth and relentless consumerism . . . Life would go on, with all its trials and tribulations—and that, after all, is precisely the point. Unless we do constrain carbon, life will very largely not go on at all.

Mark Lynas (2008, p. 302)

In the first chapter we explain why climate change is a critical issue, perhaps the most important challenge facing life on Earth. We describe the need to adopt a "climate change perspective" that recognizes the rapid advance of climate change, the human systems that cause it, its unequal impacts, and the urgency of individual and collective action. We describe climate change as not a purely scientific issue, but one that is critical for English language arts in that it raises social, moral, and ethical questions. Climate change requires essential language arts skills: understanding experiences of others, rethinking values, critically analyzing arguments and media representations, and reflecting on the past to better imagine alternative futures. Moreover, English teachers can help students to develop messaging skills and persuasive arguments that can contribute to change at local, national, and global levels.

In this chapter, we focus on how to begin addressing climate change in the English classroom. We share carefully selected examples from our classrooms along with comments, feedback, and suggestions from other language arts teachers. We talk about short stories, writing assignments, nonfictional essays, book chapters, and documentaries that can be quickly and easily integrated into your teaching of almost any secondary English language arts class, one or more pieces at a time as well as through the use of interdisciplinary instruction (Draper et al., 2010).

We describe a critical inquiry approach, sometimes called a critical inquiry stance, where students pose questions that matter and undertake meaningful research. Their inquiry includes reading diverse texts carefully, understanding multiple perspectives, imagining alternative futures through immersion in literature, and taking stands by writing persuasive and creative texts of various kinds. A crucial dimension of inquiry is envisioning, advocating, and enacting change. When it comes to climate change that means becoming part of the effort to educate others and to act together to save the Earth (Moore, 2013; Stephenson, 2015).

FIRST STEPS

Climate change is a daunting topic. This chapter is about first steps, and where they can take you. Step out from where you are currently teaching. The changes you make, small at first, will lead to new ideas and redesigned approaches. Subsequent chapters of the book will provide important frameworks, ideas, examples, and strategies that will help you carry forward the teaching about climate change that you will have already begun.

STARTING POINT 1: TEACH A SHORT STORY (OR STORIES) ABOUT CLIMATE CHANGE

Most English teachers teach literature at one point or another. Here we share our experiences, student responses, and teaching ideas for four short stories you could also use as starting points for addressing climate change. These four stories are all examples of "climate fiction," "cli-fi" as it is popularly known, and come from two excellent collections: *I'm with the Bears: Short Stories from a Damaged Planet* (Martin, 2011) and *Winds of Change: Short Stories about our Climate* (Woodbury, 2015). (At our request the publishers have agreed to make these stories available to you and your students for free or at a special reduced price. The stories from *Winds of Change* are found free, full text at http://eco-fiction.com/read. To access a 40-percent reduced price paper copy, or 50 percent reduced digital copy of *I'm with the Bears*, go to the Routledge site for our book http://tinyw.in/mtfl and look for the tab with code for Verso. More short story resources are described in Chapter 4.)

The twelve-page short story, "How Close to the Savage Soul" in *Winds of Change* by environmental writer John Atcheson (2015) depicts a frightening near future altered by climate change. A grandfather, a young father in our present day, takes his grandson from the fortified community where they live out to an Atlantic Ocean beach that had been beautiful and restorative. However, the water has risen and become acidic, increasing temperatures have devastated agriculture, and, outside their protected community, "adolescents without hope were turning the whole country into a real-world *Lord of the Flies*" (p. 36).

Allen's students noticed that many small aspects of the depiction of the natural environment in the story portrayed the impact of climate change. They were especially interested in the description of what the country would be like after climate change disrupts normal social order. As they discussed the story, Maddie Reeves commented on the "gated off" areas for the "privileged." Lauren Koch pointed out that the inequality of our own time becomes, in the aftermath of climate change depicted in the story, even more extreme. Jake Peters commented that the story might change people's perspectives on money: the main character as a young man was wrapped up in getting ahead financially at any cost, but as an older man he regrets his choices.

There is much secondary students can do with "How Close to the Savage Soul." As Allen's students noticed, the short story makes claims about the effects of climate change that students can research. It provides a dystopic social vision that students can discuss and evaluate. There are flashbacks to the central character's growing up, so there are possibilities for character and behavior analysis, as Jake suggests, looking at values and decisions. A motif in the story is "paying attention to warning signs," that opens up inquiry into climate change "warning signs" in today's world, and how we, in the present, might pay attention and act so as to avoid the dire future the story foretells.

If "How Close to the Savage Soul" is intense and frightening, a climate change short story that uses humor to make a serious point is "Hermie" by Nathaniel Rich (2011) in *I'm with the*

Bears. This magical realist nine-page story works well with any grade level, from upper elementary through high school. The premise is that a marine biologist is about to give a lecture at an international conference when, in the hotel bathroom, he somehow encounters Hermie, the very Hermit crab that he used to play with at a Florida beach when he was a boy. Of course Hermie can talk, and he reminds the narrator of the times they had together in childhood and informs him about how the beach and sea life have been devastated by rising sea levels, poisoned water, and worsening storms, resulting in loss of species (Stracher, 2011).

The story personalizes the impacts of environmental degradation and Allen's students found it not only "cute" but also "an interesting way to bring up climate change." Blair LaCross was struck by the premise of "nature asking humans for help." The story is an entry point for learning about global warming, and Allen's student Jessica Poling pointed out that the story might seem strange if students knew nothing about climate change. So, again, this cli-fi short story invites inquiry and research. "Hermie" is also a mentor text for place-based creative writing: students could write about either real or imaginary interactions with a place or wildlife that they knew as children and then in a realistic, or perhaps magical realistic way as inspired by the story, project into the future and explore possible impacts of climate change.

A third story, "The Audit," by Rachel May (2015) (in *Winds of Change*), also set in the near future. International agreements mandate "audits" to reduce everyone's "climate footprint." The story focuses on an upper middle class American family with three teenage children living in the suburbs. Their audit informs them:

> Your carbon footprint is 3.4 times the acceptable global mean. If everyone generated your level of greenhouse gases, 3.4 planet Earths would be required to accommodate the emissions. The terms of the Global Climate Accord require that you reduce your footprint as follows . . .
>
> May (2015, p. 43)

"The Audit" is a perfect impetus for students to examine ways to learn about their own "carbon footprint." There are several websites where students can have their carbon footprint calculated. Thus, the story is a starting point to research the "carbon budget" that scientists tell us must be adhered to in order to avoid the worst impacts of climate change. Maddie pointed out that the story shows students methods for addressing climate change in their lives. "The Audit" opens discussion about how to make value choices, and creates opportunities for both self-reflective writing and writing to influence others.

Margaret Atwood's two-page "Time Capsule Found on the Dead Planet," is climate change flash fiction. Found in a cylinder of brass on a dry lake shore by travelers from a distant world, the time capsule tells of a civilization that worshiped money and created feasts and famine, towers of glass, and "ate whole forests, croplands, and the lives of children." Clara Peeters described the story as "poetic and powerful." Blair called it "a war memorial tombstone of the Earth."

The story presents a disturbing vision of where our planet might be if climate change is not addressed. It considers the natural environment in the long view, and invites young people to think about behavior and values from a climate change perspective. The story inspires discussion for additional learning about climate change, as well as serving as an inspiration for your students writing their own climate change flash fiction!

Each of these stories illustrates key points about teaching about climate change in English. "How Close to the Savage Soul" opens the door for student critical inquiry, research, and strategies for mitigating climate change. "Hermie" suggests ways to make the issue personal and local, and suggests some possibilities for students to suspend disbelief and use their creative imagination. "The Audit" focuses on values, lifestyles, and not only the costs, but also the new, positive, possibilities that could come about as climate change is meaningfully addressed. "Time Capsule" puts human experience into a long view while fostering a sense of urgency and commitment. All of these dimensions of teaching about climate change will be developed in subsequent chapters.

Cooper Franks, a teacher in Southfield, Michigan, explains that:

> In teaching tenth-grade English in an urban district in metro Detroit, my students had little exposure to the natural world, but significant exposure to other environmental issues, such as the recent Flint Water Crisis. These short stories provided the spark to begin discussion surrounding water issues, pollution, and other environmental issues that affected the students' urban context.

Carly Fricano, a tenth-grade teacher in urban Memphis, Tennessee commented:

> I really like the idea of using a short story as a jumping-off point for a unit on climate change. My unit would culminate (or be interspersed) with Socratic seminars where I would pose an argumentative statement about a climate change issue and ask students to use evidence from both the fiction and informational texts to support their points of view, beginning with "as human beings living on this planet, we are just as responsible for the impact our actions have on the Earth as we are for the lives of others." We could also tie this topic into a bystander/upstander conversation.

Justin Boyd, a teacher in suburban Greeley, Colorado reports that:

> My eleventh-grade students read these short stories. Through class discussions, it became clear that many students felt powerless in the face of climate change. They did not believe they could have an impact. To address that at the end of the unit, I asked students to work in groups to develop either solution-oriented infographics that visually explain a complex idea about global warming or alternative energy (i.e., what could a student do to lower their carbon footprint?). This paired nicely with the short story "The Audit." (Examples of student work by Zilla & Sam at http://tinyw.in/RnBp and Vikki & Ren at http://tinyw.in/Ejem.)

Susan Waldie, a teacher in Richland, Michigan, explains that:

> When I started a lesson on climate change with my sixth-grade students in a suburban middle school some students asked, "Ms. Waldie, why are we doing this in ELA?" After sending my students on a webquest that I created to help them learn more about climate change, http://mswaldieccwebquest.weebly.com, their thinking began to change. Soon they were not only engaged in our discussions with the short story "Hermie," but outraged at how drastically their lives would be impacted. We finished by watching *The Lorax* and writing a paragraph in which many students made an oath to making small changes in their own lives to better serve our planet.

STARTING POINT 2: ASSIGN WRITING ABOUT CLIMATE CHANGE

As we suggested, the short stories above can be springboards for persuasive and narrative writing. If you are teaching persuasive writing, your students can research and attempt to persuade others about climate change or one of its aspects. As we know, students are most likely to learn writing or media skills when they are engaged with meaningful content and composing for real audiences.

After engaging in research on climate change, Allen had his students write as if they were members of a middle school or high school after-school environmental club that decided to focus on global warming. They were asked to write a letter to school administration, teachers, or parents in the community about why they need to support the creation of curriculum about climate change in the school. Cece Watry decided to write to the school board to make the case for addressing climate change across the curriculum:

> Climate change may and should be introduced in a scientific way in the science classrooms because that is where the proof is. The science is honest, naked, and extremely clear as to why climate change is such a pressing matter for humanity . . . Another great classroom to teach climate change is history. Perhaps even create a climate change history course on its own, but a unit on climate change should definitely be incorporated into history classes . . . A great place to start is the English classroom. There are a multitude of short stories and novels, including fiction, nonfiction, and so on, that can be read in class and used as a source for discussion on climate change.

Another persuasive piece Allen asked his students to do (in small groups) was to create short videos (could be posted on YouTube) analyzing the greenwashing strategy of a particular company or the position of a climate change denier. Greenwashing is a form of marketing or "spin" that deceptively promotes an organization's products, aims, or policies as environmentally friendly (Watson, 2016). Students enjoyed web searches to find examples of greenwashing and climate change denial, and sharing egregious examples (for examples http://tinyw.in/ymoj). Students can then create their own parody examples using VoiceThread or video production tools. Students can also use culture jamming and subvertising (Google it!) to exaggerate and mock patently ridiculous claims.

Creative writing offers another excellent starting point for addressing climate change. As an intro to writing poetry and short stories about climate change, Allen had his students write a series of diary entries of a middle-school or high-school student living in the year 2050—entries that showed the impact of climate change. As his student Ali Coutts points out, the assignment "places a student in the mentality of a young adult of similar age . . . [and] they can write creatively on how they think Earth would look." It also "prompts them to do some baseline research on climate change."

Maddie wrote a two-and-a-half-page story called "The Dive" http://bit.ly/2bpKSHm set in Sitka, Alaska in a climate-ravaged future where people have gone north. The story describes two young people from different parts of the country meeting each other as they watch people diving into an acidic ocean to search the remains of the city flooded by sea-level rise to retrieve lost personal effects:

> "They go with no gear to try and grab stuff that's been sitting in an acidic ocean for 2 years. They die down there if they swallow even a bit. This stuff will burn your insides up before you can even get back to land."

> "That explains the face scars, then."

After writing their stories, Maddie and Rebecca Shell noted that: "Writing cli-fi stories is a great way to help students get creative while keeping climate change in mind. Students can have free rein with this activity, or they can have a guided writing session with different themes or elements in mind."

Randall Seltz, a teacher at Jordan High School, Sandy, Utah, describes the importance of research in persuasive writing:

> Another idea I think we could apply (that I've had success with using in argumentative writing units) is having students search local, national, and international media outlets for op/ed and letters to the editor about climate change. These are really interesting and show a great deal about how different regions take the problem more seriously. For example, New Orleans residents may find climate change "more real" than individuals who live in a landlocked desert valley. I may have students respond specifically to the writer of the piece they found or work to edit the piece to make it stronger by adding evidence or more logical arguments.

Cooper Franks, a teacher at Southfield Lathrup High School, Southfield, Michigan:

> After providing students with a list of environmental issues, ranging from ocean acidification to genetically modified organisms, they were asked to craft a short story or a children's book. The products were exceptional. Each written piece was engaged with the environmental issue in a creative way, and opened up interesting conversations from the audience at the reading we held.

Jonah Koski, who teaches high school in New York City, describes how his students study urban green spaces to prepare for research and creative writing:

> I would assign my inner city students to research different ways that NYC is addressing issues of climate change/urbanization/shared green space. There are a plethora of different schools, programs, and organizations doing all sorts of urban gardening and park work that could be researched by the students, many of which are really cool and innovative. This would also draw students' attentions to elements of nature in their everyday lives that they might not be aware of, but would certainly be affected by climate change. For example, the Bronx has more dedicated green space than any other borough, and students could visit any of a million different places in the city where nature is more prevalent than housing towers.

STARTING POINT 3: ADD "INFORMATIONAL TEXT" ABOUT CLIMATE CHANGE

The Common Core Standards (2010) stress that English classes address "informational text." Nonfiction about climate change can be studied as a topic/genre on its own or it can be paired with literary works. A key starting point for you and your students is accessible, reliable, and meaningful information. New research on climate change and valuable, readable articles, books, speeches, and documentaries addressing climate change are constantly emerging. At this point we want to share a small number of trusted and respected resources that you or your students may want to draw on to get started.

Perhaps the best researched and most concerning book on climate change for a public audience is *Six Degrees: Our Future on a Hotter Planet* by Mark Lynas (2008). Written in an appealing journalistic style, the book goes degree Celsius by degree Celsius into what will happen to the Earth as the planet warms from human causes. Lynas points out that "Human releases of carbon dioxide are possibly happening faster than any natural carbon releases since the beginning of life on Earth" (p. 260). The title *Six Degrees* comes from the consensus prediction of the hundreds of scientists who work with the Intergovernmental Panel on Climate Change (IPCC) that, if the world follows a "business as usual" path, by the year 2100 it will be 4 degrees warmer, and, depending on "climate sensitivity," the Earth could warm by as much as 6 degrees. As noted in Chapter 1, the difference between 2 degrees and 4 degrees "is human civilization" (Marshall, 2015, p. 241). And if we continue with "business as usual," warming will not stop at 4 degrees. What will then happen?

The following are the effects with each increase in degrees:

– *One Degree* and *Two Degrees*, now inevitable, entail droughts, over-taxed aquifers, major agricultural impacts around the world, severe famines, severe flooding from torrential rains, fires, death from heat stroke, a melting polar ice cap, rising seas inundating large cities, and the extinction of a third of all species.

– *Three Degrees*, one degree hotter than hoped for in the Paris Climate Agreement, will result in eventual 25 meters of sea-level rise, even more devastating drought and flooding, the end of the Amazon rain forest, huge hurricanes, the Sahara extending as far north as France, tropical temperatures that result in disaster; as Lynas notes:

> With structural famine gripping much of the subtropics, hundreds of millions of people will have only one choice left other than death for themselves and their families: They will have to pack up their belongings and leave. The resulting population transfers could dwarf those that have historically taken place owing to wars or crop failures.
>
> Lynas (2008, p. 180)

The 3 degrees' increase will also result in freeing substantial methane from a warming tundra. Methane, eighty times more powerful as a greenhouse gas than CO_2, could create a runaway warming scenario beyond human ability to control.

– *Four Degrees* will result in tremendous heat waves hotter than anything in the millions of years of human evolution, the loss of all polar ice, collapse of food production in China, the western half of India, southern Africa, Australia, and the western United States, and large areas surrounding the Mediterranean Sea necessarily abandoned.

– *Five Degrees* and *Six Degrees* will result in the Earth returning to a time when the Antarctic was covered with forest and vast swaths of the Earth were simply un-inhabitable. Six degrees caused the Permian extinction when 95 percent of life on Earth, on land and in the seas, was wiped out likely by exploding fireballs of methane released from sea beds—"a major oceanic methane eruption . . . would liberate energy . . . around 10,000 times greater than the world's stockpile of nuclear weapons"

Lynas (2008, p. 257)

Allen's student Ali Coutts says of the book, "By the time I got to the sixth chapter it has a post-apocalyptic feel to it, almost as though I am reading a fiction novel." Teams of students can read individual chapters and use a jigsaw or other approach to report back to the class about what climate change looks like at different temperatures. This source, like any on the topic, can lead to further questions and research (Moore, 2014; Stephenson, 2015).

Bill McKibben has been called America's leading environmentalist. Allen's students particularly liked Chapter 1 of his book *Eaarth* (2010) (for a pdf of this chapter http://tinyw.in/65B5). McKibben doesn't predict the future; instead he focuses on how climate change has already impacted Earth in the present day. He argues that, "The world hasn't ended, but the world as we know it has—even if we don't quite know it yet" (p. 2). He explains,

> This [the present day] is one of those rare moments, the start of a change far larger and more thoroughgoing than anything we can read in the records of man, on a par with the biggest dangers we can read in the records of rock and ice.
>
> McKibben (2010, p. 3)

Allen's student Shane Stover commented:

> What surprised me the most from reading this chapter, was that these effects that we were all warned about are no longer predictions but are results and are here right now. I remember learning in grade school science that the ice on the poles was starting to melt and was going to continue until we did something about it. What I did not realize was how serious and abruptly approaching this problem has become.

McKibben's essay in *Rolling Stone Magazine* (2012) "Global Warming's Terrifying New Math" is a starting point for thinking about the basic facts we need to know about fossil fuels and carbon consumption to address the problem. His 2016 essay in *The New Republic* "A World at War" sets forward what America must do to address the problem.

If you are looking for something quick and easy for your students, you won't do better than the four-page "Four Degrees," the final chapter of *Don't Even Think About It* by George Marshall (2014) (available at http://tinyw.in/PU2q). Avoiding statistics, Marshall focuses on heat waves, extinctions, and food yields. While he says that the timescales are uncertain, at 4 degrees "two-thirds of the world's major cities, and all of Southern Bangladesh and Florida would end up underwater" (p. 241) (other chapters from this book, all of them short and easy to read, are also good resources to help students think about why our society is not adequately addressing the topic of climate change).

Carly Fricano, a tenth-grade teacher in urban Memphis, Tennessee suggests:

> I can see having students read multiple informational texts and asking them to make a claim about climate change and use evidence from two–three texts to support their claim, address, and then refute a counterargument.

Randall Seltz, a teacher at Jordan High School in Sandy, Utah posits:

> I might also choose ten topics under the umbrella of climate change and assign them to different groups of students. I might include things like the Great Pacific Garbage Patch, El Niño, rising ocean levels, polar ice cap melt, ozone depletion, endangered species, and so on. I want high-interest topics that may not have an obvious connection so that once students start researching and discussing they start to build those connections and ask deeper questions. I would also

link to other topics we may have discussed during the school year, like, what are the connections between climate change and racism or socio-economics? How does climate change disproportionately affect different socio-economic populations? How does climate change affect economic opportunity? How does a scarcity in necessary resources affect morality? (E.g., is it okay to hurt others to obtain provisions for your family during a natural disaster?) I think these kinds of philosophical questions help students search for very personal meanings in otherwise difficult to comprehend data and information.

Dave Saltman, San Jose Conservation Corps and Charter School, San Jose, California explains:

The active climate-change solutions, such as solar power, constitute an important part of my largely-Latino, mostly adult-age, continuation-school-students' job-training at our program. Activities, such as pre-reading tasks (reviewing and responding in writing to headlines, subheads, captions), help students get comfortable with sophisticated topics like photovoltaics and reverse-metering that come up in nonfiction texts, and for which I scaffold vocabulary, and discuss roots and compound word meanings with them. Close-reading tasks, like setting a purpose for reading, identifying words and phrases that stand-out to them personally and why, and asking them to reflect on what they've heard or know about solar power and its role in managing climate change are used extensively as we explore a series of current periodical articles about climate change and related topics.

STARTING POINT 4: INCORPORATE DOCUMENTARIES AND IMAGES ABOUT CLIMATE CHANGE

Documentaries and images are also excellent ways to bring information about climate to the ELA classroom, something we discuss in more detail in Chapter 6. Documentaries can be combined with literature, writing, and essays to develop curricular units, or serve as the focus for "literature circles" or individual research. In addition to providing information and stimulating questions and research, students can look carefully at short clips and analyze how the documentary seeks to be effective.

The best-known documentary about climate change is *An Inconvenient Truth* featuring Al Gore (Guggenheim, 2006), that won the 2006 Academy Award for best documentary and remains a good introduction to the topic. Students can investigate to what extent Gore's claims from more than 10 years ago remain—or are more—persuasive. Allen's student, Thomas White, says,

One really interesting thing about watching this movie is seeing how things have changed since this film came out in 2006. How some things have gotten better, like fuel efficiency of automobiles and forms of alternative energy. Also seeing how some things have still trended in a negative slope, like the fact that each year has still gotten warmer and the ice caps are still melting at a record rate.

In February 2016, Gore followed up on the film with a 25-minute Ted Talk http://tinyw.in/gIvP that summarizes recent research, and describes positive news about wind and solar energy, and social movements to address climate change.

Another valuable documentary is *Six Degrees Could Change the World* (Bowman, 2008) based on Lynas' book, produced by National Geographic, narrated by Alec Baldwin, and available free online. Allen's student Brandon Loiselle comments:

> One quote from this documentary is, "the warmer it gets, the faster it gets warmer." Basically, there is a tipping point for global warming, a point of no return. Whether that point is at two or three degrees, it does not matter. If humans do not find a way to reduce the amount of greenhouse gases in the air, we will hit that point.

Maddie Reeves adds, "I think this would be a great film to show every human on the planet, because while it is sad and scary, it gets the message across, and that's what our world needs most right now."

Drop in the Ocean? Ireland and Climate Change (Whelan & Rice, 2015) http://tinyw.in/asG1 focuses on climate change in Ireland but makes global connections. By looking at different reactions to global warming by diverse people in Ireland, it opens up opportunities for students to discuss how their own country compares. Allen's student Emma Garber explains,

> The initial responses from people who live in Ireland are that they associate climate change with people suffering in Africa and never pay attention to it. They honestly feel that they have more important things to focus on in their daily lives because climate change has not directly hurt them . . . As the video continues they also interview people living in Africa who are witnessing and feeling the damages climate change is leaving on the planet . . . [and they] speak out about how outraged they are about the actions of the rich countries.

This Changes Everything (Lewis, 2015) is a documentary film based on Naomi Klein's book with the same title and addresses global inequality, the role of capitalism in the crisis, environmental activism, and possibilities for positive change to create a more just world. Allen's student Ali Coutts noted:

> In the introduction Klein proposes a single important question that attempts to be answered throughout the whole movie, "what if the problem is a story we've been telling ourselves for 400 years?" In this story, humankind sees itself as having dominion over the Earth and using it as the mother-load, constantly over consuming its resources when we should be seeing it as a mother figure, fearing its capabilities.

Three more excellent documentaries: *Chasing Ice* (Orlowski, 2012) is about the problem of envisioning climate change that uses amazing photography and videos to show the rapid recession of glaciers; *Do the Math: Bill McKibben & the Fight against Climate Change* (Nyks & Scott, 2013) http://tinyw.in/IH3L portrays McKibben's powerful description of the challenge of climate change; and, *Before the Flood,* Leonardo DiCaprio's 2016 documentary on climate change.

You can also provide students with images and graphics from online repositories such as National Geographic, NASA, NOAA, Inside Climate News, and so on (for other image resources: http://tinyw.in/JLhJ). The book, *Dire Predictions: Understanding Climate Change: The Visual Guide to the Findings of the IPCC* (Mann & Kump, 2015) contains hundreds of visual infographics, charts, and photos portraying climate change causes and effects, as well as methods for addressing climate change.

Dave Saltman, San Jose Conservation Corps and Charter School, San Jose, California:

> Because so many of my continuation students read below grade level, struggle with English as a second language, or are working with a variety of learning disabilities, I use smaller clips and animations, rather than the climate "blockbusters" we use as cultural and intellectual touchstones (i.e., *An Inconvenient Truth*) to get across more narrowly defined climate change concepts, such as "carbon footprint" and "greenhouse gases." I need to ground everything about climate change in more personal terms to convince my students to engage with the material. I may also ask them to draw or find an Internet image and to caption that image as a reading-response activity. Images, especially infographics, and animations—are incredibly useful for assisting students to assimilate the science behind climate problems and solutions—the animation of . . . the fusion reactor in France comes to mind, as do carbon-extraction graphics.

Randall Seltz, Jordan High School, Sandy, Utah:

> Knowing that my former school boundaries included the world's largest open pit copper mine (Kennecott Utah Copper Mine) changes which movies I show, as many of the parents and community partnerships my school has are connected to the mine, even if it is the number 1 contributor of pollution to the valley we live in. A significant number of students in my classroom come from families that own livestock like horses and have family members who have ranches. Knowing that, I might select a movie that is somehow linking water shortages (which we experience every summer in Utah) to an increased difficulty in sustaining a farm/ranch in the desert. When I taught ninth grade, the textbook had a text selection from *An Inconvenient Truth* and several key pieces of literature about the environment, like *The Birds* by Daphne de Maurier. The only piece of text I had any parent/student objections to was Gore's "Truth." *The Birds* is really disturbing and gory, but Gore's work was labeled as "propaganda."

ENGAGING IN CRITICAL INQUIRY QUESTIONING TO FRAME LEARNING

To engage students, you can employ critical inquiry questioning that frames students interrogation of different aspects of climate change.

Lauren Oakes describes a workshop she developed for senior high-school students at Castilleja School in Palo Alto, California: A central focus of this workshop was the use of *"What can we actually do to protect species in a changing climate?"* *"How do ecological impacts of climate change affect plants and people?"* In order to address these complex questions, students participating in the workshop needed to tackle topics including: the effects that forests have on the climate system; the ways in which climate change affects forest dynamics; the benefits, or "ecosystem services" that forests provide people; and the challenges that climate change poses to forest managers and conservation planners. The central objectives of my approach, however, were for students to develop critical thinking skills across disciplines on climate-related issues, and to engage with various topics of climate change impacts occurring in their own local environment.

The first part of the workshop focused primarily on ecological content so that students could gain a foundational understanding for later assessing how changes occurring may affect people. In lecture and discussion, we addressed questions such as, *What is the role of forests in the carbon cycle? How does climate shape forest dynamics and what kind of feedbacks do forests have on the climate system? In what ways is climate change affecting plants?* Students learned about the relationships between climate change and shifts in species distributions, invasive species, forest mortality events, and the emergence of novel plant communities.

We discussed examples of local species such as coast redwood (*Sequoia sempervirens*) that may be affected by changes in fog patterns and drought. We discussed examples of climate-induced tree death, such as aspen (*Populus tremuloides*) in Colorado, and plants like Joshua tree *(Yucca brevifolia)* experiencing range contraction and fragmentation in and around Joshua Tree National Park. Students brainstormed the many ways in which climate dynamics like changes in precipitation, snow cover, snow melt, growing seasons, and the frequency of "extreme" events could affect plant communities.

I then introduced the students to "ecosystem services," a framework that, in recent years, has been used to assess the benefits of environmental services—including the impacts of environmental changes, such as climate change—on people. The term broadly encompasses the use values, which may be derived directly through extractive or non-extractive uses of nature, such as tourism, or indirectly through intangible values, such as aesthetic appreciation. We discussed the four categories of this framework (supporting services, provisioning services, regulating services, and cultural services) in terms of forests and then students worked in pairs to assign the categories to specific services. Trees, for example, provide cultural services through spiritual values; provisioning services through wood people use; regulating services like carbon sequestration; and supporting services through photosynthesis.

To integrate these social and ecological concepts and apply them to current issues in conservation and resource management, our workshop culminated in a group exercise. I chose two species of interest in nearby California ecosystems (Joshua tree and coast redwood) and told the students they were researchers that had spent years studying the impacts of climate change on these species. They had a short amount of time to use the Internet and other resources I collected on these issues (e.g., media coverage; YouTube videos by research teams, educators, and non-governmental organizations; peer-reviewed publications; and online resources) to make arguments for adaptation strategies and mitigation.

Groups of three to five students used the following guiding questions and presented their findings to the class:

1. How has climate change affected your species of interest and its broader ecosystem, and what do you expect to see in the future?
2. What kinds of benefits (i.e., ecosystem services) are people deriving from these species? How might these services be impacted and where?
3. Based on the ecosystem services you identify, who are the stakeholders? (Think across scales, such as local, regional, or global.)
4. What recommendations would you make to stakeholders and resource managers for adaptation? Do your recommendations for adaptive practices differ between protected areas, like National Parks, and the "human-dominated landscape"?
5. Applying what you have learned, how would you argue for climate change mitigation?

Each group then developed a comprehensive "map" or diagram of the ways in which the impacts these species experienced, or might experience in the future, affect the benefits they provide people. Students made recommendations for local management strategies, such as planting trees in habitats where future climate may be more suitable.

STUDENTS' EMOTIONS, HOPE, AND ACTION

Studying climate change can also inspire uncertainty, confusion, anxiety, or helplessness. Ali Coutts admitted that, "This first chapter of [McKibben's] *Eaarth* definitely left me feeling overwhelmed and paralyzed." These various emotions students have can be used to identify issues, learn more, and figure out what to do next. Allen's student Jacob Colegio wrote,

> At first I was suspicious of a lot of McKibben's claims. I've heard both sides of the story he's telling—some say that climate change will doom us if we don't take immediate action, while others argue that such thinking is overly dramatic and climate change statistics are skewed to look more daunting than they actually are. I fell in the latter camp, either because I actually think they're overreacting or because I don't want the terrifying facts about climate change to be true, or a combination of both.

After reading that first chapter Allen wrote his students' questions on the whiteboard:

- McKibben's book was written 8 years ago. Is what he says still true? What has happened since then? Has global warming been speeding up?
- Is it possible that wind and solar could provide the energy we need?
- How does agriculture impact climate change?
- How is increased flooding related to global warming?
- Will the Paris Agreement keep warming to 2 degrees C?
- Why are people having such a hard time believing that climate change is real?
- What is happening with Arctic sea ice?
- Where does the average American's emission of CO_2 come from? How do I make a difference?
- To me, the most threatening aspect of global warming is disease ... The real question becomes, are we going to die because of chlorofluorocarbons depleting the ozone, or because of a small, itchy mosquito bite [carrying malaria or the zika virus]?
- How do people who live in poor countries feel about the fact that they aren't responsible for climate change, but will suffer the most? What can be done about that?

Rather than provide answers, Allen asked his students to research their questions on the Internet, write a post on their blogs about what they found out, and make short PowerPoint presentations to the whole class. Doing their own research and listening to each other's PowerPoints, riveted students' attention to the problem. Perhaps because they were learning from each other and their own inquiry, rather than from a teacher's lecture or even a textbook, doubts about the reality of human-caused climate change evaporated, even for students from politically conservative families.

Making sense of climate change called for taking steps to address it. In the midst of confusion students also sought hope. Jessica Poling told this story:

> Destruction of Earth seems to be McKibben's topic of choice. In fact, he proposes so many negative outcomes in life, that I am beginning to doubt every action I take. While getting my hair cut, I spent half of the time discussing global warming with my hairdresser! The other half was spent talking about cancer. It's no wonder she gave me the number of a counselor, even if the number wasn't for me. Global warming is taking over our lives

faster than we can control it. But I have decided that, like the Centers for Disease Control and Prevention, our aim should be to prevent outcomes from ever occurring, rather than try to find solutions to pick up and control what's left in the aftermath. Although a rise in temperature has already created irreversible damage to our world, there is still some fragment of hope, and I hope that in the near future, members of our society will be active creating a new, cleaner version of Earth.

Seeking to understand possibilities to make a difference Allen's student Blair watched the documentary, *The Future of Energy: Lateral Power to the People* (Mazurek, 2015) http://tinyw.in/b3KI. He describes how finding out about what others were doing gives him a sense of possibility:

[The documentary is about] the budding green energy movement occurring across the United States. Its creators searched high and low for grassroots clean energy movements in a town near you, and what they found was rather exciting. Entire cities were going green, and it was happening at a local level—exciting stuff.

Take, for example, Lancaster, California, a town that mandated that all new buildings be fitted with solar technology. This city has been able to reach nearly net zero emissions in doing so and, as mayor R. Rex Parris puts it, "we now have the ability to save the planet, increase the standard of living and the well being of everyone." This film certainly argues that green energy isn't just environmentally responsible, but also socially and economically viable. In fact, one woman in the film calls the green energy movement, "the largest social movement in human history." It seems, according to this film, that green energy will help stave off our environmental woes and help lift people out of the darkness of poverty.

The film led Blair to further inquiry leading him to read a *Huffington Post* article, "How Renewable Energy Solutions Reduce Poverty Around the World" http://tinyw.in/Zmhr.

Through posing questions and sharing their research, Allen's students came to better understand climate change and position themselves as critical thinkers ready to learn more. Sharing their research helped them update their knowledge and better understand the causes and potential solutions to climate change (National Research Council, 2012). Their inquiry took them a long way toward addressing confusion, anger, and helplessness.

As the climate change course progressed, Allen's students started publishing findings on their individual blogs and the class wiki devoted to supporting English teachers http://tinyw.in/I6f4. Since their writing was public and directed to a specific audience, their work was not only useful for themselves but potentially educating others. By the conclusion of the course their knowledge, passion, and concern had led to a series of actions in their community, actions we describe in Chapter 9. The students also thought about how their knowledge of climate change might impact their future choices so they wrote blog posts about how in the careers they envisioned for themselves they would address climate change. Critical inquiry positioned Allen's students as active learners, through acquiring knowledge and seeking to make change.

AND THE TEACHER?

Teaching about climate change should foster critical inquiry where students' questions guide further learning. Justin Boyd, teaching in Greeley, Colorado, describes the advantage of bringing the starting points in this chapter together:

Each of these four steps (short stories, writing assignments, information texts, and documentaries/images) can easily fit into the curriculum of a language arts class. This multilayered approach provides excellent source material for rich discussions, the development of critical thinking skills, synthesizing resources, project-based learning, social activism, and so on. Best of all, climate change is a topic my students can quickly buy into; they see the impact it has on their own lives each day.

Teaching about climate change raises questions for us teachers, as well. As we care about the Earth and the future our students will have on it, we have to think about our own responsibility as role models. As Allen explains:

> I shared with my students my own commitment to address the problem. I was teaching about it; we were going to learn about it together and do something. I modified my own lifestyle. I educated myself and supported candidates who addressed climate change. I attended related community events. I was determined to share my concern with other teachers by speaking at conferences and writing this book—and they were going to help me with it.

Taking the step to teach about climate change positions teachers as part of the movement to do something about it. Finding ways to reach out to that movement, to connect our teaching with others is one of the themes we explore in this book.

In reading an early draft of this chapter, Carly Fricano, cited above, describes the evolution of her thinking and her motivating awareness of climate change as a social justice issue:

> I was skeptical when I got your first email about teaching climate change. I didn't really see how I could sell it to the kids, as I don't really know much about it, and I am so passionate about teaching social justice material. I just didn't think I could fit it in. As I read the chapter it strikes me that as human beings we are just as responsible for the care and conservation of our planet as we are for taking an active role in democracy and standing up for equity and civil rights. Now, I'm super excited to check some of this stuff out and create a unit!

We hope this chapter has given you, like Carly, new ideas and enthusiasm. We also hope that it has whetted your appetite not only for first steps, but also for the rest of this book. Chapter 3 fosters further thinking about how to meaningfully frame and develop climate change in English language arts curriculum.

For additional resources, activities, and readings related to this chapter, go to http://tinyw.in/Zuov on the book's website.

REFERENCES

Atcheson, J. (2015). How close to the savage soul. In Woodbury, M. (Ed.), *Winds of change: Short stories about our climate* (p. 29–40). Coquitlam, British Columbia, Canada: Moon Willow Press.

Bowman, R. (2008). *Six degrees could change the world* [Video file]. USA: National Geographic Channel. Retrieved from http://natgeotv.com/ca/six_degrees/about.

Coates, T-N. (2015). *Between the world and me.* New York: Spiegel & Grau.

Common Core Standards. (2010). *Common Core State Standards for English language arts & literacy in history/social studies, science, and technical subjects.* Washington, DC: Council of Chief State School Officers and the National Governors Association.

Draper, R. J., Broomhead, P., Jensen, A. P., Nokes, J. D., & Siebert, D. (Eds.). (2010). *(Re)Imagining content-area literacy instruction.* New York: Teachers College Press.

Guggenheim, D. (Director) (2006). *An inconvenient truth* [Motion picture]. United States: Lawrence Bender Productions.

Lewis, A. (Director) (2015). *This changes everything* [Motion picture]. United States: Klein Lewis Productions.

Lynas, M. (2008). *Six degrees: Our future on a hotter planet*. Washington, DC: National Geographic.

Martin, M. (Ed.) (2011). *I'm with the bears: Short stories from a damaged planet*. New York: Verso.

Mann, M., & Kump, L. R. (2015). *Dire predictions: Understanding climate change*. New York: Penguin/Random House.

Marshall, G. (2015). *Don't even think about it: Why our brains are wired to ignore climate change*. New York: Bloomsbury.

May, R. (2015). The audit. In M. Woodbury (Ed.), *Winds of change: Short stories about our climate* (p. 41–52). Coquitlam, British Columbia, Canada: Moon Willow Press.

Mazurek, B. (Director) (2015). *The future of energy: Lateral power to the people* [Motion picture]. United States: Planetary Advocates.

McKibben, B. (2010). *Eaarth: Making a life on a tough new planet*. Boston: St. Martin's Griffin.

McKibben, B. (2012). Global warming's terrifying new math. *Rolling Stone*. July 19.

McKibben, B. (2016). A world at war. *The New Republic*. August 15.

Moore, J. (2014) The capitalocene: Part 1: On the nature & origins of our ecological crisis [Web log post]. Retrieved from http://tinyw.in/DVZA.

National Research Council. (2012). *A framework for K-12 science education: Practices, crosscutting concepts, and core ideas*. Washington, DC: The National Academies Press.

Nyks, K., & Scott, J. P. (Directors). (2013). *Do the math: Bill McKibben & the fight over climate change* [Motion picture]. USA: Media Education Foundation.

Orlowski, J. (Director) (2012). *Chasing ice* [Motion picture]. United States: Submarine Deluxe.

Rich, N. (2011). Hermie. In M. Martin (Ed.). *I'm with the bears: Short stories from a damaged planet* (pp. 91–100). New York: Verso.

Stephenson, W. (2015). *What we're fighting for now is each other: Dispatches from the front lines of climate justice*. Boston: Beacon Press.

Watson, B. (2016). The troubling evolution of corporate greenwashing. *The Guardian*. Retrieved from http://bit.ly/2ckcT3X.

Whelan, A., & Rice, E. (Producers/Directors) (2015). *Drop in the ocean? Ireland and climate change* [Video file]. Ireland: Trócaire.

Woodbury, M. (Ed.) (2015). *Winds of change: Short stories about our climate*. Coquitlam, British Columbia, Canada: Moon Willow Press.

Chapter 3
Creating a Climate Change Curriculum

Treat the Earth well: it was not given to you by your parents, it was loaned to you by your children. We do not inherit the Earth from our ancestors, we borrow it from our children.

Native American Proverb

[Humans] make their own history, but they do not make it just as they please; they do not make it under circumstances chosen by themselves, but under circumstances directly encountered, given and transmitted from the past.

Karl Marx (Elster, 1986, p. 277)

In the last chapter, we explored ways secondary language arts teachers begin to start teaching about climate change. As you advance your teaching about climate change, you will want to more fully and carefully develop curriculum and instruction, creating richer and extended opportunities to bring a climate change perspective to your teaching and foster your students' inquiry and activism.

Human-caused global warming has a specific history with causes and solutions deeply imbedded in our social, economic, political, and cultural systems. This chapter is divided into four sections that set forward thematic ways to frame and organize climate change teaching: (1) Indigenous and Postcolonial Perspectives; (2) Capitalism and Consumerism; (3) Environmental Literature and Ecocritical Approaches; and (4) Systems Impacting Climate Change.

Too often our curriculum in English language arts is disconnected and, frankly, irrelevant to the issues in students' lives and the world today. Organized by genres, time periods, or narrowly construed national traditions, literary works or "informational texts" are presented as "pearls on a string," without meaningful connections between them. Writing instruction covers different modes or genres, but may lack real purpose and audience. Specific standards or skills get "checked off", but we sometimes wonder, are students authentically learning?

Understanding the history and social context of climate change opens many possibilities for the development of meaningful, coherent, and relevant English language arts curriculum that not only deeply explores climate change but also fosters sincere inquiry and purposeful interceding to address it.

1 INDIGENOUS AND POSTCOLONIAL PERSPECTIVES

While our ancestors have been around for about six million years, the modern form of humans only evolved about 200,000 years ago. Civilization as we know it is only about 6,000 years old, and industrialization started in earnest only in the 1800s.

Howell (2015)

For the vast majority of time humans have lived on Earth we have lived in ways that were ecologically sustainable. Our ancestors showed remarkable ability to adapt to different environments and learned to use plant and animal resources effectively and respectfully.

As evident in their religions, myths, literature, history, and daily practices, native/indigenous peoples have considered their environments as revered, sacred spaces essential to their livelihood. This approach opposes the typical Western European/American ideological perspective on nature as something to be dominated, conquered, or controlled. In his book, *Teaching Truly: A Curriculum to Indigenize Mainstream Education,* Four Arrows (2013) explains, "Indigenous perspectives see humans as part of Nature, without placing us in a hierarchy . . . It . . . honor[s] the Earth and its life systems as 'Mother' and the larger cosmos as 'Father' in ways that demand respect for them and encourage learning" (pp. 254–255). In contrast, European and American narratives have too often portrayed conquistadors, explorers, "great white fathers," military officers, corporate executives, political leaders, as bringers of Christian salvation, civilization, development, and democracy, when instead they were conquering native peoples, plundering their land and resources, and using religious justification, ideas of racial superiority, "manifest destiny," or "nation building" to justify their destructive actions.

While Europeans considered places they went to as spaces to be conquered and controlled for commercial gain, First Nation people perceived sacred spaces as located in time. As a result, many indigenous peoples construct their identities according to their narratives, portraying their connection to spaces and time:

> In Maori [New Zealand's indigenous] culture each person has a turangawaewae (literally, a place to stand) which has nothing to do with where I currently live. This turangawaewae is about my ancestry—biological and social (we call it whakapapa)—and is a place where I belong. It is a place of identity—usually represented through marae (ancestral meeting place), an urupa (burial site), and through features of the land that surrounds these places, such as mountains, rivers, lakes, and so on.
>
> Kincheloe et al. (2006, p. 145)

In applying a climate change perspective to different literary and media representations of nature, students can examine whether humans' relationship with the Earth is depicted as one of exploitation, control, and destruction or one of harmony, interdependence, and sustainability. Arrows (2013) suggests that bringing an indigenous perspective into mainstream education "is about remembering our relationship to and our love for place. It is about letting go of our sense of superiority over and our fear of the natural world so that we can return to a life that deeply respects Mother Earth" (p. 12).

Indigenous/native peoples have shown leadership in protesting the fossil fuel companies' exploitation of lands and waters. Examples include the Standing Rock Sioux Reservation pipeline protest in North Dakota, the Nez Perce stopping rigs in Idaho, the Northern Cheyenne preventing coal development in Montana, the Lummi stopping coal export in the Pacific Northwest, native tribes winning a court victory against Shell's Arctic drilling in Alaska, and indigenous groups holding back oil interests in the Amazon (Klein, 2015).

Students can inquire into, research, and discuss questions such as:

- How have European/American colonialism, slave trade, and ongoing imperialism created "developed" and "underdeveloped" areas of the world, and how do these areas differ in terms of responsibility for and suffering from climate change?
- How does the history of colonialism impact contemporary ideas of climate justice, "climate debt," and the concept of climate change "loss and damage" payments from wealthy countries to poor countries?

- How does racism and its history continue to impact thinking about climate change consequences and solutions?
- How do cultural ideas about the role of humans in nature influence thinking about climate change?
- What can be learned from indigenous cultures about sustainable living?
- What can be learned from previous social movements and how they can impact society and policy, that is, the abolitionist movement, the movement against the rubber trade, anti-colonial struggles, civil-rights movements, indigenous-resource exploitation protests?
- How might we establish a cooperative world order to address climate change rather than one based in competition, domination, inequality, violence, and exploitation?

TEACHING ACTIVITIES FOR ADOPTING INDIGENOUS AND POSTCOLONIAL PERSPECTIVES

Students could compare and contrast native/indigenous perspectives with those of colonialists/imperialists. For example, the eighty-page young adult novella, *Morning Girl* (Dorris, 2008), portrays the life of the Taino people living close to nature on an island in the Caribbean Sea, just before, in the final scene, Christopher Columbus arrives. Students could combine *Morning Girl* with the powerful first chapter from Howard Zinn's (2015) book *A People's History of the United States* entitled "Columbus, the Indians, and Human Progress" (chapter available online: http://tinyw.in/6dIk). It could also be paired with the picture book *Encounter* (Yolen, 1996) portraying Columbus' arrival from the perspective of an indigenous Taino boy. This pairing could open into discussions of values, nature, progress, and climate change.

Other native and indigenous works for secondary teachers with environmental themes:

- *Way to Rainy Mountain* (N. Scott Momaday, 1976, Kiowa tribal history in relation to movement from the Rockies to the Great Plains);
- *Two Old Women* (Velma Wallis, 1993, Athabascan story about survival in nature; easy read and good pair with Jack London's "To Build a Fire");
- *Mean Spirit* (Linda Hogan, 1991, Osage; about preserving natural values on land exploited for oil drilling);
- *Brother Eagle, Sister Sky* (Susan Jeffers, 1991, picture book provides an adaptation of the famous speech by Chief Seattle from the 1850s);
- *Things Fall Apart* (Achebe, 1958, Ibo, Nigeria);
- *The Bleeding of the Stone* (Ibrahim Al-Koni, 2002, Taurag, Libya).

On the European side, works that could help students think about issues of colonial domination of nature and people include *The Tempest, Robinson Crusoe, Heart of Darkness*, even *Lord of the Flies*. Colonialism and destruction of the natural world is a focus of science fiction works such as *The Word for World is Forest* (LeGuin, 2010) about a planet where a logging company is destroying a nature-connected native people, or the 2009 film *Avatar* (Cameron, 2009) (the highest grossing film of all time) where a mining company threatens the existence of native peoples.

In many parts of the world colonial relationships have continued in "neo-colonial" forms. Students could examine the exploitation of land, resources, and people in formerly colonized countries for short-term profit by corporations in the wealthy countries. Rather than bringing wealth, natural resources become a "curse" on local communities where the exploitation of oil, forests, farmland, minerals, diamonds, coltan, and so on, have only led to an environmental "slow violence" that separates the enclaved rich (in both First and Third Worlds) from the outcast poor (Nixon, 2011).

To have her students at North Davidson High School in Lexington, North Carolina understand how an anthropocentric worldview serves to separate us superficially from nature, Rebecca Young had her students read Carly Lettero's (2010) "Spray Glue Goes. Maggots Stay" from *Moral Ground: Ethical Action for a Planet in Peril* (Moore & Nelson, 2010).

> This personal essay juxtaposes the ways humans treat a body after death with how nature does upon witnessing the hospital's procedural sanitizing of her grandfather's dead body, which includes "so much disposable crap" in the form of "hermetically sealed cotton swabs," "rubber gloves," "individually wrapped wipes and plastic padded sheets" (p. 104). Lettero recalls a very different memory of finding the body of a sea lion that had washed ashore on a coast of Oregon that was destroyed by vultures, bugs, maggots, and flies: "So much life spiraled out from this one dead animal. In stark contrast to my grandfather's death, nothing was wasted."
>
> Moore & Nelson (2010, p. 104)

The sensory details of these burials offer a context for exploring the times when humans place themselves above all else in nature, when we see ourselves as distinct from rather than as inclusive of other species or our environment. If literature can help us recognize the false sense of superiority we have imagined for ourselves, it can also instruct us toward a more empathic social narrative that helps us value ourselves, each other, and our environment more fully.

2 CAPITALISM AND CONSUMERISM

Capitalism is an economic system based on the private ownership of nature and natural resources and the means of transportation and production such as trucks, railroads, machinery, factories, offices, computers, and the Internet. The goal of capitalism is to generate profit for owners and shareholders. Different forms of capitalism have different degrees of private or public ownership, free markets, and regulation (Moore, 2016).

Capitalism has been an enormous stimulus to invention and production. Karl Marx and Frederick Engels writing more than 150 years ago in the *Communist Manifesto* (1848), state that capitalism "has created enormous cities, has greatly increased the urban population as compared with the rural." They argue that the power of capitalism is its "cheap prices" which "are the heavy artillery" that "batters down all Chinese walls" and "compels all nations" to accept capitalist production and exchange, and thus "creates a world after its own image."

In the twenty-first century we can now see that Marx and Engels were writing about the early stages of the Industrial Revolution. At first, when manufacturing went from hand work to machines, it was supported primarily by water power. During Marx's day and after, came the "Second Industrial Revolution," which involved the use of oil and rubber, the production of steel, the development of electricity, mechanization of agriculture, and, of course, automobiles and airplanes. Next was the "Great Acceleration" which, especially after 1950, resulted in marked increased population, energy use, fertilizers, transportation, and consumption causing enormous fossil fuel emission, deforestation, industrialization of agriculture, and increasingly adverse effects on the climate (see Anthropocene Dashboard at www.anthropocene.info/great-acceleration.php).

However, capitalism's "free market" doesn't account for the costs of environmental impacts, which are considered "externalities." For example, carbon-based fuels have enormous costs in terms of their greenhouse effects but those costs are not accounted for in the prices paid for the fuels by consumers. Those costs are "external" to the market price. For that reason some economists propose a "carbon tax" or "fee" that would allow the price of fossil fuels to more accurately reflect their true cost and discourage use. One 2015 study that accounted for various health effects and some environmental effects of the burning of gasoline indicates that a gallon of gasoline should cost at least $3.80 more than the current price at the pump (Ayre, 2015).

Capitalism and economic inequality. The capitalist system benefits specific groups more than others, particularly the owners of resources and production rather than the workers, resulting in economic inequality across nations and people (Stiglitz, 2013; Piketty, 2014). Today this concentration is dramatic, as "the eighty-five wealthiest individuals in the world have a combined wealth equal to that of the bottom 50 percent of the world's population, or about 3.5 billion people" (Oxfam, 2014). As Bill McKibben (2001) notes:

> We in this country burn 25 percent of the world's fossil fuel, create 25 percent of the world's carbon dioxide. It is us—it is the affluent lifestyles that we lead that overwhelmingly contribute to this problem. And to call it a problem is to understate what it really is. Which is a crime against the poorest and most marginalized people on this planet. We've never figured out, though God knows we've tried, a more effective way to destroy their lives (p. 5).

The owners of fossil fuel-based corporations have greatly benefited financially while the environment of everyone has been compromised. The billionaire Koch Brothers' fossil fuel companies have exerted extensive influence on the political system to oppose environmental regulations, clean energy subsidies, and development of mass transit (Matulis & Moyer, 2016; Mayer, 2016), for example, opposing President Obama's Clean Energy Program in the courts.

Owners of fossil fuel industries, who are opposed to regulations and subsidy cuts, have sponsored efforts to deny or suppress information about the adverse effects of emissions. In the 1970s, when scientists at ExxonMobil found that fossil fuel had adverse effects on the environment, ExxonMobil executives suppressed that information and, since then, have sponsored attempts to cast doubt on or deny the validity of more recent data on fossil fuel effects (Hall, 2015).

This economic inequality also results in inequality in the effects of climate change across and within countries. Low-income people and countries, with fewer resources to protect themselves, suffer greater harm from degradation of the environment. Viewed globally by national populations, the wealthiest 20 percent of the world is responsible for over 60 percent of greenhouse gases. In the United States, for example, the richest 1 percent have average emissions of 318 tons of CO_2, while the poorest 10 percent emit on average 100 times less, 31 tons (Chancel & Pikkety, 2015). Despite not being responsible for climate change, it is and will continue to be, the poorest people in the developing world contributing minimal emissions who are and will be most adversely affected by extreme weather events, heat, sea rise, and illnesses (Roberts & Parks, 2006). In a poor country such as Honduras, since multinational corporations own the fertile land, the poorer majority of the population is forced to live on riverbanks and hillsides where extreme weather events have the worst impacts (Roberts & Parks, 2006).

Adopting an ethical perspective on climate change. In part, the use of fossil fuels is driven by consumerism—purchasing goods associated with achieving an assumed happiness as celebrated through advertisements and media promotions. Advertisements for gas-guzzling SUVs associate driving SUVs with achieving social status and "freedom of the road," rather than using more efficient mass transit. As we discuss in Chapter 6, an important goal for English instruction is to foster critical media analysis of the role of advertisements and media in fostering consumption of goods and products adversely impacting the environment.

The way we understand the history of global warming matters to the ethical questions it raises. All humans are not equally responsible for climate change. Some benefited and some lost out from colonialism, slavery, the Industrial Revolution, militarism, imperialism, increasing inequality, and the concentration of wealth that have been part of capitalist development.

Students can inquire into, research, and discuss questions such as:

- How has capitalist economic development impacted climate change?
- What is the role of government intervention, policy, and law to address climate change?
- How extreme is economic inequality in our world? How does this inequality affect the causes, impacts, and solutions of/for climate change?
- How does advertising function to sell not only products but unsustainable lifestyles?
- How might we evolve our thinking about consumption and consumerism to address sustainability and climate change?
- In what ways is capitalism compatible, or can it become compatible, with democracy, human rights, and sustainability?
- How do corporations and wealthy individuals admit or deny their role in climate change? How do they influence government policy regarding climate change?
- What are corporations doing to address climate change? What else might they do?
- What can we do as students to challenge consumerist values, instant gratification, and social competitiveness and adopt values associated with sustainability?
- How does the way we understand history, the words we use, and the way we describe climate change influence our thinking?

Students in Shelli Rottschafer's composition course wrote autobiographical essays in response to nonfiction texts to describe their ethical stances toward sustainability and the environment. In response to "My Land Ethic," from Aldo Leopold's (1949) *A Sand County Almanac*, Hailey Kingele, who grew up in rural Michigan, draws on Leopold's ethical stance that "'we abuse land because we see it as a commodity belonging to us' (viii)," noting that:

> we have a certain power over nature, we do not control nor possess it. It is this generation's misconception that the Earth is just an appliance for humans to use at free will with no respect . . . The relationship one has with their biota affects the level of responsibility they feel toward it. The stronger the relationship, the more responsible they feel.

In response to Leopold's essay, "The A and B Cleavage" contrasting a group of A people who "'regards the land as soil, and its function as commodity production [versus] another group (B) regards the land as a biota, and its function as something broader' (pp. 258–259)," Sarah Ress notes how "Pope Francis has discussed our role in conserving the Earth, and urges all people to take responsibility in cleaning and restoring our planet." She supports "Sustainability Initiative and Zero-Waste Initiatives on campus, and we offer recycling and composting bins in almost every building."

Lilia Thomas posits the need to develop a "'Conservation esthetic' (Leopold, 1949, p. 280)" by:

building around certain landmarks in order for people to observe and appreciate what nature has created . . . conservation involves the understanding of how we perceive nature and what it offers. Only by understanding the deep meaning will we be able to make changes to help the environment.

TEACHING ACTIVITIES FOR ANALYZING CAPITALISM AND CONSUMERISM

Since the early stages of the Industrial Revolution and into the present day there have always been writers, artists, and intellectuals describing, representing, and objecting to industrialization, urbanization, poverty, wretched working conditions, massive inequality, and mindless consumerism.

The secondary English curriculum typically includes works that address capitalism and inequality. Of course, *The Great Gatsby* or, on the other side, *The Pearl*, could be starting points. To directly tie in climate change, imagine having students attempt to compare the carbon footprint of a modern day Gatsby, Tom, or Daisy with Kino or Juana. What if students reading *Gatsby* learned about John Muir, Aldo Leopold, Maude Murie, or other early environmentalists and wrote letters back and forth or held discussions in role with characters from the novel.

To help students gain a historical perspective on the rise of capitalism and impacts on the environment beginning in the nineteenth century, students can read *Life in the Iron Mills* (1861) (free at www.gutenberg.org). This is a pioneering short story or novella written by Rebecca Harding Davis portraying the gritty, difficult life of early factory workers and an exposé of capitalism and industrialization; students can detect environmental dimensions in the critique.

While English teachers may be familiar with applying an economic analysis to portrayals of class differences in texts such as Austen's or Dickens' novels (Appleman, 2014), teachers could extend the analysis by having students look at interviews with poor and working people in London in the 1840s found in Henry Mayhew's *London Labour and the London Poor* (at www.gutenberg.org). Stephen Crane's *New York City Sketches* from the 1890s are powerful short pieces addressing poverty and wealth (also at www.gutenberg.org). Students might inquire into similar class differences in the world today, and examine implications for climate change.

A book that directly foregrounds the relationship between capitalism and climate change and can inspire English teachers with teaching ideas is the previously mentioned Naomi Klein's (2015) *This Changes Everything: Capitalism vs. The Climate*, as well as the documentary based on the book, http://tinyw.in/uQ0T. At a retreat in Portland, Oregon, twenty-two educators from across the United States shared their experiences in building curriculum based on this book (Bigelow, Kelly & McKenna, 2015).

One participant shared a collection of stories by Pacific Island activists describing resistance to Australia's promotion of the economic benefits of their exporting coal when the Pacific Islands are currently being inundated by sea rise caused by climate change. Another New York City teacher built on Klein's description of "sacrifice zones" and the Black Lives Matter movement by having students critically examine how often energy plants producing greenhouse gases are located in low-income neighborhoods, leading students to pose questions such as, "Who lives there? Who doesn't? What is being sacrificed? Who benefits from the sacrifice?"

Given the success of efforts by corporate or political groups to deny or frame climate change as a "debatable" issue, students could read selections from *Don't Even Think About It* by George

Marshall (2015) regarding the impacts of denialism and why climate change is not adequately addressed in the media or public discussion. On his book's website, http://climateconviction.org, Marshall poses questions that could be used with students to discuss society's failure to attend to climate change:

- Why do the victims of flooding, drought, and severe storms become less willing to talk about climate change or even accept that it is real?
- Why are people who say that climate change is too uncertain more easily convinced of the imminent dangers of terrorist attacks, meteorite strikes, or an alien invasion?
- Why have scientists, normally the most-trusted professionals in our society, become distrusted, hated, and the targets for violent abuse?
- Why are science fiction fans, of all people, so unwilling to imagine what the future might really be like?

Teenagers are the target of a great deal of advertising and we need to help them think critically about consumerism shaping attitudes toward products and lifestyles that adversely impact the environment. Students can view the outstanding 20-minute *Story of Stuff* video (Fox & Priggen, 2007) http://storyofstuff.org/movies which describes extraction, production, distribution, consumption, and disposal of goods. They discuss how consumerism is related to climate change. The success and appeal of *The Story of Stuff* has led to a series of engaging short videos on cap and trade, cosmetics, shopping, and bottled water, available on the same website.

Students can also read science fiction texts on the adverse effects of consumerism, for example:

- *Brave New World* (Huxley, 2014) opens onto topics of social manipulation, consumerism, and developing sustainable lifestyles.
- M. T. Anderson's (2010) young adult novel, *Feed*, in which adolescent characters are continually receiving advertisements in their brains, offers a great source for discussions about teens and consumerism and the impact of consumerism on the environment.
- Scott Westerfeld's award winning young adult novel, *So Yesterday* (2004), portrays young people learning to question consumerism. His popular *Pretties* (2006) and *Uglies* (2008) are set in a post-apocalyptic world ravaged by climate change where superficial ideas of beauty are valued over authenticity.

3 ENVIRONMENTAL LITERATURE/ECOCRITICAL TEACHING

Nature and the natural world are an important topic in literary and cultural texts from ancient times up to the present. There is a long history in English studies of addressing nature literature and a diverse school of "ecocriticism" that has evolved to think about ecological perspectives and concerns.

Ecocriticism is the study of the way texts represent nature and treat environmental topics. Related terms include "ecopoetics," "environmental criticism," "geocriticism," "deep ecology," "ecofeminism," "green cultural studies," "animal studies," and "material ecocriticism." There are college courses on nature literature, scholars whose work focuses on ecocriticism, journals and books on the topic, and a professional organization, the Association for the Study of Literature and the Environment (ASLE), www.asle.org. You can draw on these ecocritical perspectives to help your students inquire into the deep cultural attitudes that shape our understanding and actions regarding climate change.

Ecocriticism asserts the value of addressing environmental themes and issues in literary and cultural texts. Early on, ecocriticism focused on the way that writers in the Romantic movement and other literary traditions valued communion with nature. As ecocriticism evolved, it began to address the social construction of nature, questioning binaries such as nature/culture, male/female, and how hierarchical and unequal systems such as colonialism, capitalism, and patriarchy conceive and impact nature. More recently, ecocriticism has come to focus on a global understanding of ecojustice and the impact on humans, animals, and nature associated with the "slow violence" of environmental abuse (Buell, 2005; Nixon, 2011; Iovino & Oppermann, 2014).

Ecocriticism recognizes that the meaning of any given place depends on how it is described, and those descriptions can be studied to consider social, cultural, and psychological perspectives in texts. In their place-based writing about an Australian valley, Lesley Instone and Affrica Taylor (2015) describe going beyond "pastoral-conservationist" perceptions of the valley from that of "dominant white settler narratives of 'improvement' and 'protection'" to appreciate the "ancient, multiple, complex and ongoing" history as "made and remade by many actors, human and nonhuman, not just those featured in the heroic white male settler histories of the last 200 years" (p. 135).

One key branch of ecocriticism, ecofeminism (Adams & Gruen, 2014; Shiva, 2014; Vakoc, 2014; Phillips & Rumens, 2016), highlights how perceptions of the relationship between humans and the environment are gendered in that:

> men and masculinity are associated with culture and culture is valued, whereas women and femaleness are associated with nature and both are devalued. These linked valuations lead to hierarchy, which is then used to justify the domination of women, nature, and all those so associated.
>
> Garrard (2010, p. 48)

Women are most likely to be adversely affected by climate change given that they are more likely to be poor, involved in food production and acquisition, responsible for protecting their family's children and accessing and providing water for their families, as well as more likely to be adversely impacted by floods, cyclones, or droughts than males (Garrard, 2015). Perhaps it is not surprising that women in Australia (Agho et al., 2010), Canada (Scannell & Gifford, 2013), and Iran (Salehi et al., 2015) were more concerned about climate change and making changes in their behavior than men.

To apply ecocriticism perspectives, students can address questions such as:

- How are nature, the natural environment, "wild," rural, suburban, and/or urban areas portrayed in literature or other texts?
- What is the relationship between humans and nature? Are humans part of nature or separated from it? How? Why?
- Is nature portrayed as static or a dynamic interaction of interdependent ecosystems?
- Is nature "romanticized" in literature? How? Why?
- What in nature is shown to be valuable? Is nature valued for the sake of human use (anthropocentric) or for its own sake (deep ecology)?
- Is civilization/industrialization portrayed as destructive of nature? How? What can be done?
- In the era of climate change and species extinction, what rights do or should other, nonhuman, forms of life have? What rights do humans have to impact or devastate other life forms?

- What are the issues of power, class inequality, gender, or race in the representation of nature?
- How are local natural environments related to larger and global ecosystems and how are they impacted by climate change?
- How can human beings live more sustainably in relationship to the environment and other species?
- How can depictions of nature help us better understand the causes, impacts, and/or dangers of climate change or motivate action to address climate change?

TEACHING ACTIVITIES FOR FOCUSING ON ENVIRONMENTAL LITERATURE/ECOCRITICAL TEACHING

In *Last Child in the Woods* (2008) Richard Louv describes the joy and wonder, the creative sense of pattern, and the hands-on interaction young people can find in nature. Many of our students may have had their relationship with the natural world undermined by everyday consumption practices (Weintrobe, 2013). Units focused directly on nature and the environment offer an important way to help students understand and address global warming, start "reading green," and appreciate and value the natural world.

For applying ecocritical perspectives, students can respond to canonical pastoral writing by Marlowe, Spenser, Sidney, Milton, Gray, and Pope that emphasizes the appeal of the rural life, care of sheep and other animals, and close connection with the natural world. Some of Shakespeare's frequently taught plays including *As You Like It* and *Midsummer Night's Dream* are influenced by pastoral traditions and portray nature and the "green world" as a place where the artificial urban society is restored by magic or pastoral values.

When Allen's students read the classic pastoral, "The Passionate Shepherd to His Love" (Marlowe, 1599/2011) http://tinyw.in/oRCw, they discussed how the poem constructed class and gender roles, the differences between the real life of shepherds and rural workers in the sixteenth century, and the "beds of roses/and a thousand fragrant posies" in the poem. They then considered the impact on the pastoral and bucolic setting, the poem's "valleys, groves, hills, and fields," of industrialization, urban expansion, and modernization.

In the nineteenth century as factories, machines, and industrialization were becoming more prevalent, Romanticism and Transcendentalism turned to nature and rural life as reflected in poems by Wordsworth, Coleridge, Keats, and Shelley. Their poetry portrayed modern life breaking intimate, sacred bonds with nature. It is not even a stretch to connect Wordsworth's "The World is Too Much With Us" http://tinyw.in/XXDE, the killing of the albatross, the mellow fruitfulness of autumn, or the joy of the skylark to current environmental devastation and the need for a different perspective. Henry David Thoreau's (1854/2016) *Walden*, and his essays "Walking," "Life Without Principle," and "Civil Disobedience," can all be connected to climate change and taking stands to address it (for activities developed by Allen's students on teaching contemporary environmental writers such as Aldo Leopold, Edward Abbey, Annie Dillard, Barry Lopez, Gary Snyder, Jon Krakauer, and Bill McKibben visit the website: http://bit.ly/2btMlxN).

Students could apply ecological and feminist ("ecofeminist") perspectives to different works, for instance the oft taught short stories such as "To Build a Fire," "All Summer in a Day," "The Most Dangerous Game," "The Interlopers," "The Open Boat," or "Eve's Diary," or to classic novels with a significant role for nature and strongly gendered characters such as *Lord of the Flies*, *Huckleberry Finn*, *The Scarlet Letter*, *Wuthering Heights*, even *The Hobbit* and *The Lord of the Rings*.

Advanced students may apply an ecofeminist perspective to Jane Smiley's (2003) Pulitzer Prize novel, *A Thousand Acres: A Novel*. Based on *King Lear*, the owner of an Iowa farm rescinds his inheritance of the farm to one of his three daughters, Ginny, in favor of her two other sisters. Ginny discovers that the farm's soil is contaminated with pollutants from fertilizers and nearby water drainage, related to her family and neighbors' cancer. Ginny's environmental concern about and connection to the land puts her in opposition to farming practices in Iowa in the 1970s based on use of fertilizers and pesticides. Or they could look at *Animal Dreams* by Barbara Kingsolver (2013) which portrays how the mythic narrative of conquering and subduing the American West is associated with a masculine need for control and power while ignoring environmental impacts (Wrebe, 2014).

In an activity in the *Teacher's Guide to American Earth* http://americanearth.loa.org/guide, students are asked to respond to Aldo Leopold's (1949), "Thinking Like a Mountain" from his *A Sand County Almanac*, describing his experience as a young man shooting a wolf and watching it die:

> We reached the old wolf in time to watch a fierce green fire dying in her eyes. I realized then, and have known ever since, that there was something new to me in those eyes— something known only to her and to the mountain. I was young then, and full of trigger itch; I think that because fewer wolves meant more deer, that no wolves would mean hunters' paradise. But after seeing the green fire die, I sensed that neither the wolf nor the mountain agreed with such a view.
>
> Leopold (1949) in McKibben (2008, p. 275)

He realizes that when wolves die, they no longer kill deer, who, as their population grows, eat more plants to upset the ecosystem. He is learning to generalize about how the different components of the ecosystem interact with and influence each other, generalizations essential to determining how perceptions of place are shaped by social, historical, and cultural frames.

From an ecological perspective, students could explore and adopt perspectives of nonhuman participants, as did Instone and Taylor (2015) in adopting the point of view of species living in an Australian valley. Students could critically reflect on how species are housed in zoos as objects of spectacle or represented by studying portrayals of species in children's literature where they are valued for certain human traits rather than as actual beings co-existing with humans (Matthewman, 2011).

4 HUMAN-BASED SYSTEMS IMPACTING CLIMATE CHANGE

Climate change is caused by human activity taking place within specific and interacting social systems including energy production, transportation, agriculture, housing, media, military, and government. To transition away from a carbon-based lifestyle, these systems must all be changed. Why not invite English language arts students into critical and imaginative reflection on how to understand, transition, and redesign our social systems to support a more sustainable world?

Each of these human-based systems impact fragile ecosystems described in Chapter 2 that operate according to a delicate balance in which species interact with each other. E. O. Wilson (2016a) cites the example of the wolf population in Yellowstone National Park. If there are fewer wolves due to hunting or disease, then they are less likely to eat the elks who, if their population expands, then eat the aspen trees, which reduces the number of trees for absorbing carbon dioxide. Other examples have to do with invasive species such as the fire ant, Asian termite, gypsy moth, emerald elm beetle, zebra mussel, Asian carp, snakehead, and mosquitos related to West Nile virus and the rise of the Zika disease. One effect of climate change, as well as globalization, is that these invasive species move from their natural habitats to new habitats, causing damage in those new habitats, for example in the emerald elm beetle moving to different regions and destroying elm trees in those regions.

The extinction of species due to human actions then upsets the balance of ecosystems. In an op-editorial in *The New York Times*, Wilson (2016b) notes that "we can put the fraction of species disappearing each year at upward of a 1,000 times the rate that existed before the coming of humans" (p. 5). From "1895 to 2006, 57 species and distinct geographic races of freshwater fishes were driven to extinction" (p. 5). Saving these species requires increasing areas for preservation from the "current 15 percent of the land and 3 percent of the sea to half of the land and half of the sea" (p. 5). Biologists also focus on the role of species such as invertebrates—sponges, moss animals, and worms—in polar regions who play an important role in filtering water and recycling nutrients, as well as being food for animals and fish (Freiberger, 2013).

There is evidence that people who are able to think in terms of human-based systems are more likely to recognize the risks posed by climate change and support policies to address it (Lezak & Thibodeau, 2016). Engaging students in such analysis fosters career-readiness and prepares young people for leadership as twenty-first-century change-agents.

Noah Zeichner (2015), a tenth grade teacher at Sealth High School in Seattle, teaches about social systems in a way that empowers his students to take action to address climate change:

> While lowering our personal carbon footprints is important, without major systemic change, climate change will only speed up. My students this year understand how fossil fuel companies have put profit over progress. They understand why it is important to have indigenous peoples' voices at the table when climate agreements are drafted. And they understand the role that collective action can play in pressuring world leaders to lower carbon emissions.

While there are many social systems language arts students could examine and address either as a whole class or in groups, we focus here on energy production, military/conflict, housing/transportation, and agriculture. We include language arts teaching ideas with each section.

Energy production. Society needs to find alternative sources to fossil fuels to provide power for buildings, homes, businesses, and transportation. Understanding these alternatives includes research into the risks, benefits, and complications of different approaches (Ingwersen et al., 2014). For example, hydropower generates electricity without fossil fuels, but requires building dams that adversely impact rivers. Converting to alternative energy requires large investments with distant returns (Nemet, Grubler & Kammen, 2015). Without a clear sense that long-term investments will actually result in positive returns, investors and companies may be reluctant to take risks. But how else to meet the 2015 Paris Conference goals of targeted emissions reductions?

The challenge of a large-scale transition to use of clean alternative energy sources has to do with scale and time, given the disruption to current economic dependency on fossil fuels based on our consumption of goods (Smil, 2010; Maly, 2015). From a historical perspective, it takes time for a major transition to move from one energy source to another—liquefied natural gas took 150 years between its discovery in 1852 and its large-scale use. Moving off fossil fuels by

2050 to renewable energy may involve similar delays due to policies, lack of infrastructure, and funding. Continued use of coal and oil during the transition period will have negative effects on climate change (Smil, 2010; Maly, 2015). The other challenge is that wind and solar energy are much more diffuse. More of the Earth's surface is required to produce wind and solar energy than fossil fuel energy, so that without massive energy transmission grids, people in remote areas may have more difficulty obtaining this energy than people in denser urban areas (Smil, 2010; Maly, 2015).

Transitioning involves rethinking systems. Students can explore issues involved in creating a "green economy" using wind, solar, and battery/fuel cell options when the existing power grid is designed for centralized production at large fossil fuel plants. The uncertainty of relying on the marketplace to transform the energy system raises the question of government support through tax credits and subsidies, yet current US government energy subsidies go to large, established companies in the fossil fuel industry (Nemet, Grubler, & Kammen, 2015).

Transition requires not only technological innovation but imagination and commitment at the local level. Students could learn about residents of some 1,000 Transition Towns located in 40 countries that have promoted the use of wind and solar power (Hinrichs, 2014). And they can use language arts skills to advocate for conversion in their communities.

Military/conflict. The US Military budget is greater than the next fourteen countries combined and constitutes about half of the entire world's expenditure. Therefore, it is not surprising that the US Military has been described as, "the planet's single greatest institutional consumer of fossil fuels" (Smith, 2016).

According to military planners, one of the most important challenges in the future will be increasing conflicts emerging from climate change (Department of Defense, 2016). The current war in Syria, for example, arose in part because of high temperatures, droughts, and food shortages. Syrians migrated from farms into cities and in desperation joined the uprising. The civil wars in the Sudan and in Somalia have been tied to climate change. All of these conflicts have produced many climate refugees. Potential conflicts between nuclear powers India and Pakistan over dwindling water supplies, drought in Central America, complex crisis and human insecurity created by storms in Southeast Asia, food shortages and other climate change events all involve conflict.

Students can inquire into the involvement of the military in climate change and ongoing and future world conflicts. As informed citizens they can advocate that rather than spending money on expensive weapon systems, more of the military's budget could be devoted to addressing global warming challenges both at home and abroad, for example: by having the Army Corps of Engineers devise ways to cope with flooding and water access; the Coast Guard address challenges due to flooding, water access, and sea-level rise; or different branches of the armed services participate in humanitarian efforts to supply water and food, support refugees, rebuild, mitigate, and adapt to global warming in other countries. Language arts students can and should be part of imagining and enacting a more cooperative world system.

Housing/community development. Two-thirds of all emissions in the United States come from electricity and road transport in urban regions, with suburban sprawl increasing emissions due to reliance on cars and dispersed electricity needs (Organisation for Economic Co-operation and Development, 2010). Denser urban regions employ less electricity; because Japan's urban areas are around five times denser than Canada's, consumption of electricity per person is about 40 percent less in Japan (OECD, 2010). Use of individual cars in North America, as opposed to mass transit in Europe, means that North American residents produce 50 percent more CO_2 emissions than Europeans (OECD, 2010).

Many communities are moving toward mass transit and are promoting more pedestrian-friendly walking options as well as bike-trails and commuting paths. One study of 170 urban neighborhoods in 20 cities found that walkable neighborhoods tended to have higher priced homes and better schools (Boak, 2016). Students can develop persuasive arguments about the use of private cars drawing on analysis of community organization that fosters dependency on them—roads, buildings, schools, shopping malls, and so on (Shove, Watson, & Spurling, 2015).

Buildings and houses consume as much if not more energy than transportation, thus the transition away from carbon involves energy-efficient buildings and solar energy. Students could study the energy use in their school and homes to identify methods to reduce it. Drawing on Foxfire approaches to community-based inquiry and learning, students can conduct observational research on the social and cultural norms in places supporting sustainability practices (Anderson et al., 2016).

Underlying green, sustainable urban development requires that its residents share a common sense of purpose based on "the betterment of the whole in which they live" (Rose, 2016, p. 23). Jonathan Rose (2016) identifies five characteristics contributing to a more livable, sustainable lifestyle in what he calls "well-tempered cities":

- *Coherence* associated with a shared vision and plan for creating a sense of sustainable development for supporting its residents.
- *Circularity* of information, materials, and energy through use of recycling of limited water, food, or resources.
- *Resilience* to cope with challenges through construction of buildings that employ less energy and creation of green spaces for CO_2 absorption.
- *Community* to create a collective support system for residents based on shared resources.
- *Compassion* associated with caring for others that supports the need for creating a sense of community.

Rose (2016, p. 20–22)

Students could reflect on the degree to which their cities or town share these characteristics related to supporting sustainability. For example, they may note that their city or town lacks any clearly defined plan for supporting use of recycling of resources or building codes giving a lack of sense of community.

Agriculture. Agriculture is a major cause of climate change. For the average American, greenhouse gas emissions from simply eating are about the same as the emissions from energy use! Animal-based foods in particular account for 85 percent of food-related greenhouse gas emissions and 90 percent of all agricultural land use. Shifting diets away from meat could slash in half per capita greenhouse gas emissions and ward off additional deforestation, a major contributor to climate change (Magill, 2016). Industrial agriculture contributes between 20 and 25 percent of all greenhouse gas emissions, particularly through crops grown for animal feed, cattle releasing methane, nitrogen fertilizers releasing nitrogen (also a powerful greenhouse gas), transportation, and uses of biofuel. Students can learn about how their food choices impact climate change at www.eatlowcarbon.org. A powerful classroom resource is the film *Cowspiracy* (Anderson & Kuhn, 2014) which challenges environmental organizations to address animal agriculture. Available on Netflix, or for $5 at http://cowspiracy.com; there is a 15-minute short version available here: http://tinyurl.com/jqsjad8.

Agriculture will also be one of the areas most immediately and directly damaged by climate change. Droughts, increased temperatures, flooding, and ocean acidification, all caused by climate change, are expected to dramatically reduce food production, at the same time that demand is increasing due to expanding world population and changing diets. Food shortages are one of the most troubling aspects of global warming. The use of nitrogen fertilizers to increase short-term soil productivity to grow food for an increasing population, results in increased emissions from both fertilizers and transportation, and an agriculture system that differs markedly from that of the Holocene period (Williams et al., 2016).

Agriculture and human diets are critical areas of transition and invite language arts student inquiry. Allen recently taught an introductory literature course on food (syllabus: www.Allen Webb.net/engl1100spring2014food.html). Students examined fast food and healthy eating, the corporatization of the food system, working in the food industry, food justice, and climate change. They read *Dinner With Trimalchio* (from a Roman novel about the excesses of the ancient super rich), *A Modest Proposal*, *The Jungle* (and visited a meat-packing plant), selections from *I, Rigoberta Menchu* (Menchu, 2010) (about migrant farm workers in Guatemala), *And the Earth Did Not Devour Him* (Rivera, 1987) (about Mexican-American migrant farm workers), *The Hunger Games*, and, in literature circles, various classic and young adult novels with food themes. Students wrote personal essays about their relationship with food, literary analysis papers, undertook food action projects, and created TED talks. In teaching this class, Allen joined a movement in English studies to address food and culture.

Lina Yamashita teaches about food in her undergraduate class at UC Davis, "Making Visible the People Who Feed Us: Labor in the Food System."

The farm-to-fork system has a variety of environmental impacts and depends on the labor of people who produce, process, distribute, sell, and serve food. In the United States, food workers constitute one-sixth of the workforce and contribute over $2.2 trillion in goods and services annually (Yamashita & Robinson, 2016). Most existing food education programs, such as school gardens or farm-to-school programs, do not focus on the people behind food or on the social inequities that shape their experiences (Yamashita & Robinson, 2016). I taught my course to make noticeable and humanize food workers, particularly those who tend to be less seen, through multicultural texts about or by workers that highlight their diverse experiences.

I used an activity called "4 corners." Each corner stands for a stance—strongly agree, agree, disagree, and strongly disagree—and students move to one of these corners for a given statement, such as "tipping should be abolished" or "we should all become vegetarians or vegans." Before having students walk to the corners that represented their stances, they write a sentence or two to support each stance, drawing on evidence from reading or their prior knowledge. I encouraged students to respond directly to one another. Ultimately, students recognized the existence of diverse perspectives and learned to engage in evidence-based debates.

SIZE AND STEPS TOWARD ADDRESSING CLIMATE CHANGE

Climate change is a major, daunting issue. It emerges out of historical, cultural, and social contexts that call out for inquiry, careful thought, and response. This chapter provides many ways language arts teachers can develop meaningful curriculum to address the contexts of climate change.

Our students inherit and will live their lives in a climate changed world. They deserve to understand their world deeply and meaningfully, to consider large social and cultural values, ethical questions, and ways we can transform how we now live in order to save life on Earth. The subject of climate change, and our students themselves, are worthy of the time you spend transitioning your teaching.

The best way to respond to big challenges is by taking small steps, steadily, in the same direction. The last chapter set out first steps. This chapter gave ideas about how and where to keep walking. The next chapter takes another step in climate change teaching, drawing on literature and the power of the imagination.

For additional resources, activities, and readings related to this chapter, go to http://tinyw. in/4hQO on the book's website.

REFERENCES

Achebe, C. (1958). *Things fall apart.* Portsmouth, NH: Heinemann.

Adams, C. J., & Gruen, L. (Eds.) (2014). *Ecofeminism: Feminist intersections with other animals and the Earth.* New York: Bloomsbury Academic.

Agho, K., Stevens, G., Taylor, M., Barr, M., & Raphael B. (2010). Population risk perceptions of global warming in Australia. *Environmental Research, 110*(8), 756–763.

Al-Koni, I. (2002). *The bleeding of the stone.* Northampton, MA: Interlink Publishing.

Anderson, K., & Kuhn, K. (Directors) (2014). *Cowspiracy* [Motion picture]. USA: A.U.M. Films.

Anderson, M. T. (2010). *Feed.* Somerville, MA: Candlewick Press.

Anderson, V., Datta, R., Dyck, S., & Kayira, J. (2016). Meanings and implications of culture in sustainability education research. *The Journal of Environment Education, 47*(1), 1–16.

Appleman, D. (2014). *Critical encounters in secondary English: Teaching literary theory to adolescents.* New York: Teachers College Press.

Ayre, J. (2015, March 8). With "true cost" of emissions factored in, gasoline would cost $3.80/gallon MORE than the pump price [Web log post]. Retrieved from http://tinyw.in/k6c0.

Bigelow, B., Kelly, A., & McKenna, K. (2015). Bringing climate into the classroom: Inside a teaching retreat around Naomi Klein's *This Changes Everything. Radical Teachers, 102,* 34–42. Retrieved from http://radicalteacher.library.pitt.edu.

Boak, J. (2016, January 27). Few US neighbourhoods affordable, walkable with good schools [Web log post]. Retrieved from http://tinyw.in/aDrJ.

Buell, L. (2005). *The future of environmental criticism: Environmental crisis and literary imagination.* Cambridge, MA: Blackwell.

Cameron, J. (Director) (2009). *Avatar* [Motion picture]. United States: Twentieth Century Fox.

Chancel, I., & Piketty, T. (2015). *Carbon and inequality: From Kyoto to Paris.* Paris School of Economics.

Crane, S. (1894/1966). *New York City sketches.* New York: New York University Press.

Davis, R. H. (1861). Life in the Iron Mills. *The Atlantic, 7*(4), pp. 430–461.

Department of Defense (2016). *DoD Directive 4715.21 Climate change adaptation and resilience.* Retrieved from www.dtic.mil/whs/directives/corres/pdf/471521p.pdf.

Dorris, M. (2008). *Morning girl.* New York: Paw Prints.

Elster, J., (Ed.) (1986). *Karl Marx: A reader.* Cambridge: Cambridge University Press.

Fox, L., & Priggen, E. (Directors) (2007). *The story of stuff* [Video file]. Retrieved from http://storyofstuff.org/movies/story-of-stuff/.

Freiberger, M. (2013). Biodiversity on the brink. + *Plus Magazine.* Retrieved from http://tinyw.in/UmoA.

Garrard, G. (2010). Problems and prospects in ecocritical pedagogy. *Environmental Education Research*, *16*(2), 233–245.

Garrard, G. (2015). Ecofeminism and climate change. *Women's Studies International Forum*, *49*, 20–33.

Hall, S. (2015, October 15). Exxon knew about climate change almost 40 years ago [Web log post]. Retrieved from http://tinyw.in/OgE0

Hinrichs, C. C. (2014). Transitions to sustainability: a change in thinking about food systems change? *Agriculture Human Values*, *31*, 143–155.

Hogan, L. (1991). *Mean spirit*. New York: Ballantine Books.

Howell, E. (2015). How long have humans been on Earth? *Universe Today*. Retrieved from http://wp.me/p1CHIY-9UV.

Huxley, A. (2014). *Brave new world*. New York: Harper Perennial.

Ingwersen, W. W., Garmestani, A. S., Gonzalez, M. A., & Templeton, J. J. (2014). A systems perspective on responses to climate change. *Clean Technology Environmental Policy*, *16*, 719–730.

Instone, L., & Taylor, A. (2015). Thinking about inheritance through the figure of the Anthropocene, from the Antipodes and in the presence of others. *Environmental Humanities*, *7*, 133–150.

Iovino, S., & Oppermann, S. (Eds.) (2014). *Material ecocriticism*. Bloomington: Indiana University Press.

Jeffers, S. (1991). *Brother eagle, sister sky*. New York: Penguin Books.

Kincheloe, J. L., McKinley, E., Lim, M., & Barton, A. C. (2006). Forum: A conversation on "sense of place" in science learning. *Cultural Studies of Science Education*, *1*, 143–160.

Kingsolver, B. (2013). *Animal dreams*. New York: Harper Perennial.

Klein, N. (2015). *This changes everything: Capitalism vs. the climate*. New York: Simon & Schuster.

LeGuin, U. (2010). *The word for world is forest*. New York: Tor Books.

Leopold, A. (1949). *A Sand County almanac*. New York: Oxford University Press.

Lettero, C. (2010). Spray glue goes, maggots stay. In K. D. Moore & M. P. Nelson (Eds.), *Moral ground: Ethical action for a planet in peril* (pp. 103–107). San Antonio, TX: Trinity University Press.

Lezak, S. P., & Thibodeau, P. H. (2016). Systems thinking and environmental concern. *Journal of Environmental Psychology*, *46*, 143–153.

Louv, R. (2008). *Last child in the woods*. Chapel Hill, NC: Algonquin Books.

Magill, B. (2016). Studies show link between red meat and climate change. *Climate Central*. Retrived from: www.climatecentral.org/news/studies-link-red-meat-and-climate-change-20264.

Maly, T. (2015). A brief history of human energy use. *The Atlantic*. Retrieved from http://tinyw.in/QPWJ.

Marlowe, C. (1599/2011). *The passionate shepherd to his love*. Charleston, SC: Nabu Press.

Marx, K., & Engels, F. (1848). *The Communist manifesto*. London: Workers' Educational Association.

Matthewman, S. (2011). *Teaching secondary English as if the planet matters*. New York: Routledge.

Matulis, B., & Moyer, J. (2016). Beyond inclusive conservation: The value of pluralism, the need for agonism, and the case for social instrumentalism. *Conservation Letters*.

Mayer, J. (2016). *Dark money: The hidden history of the billionaires behind the rise of the radical right*. New York: Doubleday.

McKibben, B. (2001). The comforting whirlwind: God and the environmental crisis. Sermon.

McKibben, B. (2008). *Teacher's guide to American Earth*. New York: Library of America.

Menchu, R. (2010). *I, Rigoberta Menchu*. New York: Verso.

Momaday, N. S. (1976). *Way to Rainy Mountain*. Albuquerque, NM: University of New Mexico Press.

Moore, J. M. (Ed.) (2016). *Anthropocene or capitalocene? Nature, history, and the crisis of capitalism*. Oakland, CA: PM Press.

Moore, K. D., & Nelson, M. P. (Eds.) (2010). *Moral ground: Ethical action for a planet in peril*. San Antonio, TX: Trinity University Press.

Nemet, G. F., Grubler, A., & Kammen, D. M. (2015). Countercyclical energy and climate policy for the U.S. *Wiley Interdisciplinary Reviews: Climate Change*, *7*(1), 5–12.

Nixon, R. (2011). *Slow violence and the environmentalism of the poor*. Boston: Harvard University Press.

Organisation for Economic Co-operation and Development (2010). Cities and climate change. Paris: OECD Publishing. http://dx.doi.org/10.1787/9789264091375-en.

Oxfam (2014, January 20). Rigged rules mean economic growth increasingly "winner takes all" for rich elites all over world [Web log post]. Retrieved from www.oxfam.org/en/node/4451.

Phillips, M., & Rumens, N. (Eds.) (2016). *Contemporary perspectives on ecofeminism*. New York: Routledge.

Piketty, T. (2014). *Capitalism in the 21st century*. New York: Belnap Press.

Rivera, T. (1987). *And the Earth did not devour him*. Houston, TX: Arte Publico.

Roberts, J. T., & Parks, B. (2006). *A climate of injustice global inequality, north–south politics, and climate policy*. Cambridge, MA: MIT Press.

Rose, J. F. P. (2016). *The well-tempered city: What modern science, ancient civilizations, and human nature teach us about the future of urban life*. New York: Harper Wave.

Salehi, S., Nejad, Z. P., Mahmoudi, H., & Knierim, A. (2015). Gender, responsible citizenship and global climate change. *Women's Studies International Forum, 50*, 30–36.

Scannell, L., & Gifford, R. (2013). Personally relevant climate change: The role of place attachment and local versus global message framing in engagement. *Environment and Behavior, 45*(1), 60–85.

Shiva, V. (2014). *Ecofeminism*. New York: Zed Books.

Shove, E., Watson, M., & Spurling, N. (2015). Conceptualizing connections: Energy demand, infrastructures and social practices. *European Journal of Social Theory, 18*(3), 274–287.

Smil, V. (2010). *Energy transitions: History, requirements, prospects*. Santa Barbara, CA: Praeger.

Smiley, J. (2003). *A thousand acres: A novel*. New York: Anchor.

Smith, G. (2016, January 18). The Pentagon's hidden contribution to climate change [Web log post]. Retrieved from http://tinyw.in/VZI1.

Stiglitz, J. E. (2013). *The price of inequality: How today's divided society endangers our future*. New York: W. W. Norton.

Thoreau, H. D. (1854/2016). *Walden*. New York: Macmillan.

Vakoc, D. A. (Ed.) (2014). *Feminist ecocriticism: Environment, women, and literature*. Lanham, MD: Lexington Books.

Wallis, V. (1993). *Two old women*. Kenmore, WA: Epicenter Press.

Weintrobe, S. (Ed.) (2013). *Engaging with climate change: Psychoanalytic and interdisciplinary perspectives*. New York: Routledge.

Westerfeld, S. (2004). *So yesterday*. New York: Penguin.

Westerfeld, S. (2006). *Pretties*. New York: Simon Pulse.

Westerfeld, S. (2008). *Uglies*. New York: Simon Pulse.

Williams, M., Zalasiewicz, J., Waters, C. N., Edgeworth, M., Bennett, C., Barnosky, A. D., Ellis, E. C., Ellis, M. A., Cearreta, A. H., Peter, K., Ivar do Sul, J. A., Leinfelder, R., McNeill, J. R., Odada, E., Oreskes, N., Revkin, A., Richter, D., deB; Steffen, W., Summerhayes, C., Syvitski, J. P., Vidas, D., Wagreich, M., Wing, S. L., Wolfe, A. P., & Zhisheng, An. (2016). The Anthropocene: A conspicuous stratigraphical signal of anthropogenic changes in production and consumption across the biosphere. *Earth's Future, 4*(3), 34–53.

Wilson, E. O. (2016a). *Half-Earth: Our planet's fight for life*. New York: W. W. Norton.

Wilson, E. O. (2016b). The global solution to extinction. *The New York Times, Review*, p. 5. Retrieved from http://tinyw.in/qWEe.

Wrebe, T. (2014). Barbara Kingsolver's Animal Dreams: Ecofeminist subversion of Western myths. In D. A. Vakoc (Ed.), *Feminist ecocriticism: Environment, women, and literature* (p. 39–64). Lanham, MD: Lexington Books.

Yamashita, L., & Robinson, D. (2016). Making visible the people who feed us: Educating for critical food literacy through multicultural texts. *Journal of Agriculture, Food Systems, and Community Development, 6*(2), 269–282.

Yolen, J. (1996). *Encounter*. New York: Voyager.

Zeichner, N. (2015, December 13). Paris: How I have changed the way I teach about climate [Web log post]. Retrieved from http://tinyw.in/etbL.

Zinn, H. (2015). *A people's history of the United States*. New York: Harper Perennial.

Chapter 4
Literature and the Cli-Fi Imagination

In a world permeated by insidious, yet unseen or imperceptible violence, imaginative writing can help make the unapparent appear, making it accessible and tangible by humanizing drawn-out threats inaccessible to the immediate senses.

Rob Nixon (2011, p. 13)

Fiction is how we organize our knowledge into plots that suggest how to behave in the real world. We decide what to do based on the stories we tell ourselves, so we very much need to be telling stories about our responses to climate change and the associated massive problems bearing down on us and our descendants.

Kim Stanley Robinson (Milkoreit, Martinez, & Eschrich, 2016, p. xi)

What will happen to the Earth and to human beings in a future shaped by global warming? Scientists are typically very careful about making specific predictions about future events, and, both by attitude and training, they rarely speculate on how changes in the natural environment will impact human societies. This is where fiction writers, knowledgeable about climate research, make an enormous contribution.

English teachers know about the power of literature and the imagination. This chapter shows you how to harness that power to address the topic of climate change.

CLIMATE CHANGE (CLI-FI) LITERATURE

A new kind of literature has emerged called "climate fiction" or "cli-fi" (like "sci-fi") that portrays the *human* experiences of coping with climate change. Cli-fi has been called the "hottest new literary genre" (Stankorb, 2016). Familiarity with cli-fi provides resources and ideas for teaching our students about climate change, fostering their imagination, and encouraging them to take action. As we shall see in this chapter, cli-fi also offers interesting ideas for changing the way we might teach almost any literary work.

Literature provides readers vicarious experiences as they imaginatively perceive the thoughts and actions of characters. Narratives create scenarios in the storyworld for coping with issues, challenges, and conflicts, and engaging in actions. Literature brings the reader in on an emotional level to shape and develop beliefs and attitudes.

Cli-fi literature fosters imagination about future climate change effects that might, one day, actually take place and/or it shows us future worlds that help us better understand our own.

Climate fiction foregrounds the impacts of climate change on individuals and societies in ways that are meaningful to readers. It supplements factual/scientific information to create richer and more balanced understanding of the future. Through climate fiction, readers can see multiple natural and human systems interacting and consider the consequences. For example, it can help students think carefully about capitalism and consumerism. Manjana Milkoreit (2016) explains:

> Cli-fi places the reader in plausible, emotionally wrought, complex situations in which social, technological, and natural systems condition one's experience. All of a sudden, climate change becomes viscerally more "real" than it appears in a scientific discourse. With this deeper, more intuitive understanding, different kinds of questions can be asked, for example, concerning a community's coping mechanisms in periods of disruptive change, or the ability of the international system to maintain its functionality if and when globalization goes into reverse.
>
> Milkoreit (2016, p. 179)

Milkoreit argues that climate fiction fosters "complex systems thinking" as readers imaginatively participate with characters in complex situations (p. 188).

Cli-fi is an engaging literature for the classroom. As we saw in Chapter 2, the students in Allen's class found that climate change short stories allowed them to identify with characters and imaginatively place themselves into a world different from their own, a world where the consequences of climate change could be experienced in the present. Cli-fi short stories made the issue personal, led to writing, research, and critical inquiry—and stimulated a sense of urgency.

Climate fiction can help students to think ecologically, to better understand the complex and dynamic relationship between organisms and their environment, and to care about their relationship to nature. It can be combined with more traditional nature writing. Any work of climate change fiction is ripe for student inquiry and research: are the "predictions" real possibilities? Teachers know that young people enjoy research which lets them question/challenge the books they are reading; we recommend such questions be explored with any cli-fi work. If and when students discover, by their own investigation, that seemingly fictional events are, in fact, based on probable scientific knowledge, then they are more likely to take seriously acting soon to avoid a projected dystopic future (Beach, 2015).

As you are teaching cli-fi now and in the future, there are and will be, disturbing global warming occurrences taking place. Alas, you can count on changing weather patterns, increasing heat, droughts, fires, extreme storms and rain, floods, melting ice, rising sea levels, species extinction, human migration, national and international political debate and conflict, and an increasing sense of crisis taking place while you are teaching. In this sense, cli-fi literature is relevant right now. Students can bring in information about current events in the world and talk about them in the context of the cli-fi they are reading in their ELA classes.

Climate fiction can provide a vehicle for students to think about climate justice. Cli-fi typically illustrates global warming's unequal effects, that certain populations are more vulnerable, and that economic and social inequality shapes events and outcomes. Frequently in cli-fi, the people who experience the consequences of climate change are not the same people who brought it about or failed to address it. Milkoreit points out that cli-fi fosters "exploring values and ethical dimensions of climate change" (p. 188) and lets students imagine characters' underlying, conflicted values and ethical perspectives. Cli-fi typically, in some dimension, takes on a global perspective and thus helps us discuss the responsibility of wealthy countries—whose wealth was accrued through burning carbon—to developing nations that have not established extravagant carbon-based lifestyles. Some cli-fi can help students better understand indigenous or postcolonial perspectives. These questions of climate justice are important to explore in English language arts.

Cli-fi emphasizes the dangerous consequences of ignorance, denial, and inaction. Cli-fi clarifies that something needs to be done now, in the present, to forestall what might happen in the future. It typically shows characters engaging in future adaptation and mitigation efforts, thus providing examples, models, and a sense of urgency for how society can address climate change (Whiteley, Chiang, & Einsiedel, 2016).

Cli-fi "involves the ways in which people imagine their collective social life, 'how they fit together with others, how things go on between them and their fellows, the expectations that are normally met, and the deeper normative notions and images that underlie these expectations (Taylor, 2002, p. 106)'" (Whiteley, Chiang, & Einsiedel, 2016, p. 30).

Cli-fi creates opportunities for important discussion about questions such as: What is the role of government in addressing climate change? What cultural or social habits do we now need to stop/control to preserve the planet? What can individuals or groups do to bring about a different future from that portrayed in climate fiction?

Research on the impact of environmental literature suggests that cli-fi also can make a difference. A large-scale analysis of 7,379 people sought to determine the degree to which reading three books on the environment, *Walden* (Thoreau, 1854/2016), *A Sand County Almanac* (Leopold, 1949/1986), and *Silent Spring* (Carson, 1962) influenced their willingness to engage in certain environmental behaviors (Mobley, Vagias, & DeWard, 2010). The results indicated that reading one or more of these texts did predict increased awareness and propensity to take action, even when participants' general attitudes were factored into the analysis.

The cli-fi author, Kim Stanley Robinson (2015) describes the value of cli-fi literature in changing perspectives:

> Reading fiction is a very powerful experience. So I believe that if it's done right it can change one's view. You come back to reality and you have a kind of double vision. You have your normal daily vision and then you have your science-fiction vision, the future, interposed on it or behind it, so you get a kind of 3D in time. And it helps you to make decisions about what do I do today to help the situation for my grandchildren. So the science-fiction double vision, the temporal 3D, the 4D vision is really a useful tool for figuring out what to do now. It's a philosophical tool.

While cli-fi literature can portray a bleak future for our planet, it ideally will also give readers a sense of hope for the future. As Ursula Kluwick (2014) notes, "The greatest challenge for climate change stories is how to transport the message that climate change is inevitable and already happening without crippling our power to imagine a future worth changing for" (p. 510).

CLI-FI IN A TIME OF CONSTRAINED RESOURCES

This chapter introduces you to many climate change works appropriate for the wide range of today's secondary students. We know it is often difficult to purchase new materials and fit them into already crowded curricula.

We begin with ideas about how to bring cli-fi perspectives to the literary works you are already teaching, thus repurposing texts in your curriculum to address issues of climate change. Next, we describe using picture books where only one copy, read aloud and perhaps projected with a document camera, can easily be integrated into most curriculum. From picture books we move to cli-fi poetry, short stories, and film—all easy to bring to your teaching. Next, we describe young adult literature, then novels. Lastly we draw your attention to climate testimony, sobering real-world accounts of climate change events already taking place.

You can include longer works described in this chapter in ways that minimize expense and maximize student understanding and motivation. Choice reading or reading workshops can be focused on climate change—since students typically draw from school or classroom libraries this approach is also economical. Literature circles (Daniels, 2002), where a class is divided into groups that choose books and discuss them over several class periods can include library books, or, for the price of one set of class texts, a teacher can obtain smaller sets of several different works.

With either choice reading or literature circles, students can report back via "book talks" to the class, or share video responses or recommendations using tools such as Flipgrid https://info.flipgrid.com or VoiceThread https://voicethread.com about what they have read and how their work portrays climate change. Students with diverse abilities and interests reading different texts on the same theme can share ideas and participate in common discussions. Informational text, film, and common reads of shorter works can be combined with choice reading to provide additional basis for inquiry, writing, and action taking.

Since cli-fi is a new literary field engaging a vital topic, there is a case to be made that libraries and school administrations should support purchasing these texts. Climate fiction is a potential focus for grant appeals to local or national groups, Gofundme, or other fundraising efforts. Proposing interdisciplinary study with science or social studies may also generate administrative support and resources.

BRINGING THE CLI-FI IMAGINATION TO YOUR EXISTING LITERATURE CURRICULUM

Many works we already teach have explicit climate change themes. Emerging from the 1930s Dust Bowl, *The Grapes of Wrath* (Steinbeck, 2004) is certainly a novel about the effects of climate change, destruction of agriculture, forced migration, and the struggle to reconstruct society. Nature literature from Wordsworth to *Hatchet*, from *Walden* to *Dune*, already addresses the human relationship with the environment and can be the basis for climate change research, discussion, and writing. Post-apocalyptic *Lord of the Flies* describes a loss of civil discourse and collaboration leading to the destruction of nature and burning up the island. Even classics have potential climate change themes. As mentioned earlier, *Frankenstein* (Shelley, 2003) is a study of how human's use of science can go out of control. One theme of Shakespeare's play *Macbeth* is how human behavior breaks the great chain of being impacting the natural world. Links could be made with human-caused climate change in our own day. *The Tempest* is about a human-orchestrated natural event (the storm) that disorients, upends, and reconstructs the social order. Voltaire's (1991) *Candide* can provide an excellent opportunity for thinking about how the optimistic perspective that all is for the best in this best of all possible worlds, perhaps because of a benign God or universe, profoundly and dangerously ignores what is happening with climate change.

How else might an English class bring the topic of climate change to traditional literature?

One of the most interesting books about teaching literature is Rob Pope's (1994) *Textual Intervention: Critical and Creative Strategies for Literary Studies*. Pope describes a strategy of textual intervention where students creatively "intervene" in class texts they are reading to make changes, changes that often end up illuminating aspects of the texts or society. Students might "intervene" by writing letters between characters, writing from the perspective of marginal characters, adding a missing scene, changing the gender of a character, changing the location or time period—and then discussing and writing about how their "intervention" helps them see the original text or the society it portrays differently. This kind of intervention is all the easier in the age of digital texts as classic works found in online literary archives can easily be cut and pasted into student word processing programs (Rozema & Webb, 2008). Of course, texts do not need to be digitized for students to come up with creative interventions.

We believe textual intervention is a powerful tool to allow teachers to bring the cli-fi imagination and climate change inquiry to all kinds of texts already in the curriculum. After learning about climate change from research, short essays, or documentaries, students can then intervene in traditional works. Intervention can take the form of actually rewriting or adding to an existing text, or writing ideas about how that text might be changed. Students can work individually or in groups to come up with ideas and to discuss and debate different interventions.

Students can take commonly taught texts and intervene in them by setting them in the future, a future where climate change is evident. Or they could anachronistically bring climate change to the past to explore characters' thoughts, reactions, and strategies.

Climate change fiction sometimes involves climate change events happening while characters, at least at first, are not taking adequate action to avert them. Students could intervene in works by inserting various climate change events and explore characters' thoughts as they react, or fail to react. As Huck and Jim move down the river they come upon Pap's house floating along, broken loose by a flood. Students could intervene by imagining and writing up increasing evidence of floods and climate change, and characters like The Duke and the King, Tom Sawyer, Aunt Sally, the Widow Douglass, or even Pap, could be explored/contrasted for their reactions. Holden Caulfield could learn about climate change and be frustrated with other characters in his world that hold what he considers superficial attitudes about it, perhaps until finally he and Phoebe decide to take some action. *Their Eyes Were Watching God* (Hurston, 1998) might trace a series of increasingly dramatic and realistic (to our present) climate change events impacting Janie's life in Central and Southern Florida, including her stay in the Everglades.

Climate change fiction often looks at the events of climate change and how they impact different people or groups. Students reading *Of Mice and Men* (Steinbeck, 1993) can focus on how climate change might impact farm workers like George and Lenny. Climate change events could start happening in *Animal Farm* (Orwell, 2013) with different consequences for different animals (some are more equal than others). Who knows, maybe the pigs would insist on their privileges at any cost or maybe they could join together with other farm animals to demand changes in the agricultural system that would address causes of climate change. *The Outsiders* (Hinton, 1967/2006) might be set in a distant future climate dystopia where the greasers and the socs are competing over depleted resources.

Cli-fi can also portray groups of characters banding together to do something about climate change. They could intervene in texts to explore characters acting in this way. The younger generation in *Romeo and Juliet* might come together to try to alert the adults about pending ecological disaster. Macbeth's crime could be failing to address climate change and Banquo, Macduff, and other thanes might unite to force action. Students reading *To Kill a Mockingbird* (Lee, 1988) could write or imagine future chapters where Atticus, with the help of Scout, Jem, and Dill, anxious about their future, takes on environmental legal cases or advocates for laws to address climate change against powerful people with entrenched ideas. Or students reading *Fahrenheit 451* (Bradbury, 2012) could introduce climate change events and perhaps have Montag, Clarisse, and/or Granger attempt to educate and organize other characters like Mildred and Captain Beatty about dangers and harms of climate change by creatively using some of the new technologies or form a renegade group determined to draw their society's attention to it.

Randall Seltz, Jordan High School, Sandy, Utah:

> Movies often take a story and change elements of the setting to make it more relevant or interesting to contemporary audiences. What if students reimagined different canonical texts set in an environment that has been ravaged by climate change? Reimagining *Lord of the Flies* on an island that is sinking or on fire changes how the boys would interact, possibly causing them to unite despite their differences. What if *A Midsummer Night's Dream* didn't have a forest to take place in because it had been mowed down to make things we threw away?

The possibilities for using intervention strategies to link climate change with existing literary works are clearly limited only by the imagination. Students engaging in this kind of literary study would find themselves adopting interesting and fresh perspectives on the source literary works and could discuss and write about what their interventions taught them about the original characters, societies, and settings. They would have engaging reasons for doing various kinds of specific climate change research related to the interventions they were developing. Their intervention might generate lots of creative possibilities and ideas they could play and experiment with that would require careful thinking and important imaginative work about climate change, social reactions, and what needs to be done in our present world.

PICTURE BOOKS

While some consider picture books appropriate only in the primary grades, we suggest that choice picture books can be fabulous tools for engaging students at all levels, even university. A high-quality picture book is one in which thought-provoking images and a few well-chosen words tell a meaningful story visually and with language that stimulates the imagination. Picture books offer the advantage that they can be read out loud to an entire class in just a few minutes or they can be read closely. Their brevity and aesthetic power make them ideal for encouraging personal connections and generating meaningful discussions about complex issues.

The following are a handful of examples of picture books that address environmental topics through combining fantasy, cli-fi, environmental history, indigenous oral tradition, and biography. Dr. Seuss' (1999) classic book, *The Lorax,* describes deforestation in a personal and passionate way. Since deforestation is one of the main causes of climate change, students can read *The Lorax* to open an investigation of the global deforestation crisis, the role of trees as carbon dioxide "sinks," the effects of climate stress on forests, and the impacts of over-consumption and corporate greed. Another starting point to address deforestation and species loss is Lynne Cherry's (2010) *The Great Kapok Tree*, focused on the Amazon. Cherry's (1992) *A River Ran Wild* explores the history of a river transformed by ensuing groups of humans, from Native Americans to colonial settlers, industrialists, and eventually young twenty-first-century environmentalists. It is a story that adopts an indigenous perspective and is a hopeful starting point for researching the impact of humans on a given location over time as well as efforts to reverse environmental destruction.

In *Just A Dream*, Chris Van Allsburg (1990) takes the audience on a flying bed to a dystopian future of environmental catastrophes. Combined with study of climate change, it would be a great mentor text for students writing their own cli-fi children's book. In *Brother Eagle, Sister*

Sky, Susan Jeffers' (1991) paintings accompany an adaptation of a speech by Chief Seattle from the 1850s that poetically delivers an indigenous perspective about humans' relationship to the natural world. A true story of courage and resistance from Africa, Jeanette Winter (2008) describes the life of Nobel Peace Prize recipient Wangari Maathai in *Wangari's Trees of Peace.* *Please Don't Paint Our Planet Pink* by Gregg Kleiner (2014) tells a story about what would happen if CO_2 were colored pink and people could actually see the gas that is causing climate change; it teaches about the carbon cycle as well as carpooling and community.

POETRY AND CLIMATE CHANGE

As we described in Chapter 3, there is a long history of poets responding to nature that teachers can draw on to teach ecocritically. While poets tend not to write "cli-fi," there are poets that write specifically about global warming and its impacts. Four poems to recommend are "Global Warming" by Jane Hirshfield (we include it at the end of Chapter 1), "Hurry Up Please It's Time" by John Powell Ward, "One World Down the Drain" by Simon Rae, and "The State of the Planet" by Robert Haas. All of these can be found online and used in English classes.

There are terrific poetic resources addressing global warming from authors of color. One is "Trees" by the prolific and eccentric rapper Keith Kool, aka Dr. Octopus. This rap takes an alternative approach to the usual story of climate change, starting with the loss of trees, having African American children as scientists acting to address the problem; showing connections between nature destruction, deforestation, white "civilization" or domination; cars behaving like cows; older people uncaring; and so on. Students love to talk about it; the music video of the rap is here: http://tinyurl.com/ls3se35. Lyrics are here: http://tinyurl.com/zz2k77j. Richard Williams aka Prince Ea is another rapper and spoken word artist whose work has much to tell all of us about climate change. You can find his inspiring slam poems "Dear Future Generations: Sorry" at http://tinyurl.com/oruj7ob and "Man vs Earth" at http://tinyurl.com/za3c2og.

One option for shifting the focus from only the individual experience of nature to a concern with the effects of climate change is for students to adopt the perspective of the nonhuman species or objects being affected by climate change. Based on his visit to the Arctic and experiencing the melting of glaciers, poet Nick Drake (2012):

> realized that parts of the nonhuman world could also talk back from their perspectives: I could find voices for creatures and elements as well as people; they also have stories, they have life stories, they have stories of love and survival and tragedy [fostering an] awareness of what we've done and awareness that we are the people who've changed nature, which is a phrase that, I gather, the Inuit say about us.
>
> Drake (2012, p. 74)

This led to his writing poems for his *The Farewell Glacier* poetry collection (Drake, 2012) that adopts the perspective of the Arctic ice itself:

> The idea is that ice, at least ancient ice, is like an enormous library of all the winters that have ever happened on the planet. Each winter is a page in a book in the library, and it contains the story of that year: it contains what was in the atmosphere, it contains secrets and wonders.
>
> Drake (2012, p. 84)

In the following excerpt, "I Am a Long Story," from *The Farewell Glacier*, the ice itself becomes the speaker of the poem describing how it holds a history of stories:

I am a long story,
Ten thousand feet long,
A hundred thousand years old,
A chronicle of lost time,
Back to the first dark,
Too dark for telling;
I am every winter's fall;
I am the keeper of the air
Of all the vanished summers;
I honour the shadows of sorrows
That come to lie
Between my pages;
I distil lost atmospheres
Pressed into ghosts
Kept close to my cold heart.
And as for you—
What story would you like to hear?
On your two feet, tracking the snow
Two by two, two by two, two by two;
Here is the dust and music
Of your brief cities;
Here is the ash and smoke;
Here are your traffic jams
And vapour trails;
Here are your holidays in the sun
And your masterpieces
And your pop songs.
Here are your first cries
And last whispers;
Here are your long sighs
Of disappointment.
Here is where it went right,
And where it went wrong.
Easy come. Easy go.

Students could also respond to poets' dramatic descriptions of events similar to those produced by climate change. For example, they could respond to a Gary Snyder (2003) poem, "Mid-August at Sourdough Mountain Lookout," told from the perspective of a firefighter viewing the results of a deliberately set forest fire, as portrayed in these initial lines: "Down valley a smoke haze/Three days heat, after five days rain/Pitch glows on the fir-cones/Across rocks and meadows/Swarms of new flies" (p. 3). A classic poem like Wordsworth's "The World is Too Much With Us" (1807) can help students use their imaginations to think beyond the "getting and spending" related to climate change.

CLI-FI SHORT STORIES

Cli-fi short stories are a terrific way to teach about global warming. In Chapter 2 we have described teaching four stories from two different collections, *I'm With the Bears* (Martin, 2011) and *Winds of Change* (Woodbury, 2015). These stories and others have been made available to teachers, as explained in Chapter 2.

There are other excellent short story resources. We recommend *Everything Change: An Anthology of Climate Fiction* edited by Milkoreit, Martinez, and Eschrich (2016), a collection that includes many stories with teenage protagonists or characters. These diverse stories are set in locations around the world including North America, England, Venice, China, Malaysia, and Madagascar. The stories would be useful stimuli for student research into climate change effects in other countries. One story, "The Grandchild Paradox," explores the perspective of teens in a drowning world angry at the older generation for not stopping climate change, leading to important discussion in today's classrooms. A story that raises questions about the political fallout from climate change is "Into the Storm," about a coup d'etat in Canada over the failure to address climate change. A story in this collection that young people would enjoy is "LOSD and Fount"— told from the point of view of an artificially intelligent robot about the last man on an island shrinking due to rising sea levels. This story can inspire creative writing about climate change from unusual perspectives. The collection includes a fine foreword and a good interview by/with two leading climate fiction writers, Kim Stanley Robinson and Paolo Bacigalupi. It is available in full text for free at http://climateimagination.asu.edu/everything-change.

The collection *Drowned Worlds: Tales from the Anthropocene and Beyond* (Strahan, 2016) has imaginative stories from well-known authors about impacts of sea-level rise. *Under the Weather: Stories about Climate Change* (Bradman, 2012) is written for upper elementary and middle-school students and focuses on stories of young people who are making a difference in their communities.

CLI-FI FILM

Film has the ability, perhaps beyond any other form, to transport us into other worlds. Every year there are more and more films portraying a climate-impacted future. Whether viewed by a whole class, by student groups, or individually, many are engaging starting points to imagine and research the future implications of global warming as described by Allen's students.

The Day After Tomorrow (Emmerich, 2004) is the iconic Hollywood cli-fi thriller. Scientists ignored unseasonable weather and dramatic storms; global warming leads to ice shelf collapse, sudden ocean cooling, collapse of ocean currents, superstorm, arctic conditions in North America, surviving Americans fleeing to Mexico. While popular, at the time, the film's portrayal of science was ridiculed. It is ridiculed no more. James Hansen, the world's leading climate scientist, and a team of others, published a paper "Ice Melt, Sea Level Rise, and Superstorms" in March of 2016 that describes possible events not so distant from those in the film. Students can listen to a 15-minute video of Hansen explaining the implications of his research in lay terms http://tinyurl.com/h5ae22b. Kaitlin suggests students research the question, "What are the worst storms that have affected the world? Explain the damage that was inflicted."

Chloe and Theo (Sands, 2015) tells the contemporary story of an Inuit from the Arctic who travels to New York City where he teams up with a homeless teenager (Dakota Johnson) to tell leaders about the dangers of global warming. Jessica says, "This movie is relatively short, and would be a great resource for teachers looking to discuss climate change in their classrooms but are tired of using statistics and raw data."

In *Age of Stupid* (Armstrong, 2009) climate change is explored from the perspective of one of the last humans alive in the year 2055. This unusual film uses video clips of news shows, interviews, and documentary footage to show the escalation of climate change. Maddie says the film is appropriate for all ages above a seventh-grade level.

Interstellar (Nolan, 2014) is set in a future where Earth is increasingly uninhabitable due to an increase in population and temperature. Space exploration becomes an option to save the human species. Brandon suggests students do extensive research on the climate change events throughout the movie, proving them possible or impossible.

Odyssey 2050 (Bermejo, 2012) is an animated film that would appeal to middle-school students. Aliens visiting Earth in the future are shocked to see that humans have devastated their planet. Tom believes, this film is "about getting the youth involved in the climate change movement."

Snowpiercer (Bong, 2013) is set in a post-apocalyptic future where geoengineering attempts to stall global warming have resulted in an ice age. A violent struggle for survival takes place on a train that circles the world. Angelo says, the film mocks complacency about climate change and "presents the consequences of altering the climate by extreme measures" (rated R).

Take Shelter (Nichols, 2011) is about a man who becomes obsessed by a fear of a coming storm. Cece says, "*Take Shelter* can be seen as an allegory for climate change. Curtis is constantly warning the people around him and no one listens to him or believes him; however by the end of the story when the disaster arrives people finally see it for what it is, but it's too late" (rated R).

Resources to support English teachers using the films discussed above are available at: http://ourplaceinnature.wikispaces.com/Cli-Fi+Film. For a list of movies from 2004 to 2017: http://tinyw.in/dRsR) (for films organized by topics: http://tinyw.in/igy3. More titles can be found on this book's website: http://tinyurl.com/glflxg2.

YOUNG ADULT CLI-FI LITERATURE

Young adult cli-fi portrays adolescent characters coping with climate change and typically taking action in inspiring ways. Given ecofeminist concerns about how studies of climate change often ignore the disproportionate impacts on women, it is significant that most of the protagonists in the following novels are female.

The super popular books in the young adult series *The Hunger Games* (Collins, 2008) and *The Uglies* (Westerfeld, 2006) draw on a narrative of climate change to establish their story lines. *The Hunger Games* portrays,

> the history of Panem, the country that rose up out of the ashes of a place that was once called North America. He lists the disasters, the droughts, the storms, the fires, the encroaching seas that swallowed up so much of the land, the brutal war for what little sustenance remained. The result was Panem, a shining Capitol ringed by thirteen districts, which brought peace and prosperity to its citizens.
>
> Collins, (2008, p. 18)

Teachers can help students reading these works to connect understanding climate change to the future realities the novels depict by researching claims about climate change impacts (tying the focus on food in *The Hunger Games* to climate change is described in Chapter 3). In both series we find a stark contrast between heroines and heroes who authentically care about others, and a mass of privileged, superficial, and effectively brainwashed people who accept the status quo. These books invite readers to imagine themselves understanding complex realities, adopting communal values, and taking stances to fight for others and a just social order—just what young people need to begin to address climate change today.

Another climate change young adult novel is *The Carbon Diaries, 2015* (Lloyd, 2015). 16-year-old Laura keeps a diary about living with the United Kingdom's mandatory carbon rationing. Climate events cause blackouts, water shortages, and the flooding of London from storm surge and higher sea levels. In responding to this novel, students could examine their own carbon footprint and the possible impacts of carbon rationing, or imagine daily life in their own locations in a future world similar to that portrayed in the novel.

In the young adult novel, *Love in the Time of Global Warming* (Block, 2013), the main character Penelope undertakes a quest with three companions, with allusions to Homer's *The Odyssey*, to find her family after much of Los Angeles has been destroyed by an earthquake and tidal wave. Students could contrast other quest/adventure narratives and movies with Penelope's struggles.

In *Exodus* (Bertagna, 2008) the inhabitants of Wing, a small island community in the North Atlantic Ocean, can no longer hold back the rising seas. Fifteen-year-old Mara discovers another floating city and leads members of the island to find a new home. The novel addresses deforestation and sea-level rise; based on comparisons to actual examples.

Ship Breaker (Bacigalupi, 2010) portrays a world where society has stratified, fossil fuels have been consumed, and the seas have risen and drowned coastal cities. The main character, a 17-year-old boy, scavenges beached tankers for scrap metals on the Gulf Coast. He saves a girl from a crashed tanker and attempts to reunite her with her wealthy, industrialist father who makes money by refining tar that generates large quantities of greenhouse gases.

Several YA novels focus on the very real danger of drought in a climate-impacted future. *Memory of Water* (Itaranta, 2014) portrays a young girl, Noria, who assumes the role as guardian of a secret fresh water supply for her village, which, when the secret is revealed, is then challenged by the military and local wealthy people, resulting in conflicts. *Water Wars* (Stracher, 2011) is a fast-paced novel set in a time when the ice caps have melted, rivers dried up, and water is controlled by a small elite. *Birthmarked* (O'Brian, 2014) is set in an enclave on the shores of Lake Superior, whose water has been drained by pipelines carrying it to areas in drought from climate change.

A couple more YA titles Allen's students enjoyed include *Nature's Confession* (Morin, 2014), a tale of two teens trying to save a warming planet, and *White Horse Trick* (Thompson, 2010) set in Ireland and combining magic and fantasy with drastic climate-induced storms and rainfall.

CLI-FI NOVELS

The novel is the preeminent form of climate fiction. The extended treatment of the impacts of climate change in the novel allows students to go deep into imaginative inquiry about what our future may hold—and emphasizes the importance of taking action in the present. Many cli-fi novels are long; some have mature content that may make it difficult to assign as a text to the whole class. Here we describe a number of novels which Allen's students have reviewed, that could work in high schools, most likely at the junior or senior level. Certainly, more cli-fi novels are soon to be written.

Cli-fi novels can be set in the near term, creating an emphasis on imminent climate impacts and choices that people today are making to address, or not address, climate change. Or, cli-fi novels may be set in the more distant future that emphasize the implications of climate inaction. Some cli-fi is a subgenre of highly popular post-apocalyptic fiction.

Many cli-fi texts describe forced migration due to rising sea levels or intolerably high temperatures and involve conflicts over lack of safety, food, and water. They often portray failed states or an authoritarian world in which characters have lost their basic rights and therefore must fight for resources controlled by governments and corporations whose push for economic growth and urbanization has resulted in environmental destruction (Pirzadeh, 2015).

In *Odds Against Tomorrow* (Rich, 2013), a young mathematician working in Manhattan believes that he can calculate worst-case scenarios for future ecological risks allowing corporations to avoid responsibility. However, when Manhattan is flooded due to rising sea levels and a storm surge, he finds that even the remote countryside is not a safe haven. Eventually he manages to live in a wrecked urban neighborhood and develop a different set of values.

In *The Rapture* (Jensen, 2009), heat and freak weather patterns in England influence a psychologist's work with a deeply troubled teenager able to predict future events. In a suspenseful race against time, climate scientists attempt to tell the world about a predicted apocalyptic eruption of methane hydrates caused by corporate seabed fracking. Allen's student Brandon believes, "This novel is great for getting students interested in climate change."

In Robinson's The Capital Trilogy: *Forty Signs of Rain* (2004), *Fifty Degrees Below* (2005), and *Sixty Days and Counting* (2007), scientists at the National Science Foundation, the President, and a Senate staffer seek to formulate climate change policies when storms and sea rise are impacting daily life in Washington, DC.

In Margaret Atwood's (2013) world of the *MaddAddam* trilogy, characters are coping with epidemics and floods; corporations control humans through genetics and corruption. The first novel *Oryx and Crake* (Atwood, 2004) portrays a warming post-apocalyptic world where traditional humans have been destroyed by a genetically engineered plague. The novel questions the values of corporations that use science without concern for the consequential effects on humans.

Barbara Kingsolver's (2013) *Flight Behavior* features a young wife and mother on a failing farm in rural Tennessee who encounters an incredible kaleidoscope (swarm) of Monarch butterflies. Her discovery engages religious leaders, environmentalists, and climate scientists—and changes her world. Allen's student Jessica, "would definitely recommend this book to anyone looking for a sophisticated, well-written piece of literature."

In *The Water Knife* (Bacigalupi, 2015), the entire Southwest region of the United States is coping with drought, leading to graphic violence and conflicts over access to the Colorado River. The main characters struggle to stop a corporate conspiracy from eliminating water rights for Phoenix.

In *The Admiral* (Gilbert, 2014), the majority of the planet is covered in water leaving only small bodies of land and desolation. In this adventure novel, Allen's student Angelo says that Gilbert "clearly advocates for wind power."

Another cli-fi adventure novel is *Arctic Drift* (Cussler, 2009), full of narrow escapes and running fights against trained hit-men and hired thugs in a struggle over opening up the Arctic to mining. Allen's student Lucas says that Cussler "not only discusses many factual causes and concerns about global warming, but also [tells] a tale that is packed full of suspense and adventure."

In *Arctic Rising* (Bucknell, 2012), countries are attempting to claim the oil and dump waste under the newly accessible Arctic oceans. The Gaia Corporation is attempting to reduce warming through use of sunshade mirrors to redirect sunbeams back into space, while other corporations and governments are attempting to stop the Gaia Corporation's project. While Allen's student Blair points out that the novel contains profanity and adult themes, it "does a good job addressing climate change and would be a good resource for class discussion."

Polar City Red (Laughter, 2012) is a short novel about a family that flees northward to a secret sanctuary city above the Arctic Circle. Allen's student Cece says, "*Polar City Red* brings to light the moral and physical challenges brought on by climate change."

The Sea and the Summer (Turner, 2013) is set in Australia in 2044. Characters struggle against climate change which has impacted all aspects of their life. Allen's student Rebecca describes the book as "focused on income inequality and distinctions between social classes . . . and an all-powerful government."

Ultimatum (Glass, 2009) is set in America in 2032 when sea-level rise is happening much faster than expected. The novel explores tensions and United States' negotiations with China to reduce emissions. Allen's student Shane says the book would appeal to students interested in politics.

The short dystopian work, as much essay as novel, *The Collapse of Western Civilization: A View from the Future* (Oreskes & Conway, 2014), is narrated by a senior Chinese historian in the year 2393 recounting the failures of humans to take decisive action during the decades leading up to the Great Collapse of 2093. That year witnesses the final melting of the West Antarctic Ice Sheet leading to mass migrations and wars, particularly in North/South America and Europe, and the collapse of most Western governments. Because China had actually done a better job preparing for climate change, it remains relatively stable. Students could discuss governmental, business, and community inaction and resistance to change from politicians, businesses, and community organizations.

(For a list of other recommended cli-fi novels see http://tinyw.in/zvbD.)

BEYOND CLI-FI: TODAY'S TESTIMONIALS

Cli-fi helps us imagine the future impacts of climate change. But climate change is already happening and the stories, images, and testimonials of the survivors of storms, flooding, drought, fires, and heat waves are powerful texts for teaching about the present and the future.

Testimonial accounts of climate-change-related events are often mis-presented as stories of "natural disasters." In our Anthropocene era, students need to come to see that these so-called "natural" disasters are significantly the result of *human-caused* global warming. George Marshall (2015) interviewed survivors of the 2011 Bastrop fire in Texas and 2012 Hurricane Sandy in New Jersey—both events consistent with the expected impacts of climate change—and found that while survivors wanted to share stories of pride in their communities' response, they did not want to talk about or even acknowledge climate change. Yet, our teaching needs to help our students recognize the relationship of global warming and climate-related disasters.

A powerful narrative of climate disaster and the necessity to address climate change is the testimony of Yeb Sano, Filipino representative at the 2013 UN climate talks speaking while Typhoon Haiyan was ravaging his hometown (the entire 17-minute speech is at https://vimeo.com/79117298, a written version at http://tinyurl.com/jp4n3ls, and the 7-minute version Allen shows his students at http://tinyurl.com/hnol24x).

The graphic novel *Zeitoun* (2010) by Dave Eggers is a true story about a Muslim family living in New Orleans during Hurricane Katrina. Allen's student Clara points out that, the book is "a jumping off point to further address the effect climate change has on social unrest and inequality."

Right to be Cold (2016) is a compelling memoir showing how climate change is disproportionately affecting the Arctic and what a courageous Inuit woman, Sheila Watt-Cloutier, is trying to do about it. The author was nominated for the Nobel Peace Prize. A climate change memoir about an upper middle class person learning to reduce her carbon footprint is *The Big Swim* by Carrie Saxifrage (2015). *When Glaciers Slept: Being Human in a Time of Climate Change* (Jackson,

2015) tells a story from a young man's life both about the loss of his parents and about climate change challenges and solutions.

Following the news about so-called "natural" disasters provides troubling stories, images, and videos that illuminate human-caused global warming and fit right in with the study of climate fiction.

MAGICAL THINKING

In this chapter we describe both a young adult and an adult cli-fi novel written by prize-winning author Paolo Bacigalupi. In an interview Bacigalupi talks about different information, both scientific and human, that inspires him to write. He adds, "And then you also have this other piece of data that says our leadership is completely disengaged, that they are engaged in magical thinking" (Milkoreit, 2016, p. 215). Bacigalupi's observation raises a question for us: who is more engaged in "magical thinking," the authors of cli-fi who are exploring imagined future worlds impacted by climate change, or many of our current political leaders who deny that climate change is even happening?

When it comes to magical thinking, recent climate engineering ideas also come to mind. Some people think that since humans have employed technological advances to address problems in the past, there may also be a technological fix for climate change. But the geoengineering approaches that have been put forward are fantastical, and, frankly, highly dangerous. Mann and Toles (2016) (http://tinyw.in/8SsL) describe:

- placing trillions of small mirrors into the atmosphere to reflect away sunlight;
- shooting reflective sulfate particulars into the stratosphere to mimic how volcanic eruptions cool the Earth;
- fertilizing the oceans with iron dust to create algae or "phytoplankton" to absorb more CO_2;
- creating synthetic trees to absorb CO_2 at the cost of $500.00 for each ton of carbon.

And if these truths aren't stranger than fiction, Mann and Toles note that, of course, this kind of geoengineering would be absurdly expensive, carbon intensive, and likely cause still greater problems. For example, adding sulfate particulars to the stratosphere will increase the amount of acid rain and alter the ozone hole, and fertilizing the oceans with iron dust can enhance growth of harmful algae blooms responsible for dead ocean zones. As a result:

> The proposed cure could well be worse than the disease. Indeed, it could prove fatal. Although the threat the planet is facing is huge in scale, its cause is profoundly simple: an unhealthy dose of carbon dioxide. The simplest and safest solution is to address the problem at its root cause.
>
> Mann & Toles (2016, p. 129)

These kind of geoengineering solutions to climate change are, in fact, a form of "science-based" denial: we don't have to change our ways now, we can wait for science to save us.

So there is an urgent need for teaching that does away with magical thinking, and for the truths that cli-fi has to tell about how we need to change our world in the present. Climate fiction can make the not yet real become believable. It can help our students develop their imaginations so that they will be able to bridge the gap between knowledge and beliefs described by Slavoj Žižek, "we *know* the (ecological) catastrophe is possible, probable even, yet we do not believe it will really happen" (Žižek, 2011, p. 328).

In the next chapter, we describe activities for writing about climate change, for ways you can foster your students' voices and the truths they have to tell about what is and will really happen, both through fact-based argument and imaginative creative writing.

For additional resources, activities, and readings related to this chapter, go to http://tinyw. in/YjZG on the book's website.

REFERENCES

Armstrong, F. (Director). (2009). *Age of stupid* [Motion picture]. United Kingdom: Spanner Films.

Atwood, M. (2004). *Oryx and Crake*. New York: Anchor Press.

Atwood, M. (2013). *MaddAddam*. New York: Anchor Press.

Bacigalupi, P. (2010). *Ship breaker*. Boston: Little, Brown and Company.

Bacigalupi, P. (2015). *The water knife: A novel*. New York: Alfred A. Knopf.

Beach, R. (2015). Commentary: Imagining a future for the planet through literature, writing, images, and drama. *Journal of Adolescent & Adult Literacy, 59*(1), 7–13.

Bermejo, D. (Director). (2012). *Odyssey 2050*. [Motion picture]. Costa Rica: Synchro Films.

Bertagna, J. (2008). *Exodus*. New York: Walkers Children.

Block, F. L. (2013). *Love in the time of global warming*. New York: Holt/Ottaviano.

Bong, J. (Director). (2013). *Snowpiercer*. [Motion picture]. South Korea: Moho Film.

Bradbury, R. (2012). *Fahrenheit 451*. New York: Simon & Schuster.

Bradman, T. (2012). *Under the weather: Stories about climate change*. New York: Frances Lincoln Children's Books.

Bucknell, T. (2012). *Arctic rising*. New York: Tor.

Carson, R. (1962). *Silent Spring*. New York: Houghton Mifflin.

Cherry, L. (1992). *A river ran wild*. San Diego, CA: Harcourt Brace & Company.

Cherry, L. (2010). *The great kapok tree*. New York: HMN Books for Young Readers.

Collins, S. (2008). *The hunger games*. New York: Scholastic Press.

Cussler, C. (2009). *Arctic drift*. New York: Berkley Books.

Daniels, H. (2002). *Literature circles: Voice and choice in book clubs & reading groups*. Portland, ME: Stenhouse Publishers.

Drake, N. (2012). *The farewell glacier*. Hexham, UK: Bloodaxe Books Ltd.

Eggers, D. (2010). *Zeitoun*. New York: Vintage.

Emmerich, R. (Director). (2004). *The day after tomorrow* [Motion picture]. USA: Twentieth Century Fox.

Gilbert, J. (2014). *The admiral*. New York: Christopher Matthews.

Glass, M. (2009). *Ultimatum*. New York: Grove.

Hinton, S. E. (1967/2006). *The outsiders*. New York: Penguin.

Hurston, N. Z. (1998). *Their eyes were watching God*. New York: Perennial.

Itaranta, E. (2014). *Memory of water*. New York: HarperCollins.

Jackson, M. (2015). *When glaciers slept*. Brattleboro, VT: Green Writers Press.

Jeffers, S. (1991). *Brother eagle, sister sky*. New York: Penguin Books.

Jensen, L. (2009). *The rapture*. New York: Doubleday.

Kingsolver, B. (2013). *Flight behavior*. New York: Harper Perennial.

Kleiner, G. (2014). *Please don't paint our planet pink*. New York: Cloudburst Creative.

Kluwick, U. (2014). Talking about climate change: The ecological crisis and narrative form. In G. Garrard (Ed.), *The Oxford handbook of ecocriticism* (pp. 502–516). New York: Oxford University Press.

Laughter, J. (2012). *Polar city red*. Denton, TX: Deadly Niche Press.

Lee, H. (1988). *To kill a mockingbird*. New York: Warner Books.

Leopold, A. (1949/1986). *A sand country almanac*. New York: Ballantine.

Lloyd, S. (2015). *The carbon diaries, 2015*. New York: Holiday House.

Mann, M. E., & Toles, T. (2016). *The madhouse effect: How climate change denial is threatening our planet, destroying our politics, and driving us crazy*. New York: Columbia University Press.

Marshall, G. (2015). *Don't even think about it: Why our brains are wired to ignore climate change*. New York: Bloomsbury.

Martin, M. (Ed.) (2011). *I'm with the bears: Short stories from a damaged planet*. New York: Verso.

Milkoreit, M. (2016). The promise of climate fiction: Imagination, storytelling, and the politics of the future. In P. Wapner & H. Elver (Eds.), *Reimagining climate change* (pp. 171–191). New York: Routledge.

Milkoreit, M., Martinez, M., & Eschrich, J. (Eds.) (2016). *Everything change: An anthology of climate change fiction.* Tempe: Arizona State University Press.

Mobley, C., Vagias, W. M., & DeWard, S. L. (2010). Exploring additional determinants of environmentally responsible behavior: The influence of environmental literature and environmental attitudes. *Environment and Behavior, 42*(4), 420–447.

Morin, J. (2014). *Nature's confession.* Boston: Harvard Square Editions.

Nichols, J. (Director). (2011). *Take shelter* [Motion picture]. USA: Sony Pictures.

Nixon, R. (2011). *Slow violence and the environmentalism of the poor.* Boston: Harvard University Press.

Nolan, C. (Director). (2014). *Interstellar* [Motion picture]. USA: Paramount.

O'Brian, C. (2014). *Birthmarked.* New York: Roaring Book Press.

Oreskes, N. & Conway, E. M. (2014). *The collapse of Western civilization: A view from the future.* New York: Columbia University Press.

Orwell, G. (2013). *Animal farm.* New York: Houghton Mifflin Harcourt.

Pope, R. (1994). *Textual intervention: Critical and creative strategies for literary studies.* New York: Routledge.

Pirzadeh, S. (2015). Children of ravaged worlds: Exploring environmentalism in Paolo Bacigalupi's *Ship Breaker* and Cameron Stracher's *The Water Wars. Interdisciplinary Studies in Literature and Environment, 22*(2), 203–221. doi:10.1093/isle/isu143

Rich, N. (2013). *Odds against tomorrow: A novel.* New York: Farrar, Straus and Giroux.

Robinson, K. S. (2004). *Forty signs of rain.* New York: Random House.

Robinson, K. S. (2005). *Fifty degrees below.* New York: Random House.

Robinson, K. S. (2007). *Sixty days and counting.* New York: Random House.

Robinson, K. S. (2015, February 15). Cli-Fi 2015 Audio podcast. Retrieved from http://tinyw.in/rYpm.

Rozema, R., & Webb, A. (2008). *Literature and the web.* Portsmouth, NH: Heinemann.

Sands, E. (Director). (2015). *Chloe and Theo* [Motion picture]. USA: Arctica Films.

Saxifrage, C. (2015). *The big swim.* Gabriola Island, BC: New Society Publications.

Seuss, Dr. (1999). *The lorax.* New York: Random House.

Shelley, M. (2003). *Frankenstein.* New York: Barnes and Noble.

Snyder, G. (2003). Mid-August at Sourdough Mountain lookout. In G. Snyder, *Riprap and Cold Mountain poems* (p. 3). Berkeley, CA: Counterpoint Press.

Stankorb, S. (2016). Climate fiction or "cli-fi" is the hottest new literary genre. *The Daily Good.* Retrieved from www.good.is/articles/climate-fiction-cli-fi-genre.

Steinbeck, J. (1993). *Of mice and men.* New York: Penguin.

Steinbeck, J. (2004). *The grapes of wrath.* New York: Penguin.

Stracher, C. (2011). *The water wars.* New York: Sourcebooks Fire.

Strahan, J. (Ed.) (2016). *Drowned worlds: Tales from the anthropocene and beyond.* London: Solaris.

Taylor, C. (2002). Modern social imaginaries. *Public Culture, 14,* 91–124.

Thompson, K. (2010). *White horse trick.* New York: Harper Collins.

Thoreau, H. D. (1854/2016). *Walden.* New York: Macmillan.

Turner, G. (2013). *The sea and the summer.* London: Gollancz.

Van Allsburg, C. (1990). *Just a dream.* New York: Houghton Mifflin Harcourt.

Voltaire (1991). *Candide.* New York: Dover Press.

Watt-Cloutier, S. (2016). *Right to be cold.* Toronto: Penguin Canada.

Westerfeld, S. (2006). *Uglies.* New York: Simon & Schuster.

Whiteley, A., Chiang, A., & Einsiedel, E. (2016). Climate change imaginaries? Examining expectation narratives in cli-fi novels. *Bulletin of Science, Technology & Society,* 1–10. doi: 10.1177/0270467615622845

Winter, J. (2008). *Wangari's trees of peace: A true story from Africa.* San Diego, CA: Harcourt Brace & Company.

Woodbury, M. (Ed.) (2015). *Winds of change: Short stories about our climate.* Coquitlam, British Columbia, Canada: Moon Willow Press.

Wordsworth, W. (1807). *Poems in two volumes.* London: Longman.

Žižek, S. (2010). *Living in the end times.* New York: Verso.

Chapter 5
Writing about Climate Change

Ours was a time when most forms of art and literature were drawn into the modes of concealment that prevented people from recognizing the realities of their plight? Quite possibly, then, this era, which so congratulates itself on its self-awareness, will come to be known as the time of the Great Derangement.

Amitav Ghosh (2016, p. 25)

A word after a word after a word is power.

Margaret Atwood (Nischik, 2000, p. 253)

In this chapter we examine writing, and the teaching of writing, as a way of inquiring into climate change. Rather than viewing writing simply as a vehicle to convey something already known, we consider writing a process of learning, a journey into feelings, ideas and knowledge, an exploration of meaningful questions. Certainly there are many genres for many audiences. We offer examples that are personal and expressive as well as argumentative. We believe that in this time of desperate need for awareness and action to save the Earth, all writing about global warming has a potentially public and persuasive dimension. Whether a highly personal reflection or a civic manifesto, writing about climate change calls out for audiences beyond the teacher.

This chapter is divided into three main sections that sometimes connect and overlap: place-based writing, creative writing, and persuasive writing. The writing activities we describe can be stand-alone units, elements of a writing workshop, or woven into literature or content curriculum such as already described in Chapters 2–4. These activities can be the basis for single assignments or a scope and sequence for an entire semester or year. While we give examples from middle school to high school to college, almost every example can be adapted for the grade level you teach. We describe writing about climate change consistent with the Common Core writing standards. We point to the importance of attention to genre, detail, and audience. Conventions, revision, and assessment are important to us as well, and critical to teaching writing, but they are not the focus of this chapter. There are many resources that convey best practices in the teaching of writing and we urge you to draw on them. Here our focus is on the urgent matter of meaningful ways to write about climate change.

GETTING READY

Writing offers many ways to inquire into climate change, and much of what students need to research and learn about global warming can take place as part of their engagement in any one or series of writing activities. Climate change is an important topic potentially meaningful at both personal and social levels. When students generate questions because they are engaged in an activity that matters to them, they are more likely to be genuinely curious and to undertake research for information relevant to their need. Once students are intrinsically motivated, it's important to support the development of their questions, create time for their research, and help them investigate with care and curiosity.

Depending on your situation, you may want students to read about climate change before starting the writing process. In Chapter 2, we discussed various ways for beginning this exploration using short stories, essays, chapters, books, documentaries, and images. In Chapter 4, we pointed to a wide variety of literary and reality-based texts. To better understand climate change, students can read from informational essays, websites, news articles, speeches, and books. Students need to learn to investigate their questions, to sort through search results and identify reliable sources and well-written models. A couple of examples: the site http://tetw.org/Climate_Change points to well-known climate change essays; an extensive list of nonfiction books for middle-school students can be found at http://tinyw.in/Kd5b.

PLACE-BASED WRITING

Place-based writing invites students to write about their observations, personal connections, and reflections on and about specific places (Beach, 2014). Elliot Jacobs (2011) describes place-based writing as writing with "reverence," writing as a "witness," recognizing the Earth as "holy." He sees place-based writing as important to developing connections with nature and making efforts to conserve places and communities we love (p. 52). With place-based writing, students are constructing their identity based in part on their relationship with their environment. That environment is not always "natural:"

"I identify strongly with the Bronx. It is the best place for what I like to do . . . For me, the Bronx is community gardens, the Bronx River and my friends" (Kudryavtsev, Stedman, & Krasny, 2012, p. 231).

Place-based writing can take a variety of forms and genres. lisa eddy, the high-school teacher who described Aldo Leopold's "Land Ethic" in Chapter 1, writes about a summer environmental writing course she taught for college students:

I worked for the Summer Institute for the Arts and Sciences (for gifted students) at Adrian College. It was a land-based camp that included investigation and restoration of a local Nature Conservancy site (Ives Road Fen) and I offered a writing course called "Earth-Centered Writing." Writers composed individual pieces of writing to be read and/or to be performed; a collaborative, performance piece for the end-of-camp talent show; and a literary magazine for an audience of camp participants, parents, and community members.

In writing a play about her neighborhood in Kings Cross, Australia, Bronwyn Davies describes her sensual experience, inviting

the reader to listen, not only to new possible meanings, but also to the sounds of the words, their rhythms, their poetry—to take pleasure in it, and also feel its pain. I wanted readers to feel their flesh prick, or their eyes water, as they entered the place called the Cross.

Somerville et al. (2011, p. 34)

To create her place-based text:

> Whenever I can, I participate. I talk. I listen. I walk through. I sit. I observe. I find the words to bring these folds to life in my body/my writing. I dwell on the times I have been in the Cross in the past; memories stretching back fifty years; intense passionate memories; my own search for lost time.
>
> Somerville et al. (2011. p. 35)

One essential component of place-based writing is the use of concrete descriptive details, something students acquire from reading writers' effective use of descriptive language. For example, in reading the following passage from Sandra Steingraber's (2010) description of fracking in her upstate New York town contained in an anthology of writing about energy (Slovic, Bishop, & Lyndgaard, 2015), students can note her use of specific, detailed descriptions:

> For this method, a drill bores down and then turns sideways. Explosives are detonated along the horizontal pipe, shattering the shale bedrock above and below. A pressurized slurry of water, sand, and chemicals goes down next. The water forces open the shattered rock, the sand grains keep it open, and the chemicals inhibit corrosion, kill algae, and reduce friction so that the released gas can flow up the pipe. Some of the water and chemicals forced into the fractured shale flows back up. And some of the water and chemicals—40 to 85 percent—stays in the ground. A single fracking operation requires drill rigs, a compressor station, a network of pipelines, an access road, 2 to 8 million gallons of fresh water, 10 to 30 tons of chemicals, and about 1,000 tanker truckloads of water and toxic waste. About 4,000 wells are envisioned for my county alone (np).

Place-based writing can also take on critical perspectives and address social change and transition. Teaching in Detroit, David Seitz talks about place-based, genre-focused writing that involves critical analysis of his students' urban community; his students:

> choose to interview their grandparents about the losses of a viable, walkable downtown life; their parents about the relationship of their workplaces to their home communities; people with institutional roles in the town, such as teachers, coaches, or ministers, about the local effects of demographic shifts. . . .
>
> Seitz (2014, p. 253)

A powerful aspect of place-based writing is that it develops passion and understanding of nature, something that can occur in rural, urban, and social "places."

There are many different ways to use place-based writing to inquire into climate change. Allen had his students do paired writings about a specific place. First they wrote about observations in the present day, then about how that place might change over the next 50 years based on what they knew about climate change. Brandon Loiselle wrote the assignment as a series of journal entries about a piece of land his family owns in Northern Michigan, a spot he had known since childhood. For each journal entry, he cited a specific date and season. He used descriptive details that convey how much he cared about the location and he wrote in sort of perpetual present tense that suggested continuity with the past,

> There is still snow on the ground, from the snowfall this afternoon. Although the land appears abandoned, I am able to make out signs of life . . . Little paw prints in the melting snow, squirrels running about, birds singing as they fly above. In the water, the geese rest peacefully. The trees revealing evidence of a new beginning. The water only to be disturbed by the occasional gust of wind, stirring and sending ripples across the surface. If you look closely, you can see the reflection in the water, mirroring its surroundings.

In his imaginative journal from 50 years in the future, he wrote,

I haven't seen a hint of snow in months. The trees in this area are dying . . . The lake's edge has receded and is now just a mucky eye sore. There are no longer squirrels running about and there are no longer birds flying above.

Allen's student, Thomas White, wrote about a park near where he currently lives and a trip he took there with a friend to play catch. Thomas' piece is more descriptive than narrative (although some storytelling could enrich this kind of writing). Unlike Brandon, he did not give his writing a specific date, though it also appears to take place in early spring (the time of year when the students were completing the assignment). He wrote,

The trees are still bare but bring brown and black to the color spectrum that draws my eyes. The sun shines bright with its goldish brilliance, warming the atmosphere. The sky is baby blue with streaks of white from the clouds that preside. The previous day the color pallet changed completely as the sky turned grey and all that can be seen is white from the day's snow.

In his description of the future of this park he noted,

With the current world temperature rising, the seasons might change . . . There could be little to no snow . . . some of the species of animals other than birds might die off . . . The grass might die out because drought might occur more often . . . Stronger storms might destroy some of the vegetation, like trees in the park that are home to many different animals . . . humans might no longer use the park.

After engaging in this type of writing, Brandon and Thomas reflect together about the writing process. We find their comments insightful:

This project truly connects the person with his/her surroundings. As the student begins to describe our earth they will realize how delicate the earth actually is. The student is able to . . . experience climate change on a deeper, more personal level. It is an interesting way of writing and getting to know more about climate change because it can be done over a period of time, where changes might be seen.

A variation of this assignment that Allen's students experimented with is writing not from their personal perspective but from the perspective of an animal or plant. This assignment fosters students' use of their imagination to think more deeply about the impact of global warming on other species. This is an important focus given that we are in the period of Earth's Sixth Great Extinction, and the first human-caused, where 140,000 species are now going extinct every year. One of Allen's students, Lucas Wilkins, took a particularly creative approach to the assignment. He wrote from the perspective of the Loch Ness Monster, a creature, he explained, who "witnessed with the dinosaurs and others before them." Lucas' Monster takes the long view:

Do not be saddened at the thought of your race and all its so called accomplishments being erased from history, for we will not forget and you will live on in our stories. Our young will be told of your once large cities and mysterious contraptions that belched out poisons and hurled the earth towards the brink of destruction. They will learn how you ignored the warning signs and gave no regard for the well being of the earth. All of this and more they will be taught and you can be certain you will not be forgotten as you have forgotten us.

Lucas writes from the future to communicate back to the present. He invokes a tragic tone to spur the present day audience to action.

An interesting example of place-based writing was developed by the National Park Service to foster Glacier National Park visitors' concern about the effects of climate change (Barrett & Mowen, 2014). Visitors engaged in a "Goodbye to Glaciers" program by creating poems or songs based on a plot diagram of exposition ("How glaciers carved the landscape of Glacier National Park"), rising action ("How climate is changing on a global scale and is being accelerated by human processes climax"), falling action ("Playing our part: What we can do to reduce our impact on the planet"), climax: ("Focusing on the impacts of climate change at Glacier National Park"), and resolution ("Summarize the content of the program by singing 'I am a Glacier,' or poetically reciting the lyrics.") (Barrett & Mowen, 2014). Visitors said that they enjoyed participating in the project, 69 percent indicating that their participation helped them recognize the impact of climate change.

The use of images can serve to foster attention to specific details in writing about place. Participants on the WalkMyWorld http://walkmy.world site draw on images of specific places to create concrete written descriptions of those places evoked by the images. The National Museum of Wildlife Art provides resources and magnificent artwork at the museum in Jackson Hole, Wyoming and online www.wildlifeart.org. As part of a project working with Yup'ik students in Alaska, Lauren McClanahan (2010) asked students to take photos of evidence of the effects of climate change. Students then used these photos to write about the effects of climate change in order to create digital recordings for use in a soundtrack for a video about their local place.

Students can write about urban, suburban, and rural spaces and issues of sustainability. Students examined how suburban culture is created by popular culture/media representations of products and practices associated with suburban life (Hothem, 2009). This included a focus on the automobile as a popular cultural expression of mobility, status, individuality, and convenience that ignores sustainability and emissions, congestion, and diminution of walking and use of mass transit. Students also examined maps and aerial photos of suburban sprawl to identify how in suburbia the location of roads, strip malls, and schools create dependency on cars.

With climate change in mind, students can investigate the relation of their local place to carbon extraction and energy use. Where does their electricity come from? What kind of CO_2 releases and other pollutants are involved? Who suffers the consequences? What alternatives are possible? Often people do not even know about energy sources in their communities. People living near the Kalamazoo River in SW Michigan had no idea that a major tar sands pipeline from Canada passed through their area, until the pipe broke in July 2010, creating the largest on-land oil spill in North America. The research of secondary English students doing place-based writing and research can reveal local information important to understanding climate change and environmental issues relevant to the safety of their communities.

In writing about their experiences with different environmental spaces, students can consider larger institutional forces and conflicts over climate change messaging and values. For example, in writing about local fracking mines, students can examine the role of the fossil fuel industry in promoting fracking as "good for the economy," when, in fact, fracking has resulted in leakage release of unburned methane:

> These leaks are big enough to wipe out a large share of the gains from the Obama administration's work on climate change—all those closed coal mines and fuel-efficient cars. *In fact, it's even possible that America's contribution to global warming increased during the Obama years*. The methane story is utterly at odds with what we've been telling ourselves, not to mention what we've been telling the rest of the planet. It undercuts the promises we made at the climate talks in Paris.
>
> McKibben (2016)

From a climate change perspective, effective place-based writing connects people's observation, research, and experiences with their values to foster institutional and cultural change.

Michele Hollingsworth Koomen, who teaches at Gustavus Adolphus College, in St. Peter, Minnesota, describes her use of writing activities for a 2-day mini-unit funded by the InTEgrate project, http://tinyw.in/n5Yl, that supports teachers' curriculum planning addressing climate change.

Part 1: Describing environmental changes

Advance organizer writing prompts: Have you ever walked across a frozen lake or river? Explain your experience using your five senses. In her book, *Orlando: A Biography*, Virginia Woolf (1993) writes about the Great Frost that occurred during the winter of 1683–1684:

> The severity of the frost was so extraordinary that a kind of petrifaction sometimes ensued; and it was commonly supposed that the great increase in rocks in some parts of Derbyshire was due to no eruption, for there was none, but to the solidification of unfortunate wayfarers who had been literally turned to stone where they stood . . . The King directed that the river, which was frozen to a depth of twenty feet and more for six or seven miles on either side, should be swept, decorated and given to all the semblance of a park or a pleasure ground, with arbors, mazes, alleys, drinking booths, etc. at his expense (p. 26).

Discussion prompt: What happened during the Great Frost according to Woolf? How does the King's decree compare to winter celebrations or events that you have experienced? What are some similar changes in the environment portrayed in texts you are reading. For example, drawing on the dried-up Colorado River bed in "The Tamarisk Hunter" to generate your own descriptions of environmental changes in your own regions.

Part 2: Weather and Climate

Writing or discussion prompt: What is the difference between weather and climate?

Possible responses: Weather generally describes short time frames: minutes, hours, days, and weeks. Weather may include the following conditions: sunshine, rain, cloud cover, winds, hail, snow, sleet, freezing rain, flooding, blizzards, ice storms, and thunderstorms.

Climate refers to the statistics of weather: the average pattern for weather over a period of months, years, decades, or longer in a specific place.

Writing or discussion prompt: Was the Great Frost weather or climate?

Writing or discussion prompt: What are some impacts of warming for London and the Thames River? Models show progressive increases in both summer heat island intensity and frequency with detrimental effects on air quality, summer electricity demand, and comfort in the city's buildings and transport network. Warmer temps reduce the amount of water available and increase demand in summer, causing changes in biodiversity and more flooding.

CREATIVE WRITING

So far in this book we previously described several ways students can use creative writing to inquire into global warming. In Chapter 2, we report on Allen's students writing flash fiction and cli-fi short stories. Chapter 4 made the case for the power of the literary imagination to address climate change, and we suggested students create their own climate-themed picture books. Already in this chapter there have been examples of place-based plays, fiction, and poetry. There are many more possibilities.

Allen's students engaged in a number of climate change related creative writing experiments. Clara Peeters and Emma Garber wrote climate change poetry inspired by particular images. Clara wrote a poem as a series of three haiku responding to Salvador Dali's haunting painting "The Anthropormophic Cabinet" http://tinyurl.com/h432kyc, a painting of a woman in mute protest whose body, apparently ravaged by heat and time, is full of half-opened drawers.

Air unbreathable
Lungs scratch against each other
Akin to stuck drawers,
Airborne pollutants
Widen fissures inside us
Smoggy atmosphere,
My body is not
A storage vessel for your
Forgettable toxic waste.

Emma wrote several poems inspired by common climate-change images found online. A picture of a melting Earth inspired this stanza,

The Earth is not as strong as we thought.
The damage is done, the heat is too strong.
Money was all that mattered, but lives can't be bought.
We thought we were invincible, but that idea is long gone.

Blair LaCross wrote a comedic film script about a UN climate change summit meeting http://tinyurl.com/gnyr28e. Aly Coutts wrote a diary from the point of view of a student living in 2050 http://goo.gl/p0qv4T. Rebecca Shell's story, "The Candle" http://bit.ly/2aK24dX portrays an older man mourning the losses in a dying Earth by lighting a candle in a church to celebrate the survivors who are still living. Allen had several other creative writing ideas that his students did not try out, but that could be engaging:

- Write a song or songs that could be used in the movement to address climate change.
- Create a climate change cookbook with recipes and information about the relationship of food and agriculture to climate change (the cookbook could either be for the present or set in the future).
- Create a newspaper (or other news source) at a date in the future that reports on future climate change events.
- Describe and design a climate change clothing line, could be set in present or in the future.
- Write a proposal pitching a climate change app to a technology company. (Could be set today or in the future. Could be an app used in the cli-fi short story, "The Audit.")
- Write a proposal pitching a video game with climate change themes to a game company.

Another teacher used diaries and short stories in an engaging way. After reading the young adult fiction novels written in diary form, *The Carbon Diaries 2015* (Lloyd, 2008) and *The Carbon Diaries 2017* (Lloyd, 2010), Nicola Toth's students recorded daily diaries about their energy use (Toth et al., 2013). In writing their diaries, students decided for themselves what experiences to include. Next, they used their diaries to create short stories addressing, among other things, the energy use of household and personal appliances, portable devices, computers, gaming, lighting, transportation, heating, etc. In discussions of their diaries and stories, students expressed concerns about the impact of reduced sources of energy for future generations and the costs of saving energy. They identified barriers to making any changes in their use of energy: their own familiar, habitual lifestyle; being detached from the problem; not having to pay energy bills; and, the design of appliances—for example, televisions that are left on.

Based on their reading of cli-fi novels and short stories such as those described in Chapter 4, students can create their own stories set in the future where characters cope with the effects of climate change. As they do so, students might be encouraged to focus less on doomsday, disaster scenarios, and more on portraying characters using their collective imagination to generate mitigation and adaptation strategies, perhaps even strategies that may be relevant to making change in the present. Renata Tyszczuk (2014) describes these as "precautionary tales" that are set

> in an uncertain world [so that] it is not necessarily important to know how it all ends; the story is really about the "getting there", however messy, halting, incremental, sideways and unfinishable the journey. What matters is how we respond to what the world throws at us and what enabling stories, cautionary tales included, we continue to tell.
>
> Tyszczuk (2014, p. 57)

In creating narratives and poems about climate change, students can engage audiences by using links, visual images, audio recordings, videos, and graphics. Language arts is a great place to learn digital storytelling, and digital stories about climate change have potential for impact (for resources http://tinyurl.com/lhyglfh and the Center for Digital Storytelling www.story center.org). Students can also create their own audio/images productions using online tools such as VoiceThread, ShowMe, or Explain Everything. In creating her "SoundWalk," *Wood Wolf Girl* http://tinyw.in/FdpR Cornelia Hodgland (2016) drew on Little Red Riding Hood's walk in the woods to have students create their own versions addressing environmental problems using poetry, narrative, and sound. To create videos based on poems or rap lyrics, students can view *Take Aim at Climate Change* http://tinyw.in/pTWL or a video of three poets, Deanna Rodger, Ray Antrobus, and Zia Ahmed (Rhyme & Reason: Reflections on Climate Change: http://tinyw.in/uImt. Chapter 6 more fully explores using new media to address climate change.

PERSUASIVE WRITING

Effective persuasive writing depends on having meaningful topics and a clear sense of audience. With persuasive writing we continue to see writing as a form of inquiry, an exploration that leads to continued improvement in the formulation and development of arguments and evidence.

Students are more likely to be engaged in persuasive writing when they perceive it as a dialogic interaction in response to others' positions (VanDerHeide, Juzwik, & Dunn, 2016). In the classroom, students share arguments with each other. In this way they are exposed to alternative perspectives that they can consider when thinking about their audiences (Newell, Bloome, & Hirvela, 2015). In teaching writing at Jordan High School in Sandy, Utah, Randall Seltz describes having his students enter into actual ongoing arguments:

They search local, national, and international media outlets for op/ed and letters to the editor about climate change. These are really interesting and show a great deal about how different regions take the problem more seriously, for example, New Orleans residents may find climate change "more real" than individuals who live in a landlocked desert valley. I may have students respond specifically to the writer of the piece they found or work to edit the piece to make it stronger by adding evidence or more logical arguments.

Eleventh-grade students sharing their arguments on the topic of climate change in an online forum were more likely to share evidence with each other and reflect on the quality of their supporting evidence than students who were not interacting on the forum (Iordanou & Constantinoum, 2015). Students reflected on the quality of their evidence because they were responding to each other with statements such as, "Give us some evidence" or "You have not provided evidence" (p. 307).

In thinking about their audiences, students could consider advice formulated in a talk by climate scientist, Katherine Hayhoe (Urevig, 2016). She points out that audiences have:

– *Polarized stances* on climate change, that students need to consider that their audiences may think differently than they do about climate change. While students may assume that citing a lot of scientific data may serve to convince skeptical audiences, it may be the case that concrete narratives or personal examples may be more rhetorically effective.
– *Knowledge* as shaped by their personal beliefs that serves to filter that knowledge. Students can then identify those beliefs with which their audiences may identify—for example, a belief in the value of economic growth, to then argue for the benefit of economic growth through development of clean energy jobs.
– *Shared values*, for example, a shared value in the importance of family and future generations, leading to arguments on the significance of climate change as impacting these future generations.
– *Need for solutions* through collaborative policy efforts or benefits of alternative strategies.

In developing persuasive writing assignments for his language arts students studying climate change, Allen focused on audiences beyond the classroom. His students wrote:

– A *guide* for high-school or college students who want to become involved in local area climate change activities and organizations, as did Ryan Powers http://tinyurl.com/hba3qe2 informing students about local and national groups, such as Citizens' Climate Lobby https://citizensclimatelobby.org.
– An *email* to a person or group engaged in changing lifestyles to address climate change, explaining why students like what they are doing, asking questions, and seeking information about how to improve their own practices, as did Shane Stover in writing to the Sierra Club http://tinyurl.com/jofwvag.
– A *memo* to school administrators, teachers, and parents in a community about why they need to support the creation of curriculum about climate change that includes examples of recommended curricular materials in different subject areas, as did Cece Watry http://tinyurl.com/gltrt6j as a representative of "Students Combating Climate Change."
– An *amicus brief* for a current lawsuit or court case addressing climate change from the point of view of a specific group or organization, as did Kaitlin Braunschweig http://tinyurl.com/zfj8kcn addressing whether students have standing in a lawsuit against the government in climate change.

- An *online multimedia poster* (at a site such as Glogster) about a specific aspect of climate change, which Jessica Poling created http://tinyurl.com/z3we55e.
- *Class blog* available to the public or *letters* or *op ed essays* to their school or local newspaper (for a unit on writing editorials: http://goo.gl/ZTT36E).
- An *analysis of songs* that are used or could be used in the climate change movement. What makes them effective? (See Angelo Negrito's analysis http://tinyurl.com/z7a9hvv.)

Allen had some other ideas that his students have not yet tried:

- As leader of a local chapter of 350.org, identify a company or organization responsible for significant carbon or methane pollution in your area. *Write a letter* to the president/board of that company about why they should change their practices and what your group might do if they do not comply. Draw on research and make arguments with evidence.
- Create a *conversation* between two junior high-school students and their parents. The students want to join the young people who are suing the government over failure to stop greenhouse gases. Draw on research into that lawsuit.
- Create a *short video* that analyzes the greenwashing strategy of a particular company or critiques the position of a climate change denier. Post on YouTube.
- Create an online stash of *"rank memes"* related to climate change.

In selecting issues to address, students may be more engaged in writing about mitigation or adaptation efforts related to their own local region that will impact their own lives. For example, students in Elizabeth Giddens' (2011) composition class wrote about "how locally grown foods could be served in the university cafeteria, the state's water crisis and political and personal responses to it, and how guidelines for green buildings are best adapted to Georgia's hot and humid climate" (p. 45). Students prepared for writing their reports by creating an issue diagram that identified the different stakeholders and their positions on the issue, for example, scientists, the general population, fossil fuel company employees, etc. Doing so helped students consider counter-arguments to their claims.

There is value in going in depth. Analysis of a project in which first-year college writing courses at Southern Illinois University only addressed the topic of sustainability found that focusing on that single topic enhanced the quality of students' writing, and that acquiring knowledge about the topic contributed to their revising and resulted in improved writing (Hembrough, 2016). As one student noted, "after a couple papers when I was more familiar with the topic, I was able to start expanding my word choice and get more creative."

Learning to carefully analyze arguments can help students become more sophisticated thinkers. For example, they might analyze statements by climate change denying politicians. Senator Marco Rubio states that he opposes laws for cutting carbon emissions:

> If in fact sea levels are rising . . . we should spend money to mitigate that . . . as a policy maker, you have to show me whether the laws you want me to pass will actually impact the issue that you are raising. I have people that come to me and say: we want you to pass these laws on carbon emissions, and I ask them, well how many inches of sea rise will it prevent?
>
> Fragoso (2016a)

Senator Rubio frames the problem of sea rise in hypothetical terms—"if in fact sea levels are rising," when, in fact, with a projected sea rise of 6 feet by the Intergovernmental Panel on Climate Change (IPCC), 30.5 percent of homes in Miami would be lost (Fragoso, 2016b). By posing an overly precise question, he suggests we cannot know what difference restricting carbon will make. Critically analyzing his argument indicates he is failing to recognize the relationship between increased carbon emissions and sea rise.

A risk of creating fear about future climate change is that doing so may generate hopelessness or apathy. Some people maintain that arguments will be more effective if they highlight citizens engaged in positive community-based, concrete actions and solutions (Wibeck, 2013). For example, students might argue for creating more bike lanes, walkable sidewalks, and mass transit in their community to reduce car traffic and foster healthy lifestyles. That kind of argument is more likely to appeal to their audience's emotional sense of physical well-being. At the same time, it is important to be accurate and honest about climate change since many people do not understand its danger.

For her composition class, Emily Polk's students write feature news stories about communities' struggles with climate change. Their writing is based on a careful process of research and rhetorical analysis, and an immersion in climate change writing. Their writing is situated in ongoing discussion and attentive to cultural and social contexts. At the end of the class they actually submit their stories for publication. She describes her class in a short video: http://tinyw.in/ybwi. Emily explains about her class:

In our class, students are asked to engage critically in popular media stories about climate change and research and write their own feature-length article. We begin the class by considering some basic questions of our time: How do we tell the many global stories in such a way that makes an impact and evokes some kind of change? How do we communicate so that people are moved to act—personally and/or politically? How can we write stories that both mirror and shape the ways in which people are living with and responding to climate change? Students seek answers to these questions by writing their own climate change story about a specific issue, site, or community, which they prepare to submit to a popular publication at the end of class.

We prepare for this writing process by analyzing a range of current research on communication practices that have been effective in motivating people to care about and act on climate change issues. We combine this foundational research with rhetorical analyses of popular (multi)media focused on climate change. These articles, videos, and blogs address themes like climate change and the personal story, climate change and creative art, climate change and technology, climate change and social justice, among others.

Of every text, we ask the same rhetorical questions: Who is the audience for the piece? What was the piece *trying to do*? How did the author do it? We talk about the impact of the piece—both intended and consequential and the relationship between impact and distribution platform, between the authority of the author and the audience, between the strategies that move us to *feel* the issue and the strategies that help us to *understand* it (showing vs. telling/evoking vs. explaining), and perhaps most importantly, students are asked to consider the ways in which the contexts of their own lives inform their reading of the story.

This is a particularly important consideration given the wide range of backgrounds of my students. They are from Ghana, Botswana, Thailand, India, and various parts of the United States, from off-the-grid Alaska to Tulsa, Oklahoma. By asking them to consider the personal social, cultural, political factors that are informing their interpretation and analysis of the texts, they practice conceptualizing the relationship between author, reader, and text as dynamic and relational, something that many of them noted they do not do consciously.

This conceptualization is crucial to students as they develop their own climate change story ideas and "pitch" them to a publication of their choice. This pitch is written in the form of an actual query letter, and is our first major assignment. The majority of students developed pitches with topics focused on their own community's struggles with adapting to climate change. Natty pitched a story about environmental health interventions for undocumented-hill-tribe youth on the border of Thailand and Burma. Maria wrote about renewable energy cooperatives run by and for marginalized communities in Oakland, California. Tamer wrote about the role of climate change photography in Ghana, and Meghan wrote about the first wave of Pacific Island climate refugees who have resettled in the Bay Area, among many others.

Writing the query letter encourages students to practice persuasive writing in a way that feels meaningful to them. They must essentially figure out a way to structure their pitch so that they can simultaneously attract the attention of the person reading it *and* convince them that this is a significant story worth publishing, all while writing in the voice and style of the publication. Students must use various rhetorical strategies to set their story apart from the others while also establishing their own authority to tell the story.

We find Emily's writing class focused on climate change inspiring. Her students become involved in the most vital issue of our time. They draw on their local knowledge, their learning about climate change, their research, their study of rhetoric, to write in public forums and make a difference.

Students can also benefit by writing from the perspective of people adversely impacted by climate change. In a geoscience college course on climate change, students were assigned to write a blog about climate change effects on a particular country (Schuenemann & Wagner, 2014). Through this process, students increased their awareness of how much people in developing countries would be harmed by climate change. As one student explained:

> It [the blogs] helped me gain a different perspective on how other nations are affected by changes in climate and global warming. I was able to learn how other countries plan to help mitigate the problem and countries' beliefs and opinions on the various topics of global warming.
>
> Schuenemann & Wagner (2014, p. 372)

A resource to help students understand the perspective of people from developing nations is the People's Agreement of Cochabamba http://tinyurl.com/n86pohf formulated in 2010 in Bolivia by representatives from 100 countries. This document affirms the knowledge of indigenous people and calls on the developed countries to honor their climate debt by "restoring to developing countries the atmospheric space that is occupied by their greenhouse gas emissions," "assuming responsibility for the hundreds of millions of people that will be forced to migrate due to the climate change caused by these countries," and creating an Adaptation Fund that addresses the "impacts and costs of climate change in developing countries."

After his students had spent significant time studying climate change and considering issues of fairness and justice, Allen had them all write their own "Climate Change Manifesto." The word "manifesto" comes from Latin, meaning "clear or conspicuous." It is a public declaration of the views of the issuer on a matter of great public importance. Allen explained to his students that a manifesto typically includes (1) a history of the issue, (2) a prescription for change, (3) a section which distinguishes its approach from other approaches, (4) a call to action, and (5) a specific vision of how a future society should be organized. Wikipedia https://en.wikipedia.org/wiki/Manifesto has links to many examples of manifestos, including the Declaration of Independence. Allen's assignment told students,

> You are writing about the greatest issue human beings have ever faced. Show that you have a serious knowledge of the facts, history, politics, theories, issues, and ethics in question. Choose an audience that has meaning to you and use language that will draw others to your position. Be thoughtful, courageous, passionate, and visionary.

Allen shared with his students a draft of the first chapters of this book and told them that this book was a "manifesto" written to secondary English teachers. His students were encouraged to choose a particular audience. Several wrote to other students like themselves. Travis Hosna wrote to the business community. Jake Crow wrote to English teachers. Many included charts, images, and links. Some were quite creative. Alice Kinney wrote a poem to children, told from the point of view of a bird,

> I'm a sparrow named Sal, and I've flown across seas.
> I've flown over deserts, and forests, and snow . . .
> But lately my flock and I have seen
> This world we love become less clean . . .
> Our snowcaps are melting and our reefs are bleached
> It's becoming quite clear that the limit's been reached . . .

At first the students struggled with a genre that was new to them. It was a challenge to decide where to focus when writing about such a large topic when they weren't accustomed to formulating their own opinion in a public voice. The results, however, are impressive, and, after writing, the students showed a marked increased level of confidence in expressing their ideas (the manifestos are online at http://tinyurl.com/gwu8cm3).

WRITING, DOES IT MATTER?

In Chapter 1 we described a climate change perspective that urges us to recognize the importance of the problem, overcome individualism and adopt a global perspective, create solidarity, strive for climate justice, and envision and enact change.

We believe that as students inquire into climate change through place-based writing, they will more deeply connect with the world around them and take a step away from isolated individualism. Place-based writing can help students better understand climate change as it impacts places and communities that they know and love. As students engage in creative writing, they use their imagination to grasp climate change in ways both intimate and expansive, in the present and in the future. Taking the perspective of others creates mutual understanding and common interest. Persuasive writing focuses on audiences. What do I have to say? How can I convince others? How do I appeal to them intellectually, emotionally, and to their sense of fairness and justice?

The next chapter takes writing another step, more fully into the remarkable capacity for digital media communication for employing persuasive writing, as well as engaging students in critical analysis of media representations of climate change.

For additional resources, activities, and readings related to this chapter, go to http://tinyw. in/WNiN on the book's website.

REFERENCES

Barrett, A., & Mowen, A. J. (2014). Assessing the effectiveness of artistic place-based climate change. *Interpretation Journal of Interpretation Research, 19*(2), 7–24.

Beach, R. (2014). Engaging students through place-based education. *Ubiquity: The Journal of Literature, Literacy, and the Arts, 1*(1), 122–137. Retrieved from http://ed-ubiquity.gsu.edu/wordpress/.

Common Core State Standards (2010). *Common core state standard for English language arts.* Washington, DC: National Governors Association.

Fragoso, A. D. (2016a, October 18). As climate change floods Florida, Marco Rubio refuses to acknowledge science [Web log post]. Retrieved from http://tinyw.in/yQ1Y.

Fragoso, A. D. (2016b, August 3). Sea level rise could put millions of U. S. homes underwater by 2100 [Web log post]. Retrieved from http://tinyw.in/hkxa.

Ghosh, A. (2016). *The great derangment: Climate change and the unthinkable.* Chicago, IL: University of Chicago Press.

Giddens, E. (2011). Encountering social-constructivist rhetoric: Teaching an environmental writing and literature course. In G. Garrard (Ed.), *Teaching ecocriticism and green cultural studies* (pp. 37–48). New York: Palgrave Macmillan.

Hembrough, T. (2016). Writing strategies for action: A case study about an interdisciplinary curriculum of sustainability and ecocomposition in first-semester composition and other FY courses. Paper presented at the meeting of the College Composition and Communication Conference, Houston.

Hodgland, C. (2016). Sound ecology in the woods: Red Riding Hood takes an audio walk. In W. Arons, & T. J. May (Eds.), *Readings in performance and ecology* (pp. 181–190). New York: Palgrave Macmillan.

Hothem, T. (2009). Suburban studies and college writing: Applying ecocomposition. *Pedagogy, 9*(1), 35–59.

Iordanou, K., & Constantinoum, C. P. (2015). Supporting use of evidence in argumentation through practice in argumentation and reflection in the context of SOCRATES learning environment. *Science Education, 99*, 282–311.

Jacobs, E. (2011). Re(Place) your typical writing assignment: An argument for place-based writing. *English Journal, 100*(3), 49–54.

Kudryavtsev, A., Stedman, R. C., & Krasny, M. E. (2012). Sense of place in environmental education. *Environmental Education Research, 18*(2), 229–250.

Lloyd, S. (2008). *The carbon diaries 2015.* London: Hodder Children's Books.

Lloyd, S. (2010). *The carbon diaries 2017.* London: Hodder Children's Books.

McClanahan, L. G. (2010). First person singular: Documenting climate change through first-person narratives. *Green Teacher, 88*, 3–6.

McKibben, B. (2016, March 23). Global warming's terrifying new chemistry [Web log post]. Retrieved from http://tinyw.in/jzzo.

Newell, G., Bloome, D., & Hirvela, A. (2015). *Teaching and learning argumentative writing in high school English language arts classrooms.* New York: Routledge.

Nischik, R. (2000). *Margaret Atwood works and impact.* Rochester, NY: Camden House.

Schuenemann, K., & Wagner, R. (2014). Using student-generated blogs to create a global perspective on climate change. *Journal of Geoscience Education, 62*, 364–373.

Seitz, D. (2014). Place-based genre writing as critical expressivist practice. In T. Roeder & R. Gatto (Eds.), *Critical expressivism: Theory and practice in the composition classroom.* Anderson, SC: Parlor Press.

Slovic, S., Bishop, J. E., & Lyndgaard, K. (Eds.) (2015). *Currents of the universal being: Explorations in the literature of energy.* Lubbock, TX: Texas Tech University Press.

Somerville, M., Davies, B., Power, K., Gannon, S., & de Carteret, P. (2011). *Place pedagogy change*. Rotterdam, the Netherlands: Sense Publishers.

Steingraber, S. (2010). Shale game. *Orion Magazine*. Retrieved from http://steingraber.com/shale-game.

Toth, N., Little, L., Read, J. C., Fitton, D., & Horton, M. (2013). Understanding teen attitudes towards energy consumption. *Journal of Environmental Psychology, 34*, 36–44.

Tyszczuk, R. (2014). Cautionary tales: The sky is falling! The world is ending! In J. Smith, R. Tyszczuk, & R. Butler (Eds.), *Culture and climate change: Narratives* (pp. 45–57). Cambridge, UK: Shed.

Urevig, A. (2016, May 4). 6 things we learned about changing people's minds on climate [Web log post]. Retrieved from http://tinyw.in/1ymW.

VanDerHeide, J., Juzwik, M., & Dunn, M. (2016). Teaching and learning argumentation in English: A dialogic approach. *Theory into practice, 55*(4), 287–293.

Wibeck, V. (2013). Enhancing learning, communication and public engagement about climate change: Some lessons from recent literature. *Environmental Education Research, 20*(3), 387–411.

Woolf, V. (1993). *Orlando: A biography*. New York: Harcourt Brace.

Chapter 6
Critical Media/ Digital Analyses of Climate Change

Crucially, mass media play an instructional role by defining the status quo, setting the agenda for our socio-economic system, defining what to think about, and recursively reinforcing non-sustainable cultural beliefs.

Antonio López (2014, p. 72)

Yet, even as media images have made the environmental crisis visible to a mass public, they often have masked systemic causes and ignored structural inequalities.

Finis Dunaway (2015, p. 2)

As climate change becomes the biggest crisis to affect life on this planet, we are seeing corporations and politicians spinning facts and emotions to create doubt about the science and reframe the discourse. Neoliberal ideology, unregulated capitalism, rampant consumerism, sensationalized journalism, and the extraction and burning of fossil fuels are combining to create an environmental catastrophe that is changing everything (Klein, 2014). The media messages about these issues are an ideal space for students to critically analyze the media's use of assumptions, actions, and inactions. Using a framework of critical media literacy, educators can guide students to question and create their own media messages about environmental justice and sustainability.

To encourage students in the English language arts classroom to use their critical capacity, imagination, and creativity to explore and respond to climate change, we need to break from the confines of the printed page and unleash the potential that lies beyond the margins. By incorporating ideas from critical media literacy, we can enhance students' reading and writing skills with all types of texts (movies, music, videogames, photographs, social media, books, etc.), deepen their understandings about the power of literacy, and stoke their creative spirits to learn about, as well as challenge, dominant narratives about our relationship with the natural world.

In 2015, Pew researchers found that 92 percent of American 13–17-year-olds go online daily, "including 24 percent who say they go online 'almost constantly'" (Lenhart, 2015). Just 4 years earlier, researchers reported that 8–18-year-olds in the United States spent more than 10 hours a day exposed to various forms of media, such as television, film, music, computers, video games, and print (Rideout, Lauricella, & Wartella, 2011). With the popularity and accessibility of cell phones and new mobile devices, youth are communicating and socializing every day in numerous ways using texting, tweeting, tagging, blogging, posting, pinning, instant messaging, photographing, podcasting, and sharing all types of texts. It is significant that the introduction to the Common Core State Standards specifically mentions the need for students to read and write with digital texts and "use technology and digital media strategically and capably" (Common Core State Standards, 2015, p. 7). According to a report by the National Environmental Education and Training Foundation (2005), "children get more environmental information (83 percent) from the media than from any other source" (Coyle, 2005, p. x). Since social media, smartphones, and the Internet have become the dominant conveyors of information and students' preferred option for communication and entertainment, English teachers should be integrating these tools and practices into the classroom with theory and pedagogy that support critical thinking.

A CRITICAL MEDIA LITERACY FRAMEWORK

In *Greening Media Education: Bridging Media Literacy with Green Cultural Citizenship*, Antonio López (2014) warns that there are a lot of people in environmental education who think that "media and technology are anti-nature" and that "the general practice of media literacy marginalizes ecological perspectives" (p. 1). However, it does not have to be this way. Critical media literacy can be an important framework for uniting information communication technologies (ICTs) with environmental justice.

Teaching students to think critically about the messages they read, hear, see, and create requires an understanding of what it means to be literate in the twenty-first century that is inclusive of all types of information and entertainment. It is important to recognize the potential and limitations technology and media bring to education, especially for developing a critical engagement with environmental issues, because many neoliberal education reforms support using technology and media to improve the efficiency and effectiveness of non-critical practices. Too often computers, cameras, and cell phones are used as appealing new tools to make the same old teaching practices just *look* better. However, when media, technology, and popular culture are embraced through critical media literacy pedagogy, there is far greater potential for education to become truly critical and empowering (Share, 2015).

Climate change education needs media literacy because for decades informal science education has worked with a deficit perspective and failed to promote critical thinking. A one-way transmission model, known as the Public Understanding of Science (PUS) approach, has not been effective at educating the public about the seriousness of climate change (Cooper, 2011). Caren Cooper writes, "In order to be climate change literate, the public must first be media literate" (p. 235). The PUS approach is giving way to the Public Engagement in Science (PES) model of education that is more in line with media literacy and empowerment education because it promotes critical thinking and an inquiry model of questioning.

Even though media education has not always supported sustainable practices and environmental perspectives (López, 2014), *critical media literacy* provides the potential to make English language arts more transformative because it promotes social and environmental justice through critiquing dominant ideologies. Evolving from cultural studies, critical media literacy aims to *expand* our understanding of literacy to include reading and writing all types of texts, as well as *deepen* analysis to more critical levels that question the relationships between media and audiences, information and power. Critical media literacy is defined less as a specific body of knowledge or set of skills, and more as a framework of *conceptual understandings* (Buckingham, 2003). Based on the work of many scholars and organizations around the world, the following is a list of six critical media literacy conceptual understandings and corresponding questions (see Table 6.1) (Funk, Kellner, & Share, 2016).

These questions can be useful tools for students trying to make sense of the messages about climate change since there is an abundance of misinformation in much of the commercial media. When students are encouraged to read and write beyond the boundaries of print into visual, aural, and multimodalities, they can expand their access and communication potential.

TABLE 6.1 Conceptual Understandings for Critical Media Literacy

Conceptual Understandings	Questions
1. **Social Constructivism** All information is co-constructed by individuals and/or groups of people who make choices within social contexts.	**WHO** are all the possible people who made choices that helped create this text?
2. **Languages/Semiotics** Each medium has its own language with specific grammar and semantics.	**HOW** was this text constructed and delivered/accessed?
3. **Audience/Positionality** Individuals and groups understand media messages similarly and/or differently depending on multiple contextual factors.	**HOW** could this text be understood differently?
4. **Politics of Representation** Media messages and the medium through which they travel always have a bias and support and/or challenge dominant hierarchies of power, privilege, and pleasure.	**WHAT** values, points of view, and ideologies are represented or missing from this text or influenced by the medium?
5. **Production/Institutions** All media texts have a purpose (often commercial or governmental) that is shaped by the creators and/or systems within which they operate.	**WHY** was this text created and/or shared?
6. **Social & Environmental Justice** Media culture is a terrain of struggle that perpetuates or challenges positive and/or negative ideas about people, groups, and issues; it is never neutral.	**WHOM** does this text advantage and/or disadvantage?

Before the printing press, storytelling was a multisensory experience, place-based and rich in expression, interaction, and relationships. Many of these old qualities of personal interactions are possible with new media that incorporate sounds, visuals, and movement. Teachers can have students compare and contrast different versions of stories about humans interacting with nature (found in books, cartoons, movies, websites, songs, or video games). Then students can collaboratively create media with their own alternative perspectives or different endings of the same story (taking the form of comic strips, memes, podcasts, digital stories, or photographs). Students can also analyze movies that explore environmental issues to learn about production techniques as well as questioning the way characters, concepts, and places are developed and represented. They can then create their own texts (as advertisements, blogs, animation, zines, movie trailers, books, or social media) to retell or repurpose the story from different points of view. The possibilities for creating various types of texts open the potential for students to be more creative, expressive, and critical than is likely when they are bound to the printed page.

It is also important for English teachers to recognize that digital reading and writing require many of the same skills as print-based literacy, yet when reading and writing are digital and networked, some important dimensions change. Digital texts gain new potential to be *multimodal* (combining different formats), *hyperlinked* (connecting with other media and building new relationships), and *interactive* (allowing for sharing, remixing, and participation) (Beach, 2009). Digital reading and writing do not occur in isolation; they are embedded in mediated environments and networked publics that have unique qualities, especially in relation to notions of *persistence*, *visibility*, *spreadability*, and *searchability* (boyd, 2014). These changes can allow greater freedom and creativity for students to read and write the word and the world (Freire & Macedo, 1987), supporting new critical analytical skills and producing alternative messages, especially when making sense of complex issues like climate change. They can also create new challenges; as contexts collapse, digital texts travel the cybersphere to audiences unknown.

ECONOMIC AND POLITICAL CONTROL OF MEDIA COVERAGE OF CLIMATE CHANGE

In the twenty-first century, a small handful of enormous media corporations are the dominant storytellers of our time, often repeating the same story, at the expense of countless different perspectives and creative ways of thinking. When it comes to news reports, TV, movies, and podcasts about climate change, students often encounter messages that are framed more as spectacles and controversies than meaningful and enlightening information. Many of these storytellers are actually story-sellers, more interested in peddling their perspectives and products than informing, inspiring, or questioning dominant systems.

A major structure shaping commercial media in a capitalist economy is that they depend on advertising, which, in turn, requires endless consumption. Our consumerist ideology requires what Lewis and Boyce (2009) argue is a "need to acknowledge the role that advertising plays in *creating a set of cultural conditions* that makes us less inclined to deal with climate change" (p. 8). Naomi Klein (2014) asserts that we need to change the consumption economic system through "de-growth" reductions. Executive Director of Greenpeace USA, Annie Leonard, agrees with the need to change our unsustainable dependence on consumption and consumerism and calls for transformational solutions that will change our economic goals. In the online video, *Story of Solutions*, Leonard explains that in order to make real changes to the system we need to change the game; that we can do this by shifting the goal from working for "more" stuff to working toward "better" solutions that will improve the quality of life for everyone (Leonard, Sachs, & Fox, 2013).

The economic system is also supported and influenced by political systems; the effects of campaign donations to candidates by corporations and lobbying organizations can be seen in policies favoring the agendas of large donors, often related to the support of the fossil fuel industry (Howe, 2014). The lobbying organization, *Americans for Prosperity*, funded by the Koch Brothers, owners of Koch Industries, successfully lobbied 156 largely Republican members of Congress to support a "no climate tax" pledge, given that such taxes on emissions would adversely affect their profits (Mayer, 2016). One reason for their opposition is that Koch Industries was identified by the EPA in 2012 as the largest producer of toxic waste in the country (Mayer, 2016). Students can learn a lot by investigating who owns the commercial media, something they can do at various websites: http://tinyurl.com/86r4dck, http://tinyw.in/eyQO, and http://tinyw.in/Vkte.

USE OF DOCUMENTARIES AND VIDEOS

English language arts teachers can also employ documentaries, videos, and cli-fi films to portray different aspects of climate change. Chapter 2, Starting Point 4, has important suggestions for climate change documentaries and images. Chapter 3 describes the powerful Story of Stuff and related videos in the section on Capitalism and Consumerism. Chapter 4 has a relevant section on cli-fi films.

LIMITED MEDIA COVERAGE OF CLIMATE CHANGE

Media stories about climate change are too often under-reported and when they are represented in mainstream media, they tend to be sensational and controversial. Seldom are commercial media messages helpful for understanding the complexity of climate change in a way that motivates people to care and act. Analysis of TV news coverage of climate change by ABC, CBS, NBC, and Fox, found that they devoted only 146 minutes during 2015 to climate change, despite the Paris climate summit, the EPA's Clean Power Plan, Pope Francis' papal encyclical, and other 2015 stories with the focus largely on extreme weather events and few, if any, references to impacts on national security, health, or economic growth (Media Matters for America, 2016). Analysis of coverage on Sunday news talk shows found that half of the coverage was driven by politics; 19 percent on discussions of scientific findings; and 29 percent on climate change's impact on extreme weather events or wildlife (Kalhoefer, 2015). Most of the reporting provided a false balance related to framing the issue as "debatable" or "controversial". For example, a February 16, 2014 *Fox News Sunday* program featured George Will critiquing Obama's focus on climate change

> because "the climate is always changing," and *Wall Street Journal* columnist Kimberley Strassel argued that the term "global warming" became "climate change" because "you couldn't prove that there was much global warming anymore . . . as the temperature didn't change."
>
> Kalhoefer (2015)

There is also wide variation across media outlets in the degree of media coverage of climate change. Analysis of reporting of climate change between 2000 and 2015 by the *Washington Post, Wall Street Journal, New York Times, USA Today,* and *Los Angeles Times,* found that the *Wall Street Journal* and *USA Today* had consistently little or minor reporting while the *New York Times* and *Los Angeles Times* had far more coverage, particularly from 2007 to 2010 and then again in 2015 (Daly et al., 2015). Language arts students can do their own investigations about current media coverage. They can conduct quantitative research by counting the number of articles and news broadcasts on climate change and also qualitative research by evaluating the bias and construction of the reporting. *Fairness & Accuracy in Reporting* (FAIR) http://fair.org is a non-profit organization that provides regular critiques of media coverage that can be useful for students to view specific examples of news reporting through a critical lens. For an historical perspective, *Project LookSharp* provides free lesson plans about the history of global warming in the media from the 1950s up to 2010 (Lesson 8 in the Teacher Guide: http://tinyw.in/KFLW).

The fact that some news media and politicians still question the science of climate change makes the need for a media literate populace more essential than ever. While the debate in the scientific community ended decades ago, the popular discourse in commercial media is heavily influenced by public relations companies receiving large amounts of money from the fossil fuel industry (Oreskes & Conway, 2010). For students swayed by this deception, there are many resources available to critique climate deniers and triangulate the vast amount of scientific evidence. There are also resources to support teachers to guide their students to critically analyze the news such as Project LookSharp's (2010) *Media Construction of Global Warming: A Media*

Literacy Curriculum Kit, the National Center for Science Education's website and resources *Dealing with Denial* http://tinyw.in/BDkI, and the *Scientific Trust Tracker* http://tinyw.in/meMw.

It is essential that students adopt a critical stance, given the history of the fossil fuel industry covering up information on the adverse effects of fossil fuels. Beginning in the 1970s, the fossil fuel industry launched a public relations campaign to silence or censor their companies' own scientists' warning about emissions effects, as well as providing support for scientists who voiced denials regarding human causes of climate change (Oreskes & Conway, 2010). They also lobbied Congress and state legislators to oppose adding subsidies for alternative clean energies, as well as fought against a carbon fee or tax as proposed by the Citizens Climate Lobby http://citizensclimate lobby.org. In a carbon fee program option, carbon producers contribute to a fund that returns money to the public to reward individuals for their energy efficiency, given the high level of waste associated with energy consumption (Hansen et al., 2013; http://tinyurl.com/ne596pg).

THE MYTHS OF UNIVERSAL VULNERABILITY AND UNIVERSAL RESPONSIBILITY

For years, environmental problems in the United States have been represented in mainstream media as issues of *universal vulnerability*, as if everyone were affected equally by environmental dangers. This hid the fact that low-income neighborhoods, especially communities of color, have been impacted with far worse consequences of environmental hazards than middle and upper class areas. When one takes into consideration issues of age along with class and race, it becomes very apparent that the inequality of the effects of climate change put poor children of color on the front line. Frederica Perera (2016) reports, "While air pollution and the adverse health impacts of climate change affect us all, they are most damaging to children, especially the developing fetus and young child and particularly those of low socio-economic status, who often have the greatest exposures and least amount of protection." The effects of climate change are also worse for people living on islands like the Maldives where rising sea levels are causing increasing flooding and putting the entire nation at risk (Berge, Cohen, & Shenk, 2011). Students need to understand that climate change is a problem that affects everyone, but not equally.

Another trope often repeated in commercial media is the notion of *universal responsibility*; the idea that we are all equally responsible for the environmental damage. While it is important that everyone feel a sense of responsibility and desire to improve the environment, it is also essential that corporations, governments, non-sustainable economic practices, and unjust ideologies be held accountable for the majority of the harm they are causing to the environment. During a heyday for the environmental movement in the 1970s, one of the classic environmental commercials was known as the "Crying Indian" that was created by an organization called *Keep America Beautiful.* This popular television commercial is fraught with problems, from the actor playing the Native American actually being Italian American to the organization funding the ads being more concerned with selling beverages and packaging than environmental change. With the tagline, *People start pollution. People can stop it,* this one commercial reframed the public discourse in the United States from corporate environmental devastation to a litter campaign in which all Americans can fight environmental pollution by simply picking up their trash (Dunaway, 2015). ELA teachers can download this commercial from YouTube http://tinyurl.com/ cye6k5l and have their students answer the six critical media literacy questions listed above after watching the commercial several times. Deep reading benefits from students viewing videos numerous times to uncover elements that are often missed the first time, such as the influence of sounds, editing, and considerations of what is missing. It is also helpful for students to critique media by considering the historical, cultural, and social contexts from when the texts were created, disseminated, and how they can be interpreted today in our own contemporary context.

One challenge in media representations of climate change is what Rob Nixon (2013) describes as the problem of "slow violence." Much of news media and movies appeals to audiences through sensationalizing momentary visual spectacles as dramatic entertainment. However, what is rarely portrayed is the "slow violence"

> that is neither spectacular nor instantaneous but instead incremental, whose calamitous repercussions are postponed for years or decades or centuries . . . Stories of toxic buildup, massing greenhouse gases, and accelerated species loss because of ravaged habitats may all be cataclysmic, but they are scientifically convoluted cataclysms in which casualties are postponed, often for generations.
>
> Nixon (2011)

As a result, climate change gets very little coverage, as evident in an analysis of CNN coverage during a week in 2015 that experienced record breaking temperatures when they aired five times more oil industry advertising than coverage of climate change (Kalhoefer, 2016). Nixon (2011, 2013) notes the lack of media representation of "slow violence" is particularly evident in poor southern hemisphere countries such as Ecuador where there are few, if any, regulations on oil drilling or the building of a dam in Brazil that displaced 40,000 mostly indigenous people and flooded 200 square miles of forests—furthering the deforestation of Brazil.

IS SEEING BELIEVING? USE OF PHOTOGRAPHY AND INFOGRAPHICS

In 1968, a photograph from the darkness of space showing a blue planet Earth rising over the moon, vitalized the environmental movement. Other images of birds covered with tar from oil spills or baby seals being clubbed to death on ice floes outraged the public and triggered emotional responses; even if only momentarily, they viscerally tugged at the heartstrings in a way that only photographs can. Vicki Goldberg (1991) asserts,

> Photographs have a swifter and more succinct impact than words, an impact that is instantaneous, visceral, and intense. They share the power of images in general, which have always played havoc with the human mind and heart, and they have the added force of evident accuracy.
>
> Goldberg (1991, p. 7)

Viewing these images has differently impacted people's attitudes and willingness to take actions. Images of climate change effects, for example, aerial views of flooding, led many people to believe that climate change is important (O'Neill et al., 2013). At the same time, some of these same images actually undermined some people's sense of self-efficacy that they could address climate change, while other images portraying energy futures enhanced feelings of optimism and empowerment.

Teachers can find numerous images and visual presentations about climate change on the Internet (see our wiki for links). There are a variety of sources today for students to view the visual effects of climate change, such as the time-lapse photography by James Balog in which he shows and discusses the results from his *Extreme Ice Survey* in his TED Talk online (Balog, 2009) and in the documentary *Chasing Ice* (Pesemen, Aronson, & Orlowski, 2012). NASA has several movies and interactive tools online that visually demonstrate the effects of climate change, such as the *Climate*

Time Machine, Global Ice Viewer, Images of Change, Eyes on the Earth 3D, and other programs that allow users to move their cursor and see changes on planet Earth over time http://tinyw.in/orCD. The Climate Reality Project provides infographics that simplify complex ideas with images and few words, making it an excellent tool for English language learners and all visual learners (*Telling the Story: Eight Great Infographics on Climate Change*, http://tinyurl.com/hokjbhf).

A major developer of interactive simulations is Climate Interactive www.climateinteractive.org which provides scientific information to students through appealing interactive simulations, for example, the *Climate Scoreboard* www.climateinteractive.org/tools/scoreboard uses a graphic to show how different nations' contributions could reduce greenhouse gas emissions by 2100.

Another effective set of animations created by Ed Hutchins portrays temperature increases since 1850 to the present http://tinyw.in/vmdP which was included in a video shown at the opening of the 2016 Olympics in Rio to portray how close we are to a 1.5-degree Celsius temperature increase.

STUDENTS CREATING VISUAL IMAGES

One of the best ways to teach students to read visual imagery is through creating visual images. The production process can also be an ideal method for students to demonstrate their understanding of climate change issues and share their concerns with others. Justin Boyd had his eleventh-grade students in Colorado work in pairs to create their own infographics about climate change using Piktochart (see examples of student work by Vikki & Ren at http://tinyw.in/Ejem). There are numerous websites to help students make their own infographics and visual thinking maps, such as Piktochart http://piktochart.com or Glogster http://tinyw.in/h4Xr. Educational Technology and Mobile Learning's website lists eighteen free programs for creating mind maps: http://tinyurl.com/7luyqeb (see *multimodal maps, simulations, and infographics* on the website).

CIVIC ENGAGEMENT WITH DIGITAL MEDIA

While adults may be accessing information about climate change through print or TV news outlets, young people are more likely to obtain their news through online social media outlets such as Facebook and YouTube (Newman et al., 2016). Given the popularity of social media for students sharing information and ideas, students employ different social media platforms to communicate their perspectives on climate change. Young people in Africa share their efforts to foster sustainability using the Climate Wednesday site www.climatewed.org (Joseph, 2016). Through use of Twitter, Facebook, Pinterest, and other platforms, users can share narratives and videos with hashtags describing their specific actions for fostering sustainability.

Adolescents are increasingly turning to digital media to voice their perspectives on issues, as documented in the book *By Any Media Necessary: The New Youth Activism* (Jenkins et al., 2016; http://tinyw.in/aFEM). Reports from the *Journal of Digital and Media Literacy* www.jodml.org. Jenkins et al. (2016) document how students are learning by using social media in their participatory culture are potential resources and strategies for their participation in political actions and collective activism. For example, students can employ what Eric Gordon (2013) defines as the "civic web" to share visual data about local environmental impacts. They can use the Community viz http://placeways.com/communityviz software to document local environmental impacts on their community or Trash Track http://senseable.mit.edu/trashtrack to track the movement of trash as it left Seattle, Washington or Monitour http://senseable.mit.edu/monitour to see the paths of e-waste across the world.

Students are more likely to use digital media tools for civic engagement when they:

– Experience being an active member of a diverse online community such as Youth Voices http://youthvoices.net for sharing their ideas with students from across the globe.
– Analyze the content on certain sites in terms of exposure to alternative perspectives.
– Engage in productive dialogue about certain issues in a respectful manner.
– Share their views and opinions regarding needed social and political change.

Hodgin (2016)

CRITICALLY QUESTIONING VISUAL REPRESENTATIONS

Before children can speak, they are surrounded by visual images that become even more ubiquitous as they get older. This omnipresence of visual representations beckons educators to help students think critically about visual aesthetics, design, and the influences of images to shape our information, ideas, and the basic notions of what is considered "normal" or "common-sense" (Hall, 2003). Images communicate within ideological systems and connote different meanings to different people depending on the contexts; they are always embedded in hierarchical relationships of power. Stuart Hall (2003) explains that dominant ideologies shape our notions of what seems "normal" and "tend to disappear from view into the taken for granted 'naturalised' world of common sense" (p. 90). This naturalizing of ideas, assumptions, and beliefs gains power with visual images when they are assumed to be objective or go unexamined.

Visual images and media messages are social constructions created by people with all their subjective biases and, whether they are intended to or not, all information advantages some at the expense of others. Therefore an important job for English teachers is to help students question all media and the ideological messages they convey. The sixth critical media literacy question is intended to help students understand this concept and inquire about who benefits and who is disadvantaged by the text, related to representations of climate change.

In her seventh grade English/Social Studies class in East Los Angeles, Fedora Schooler taught an 8-week unit combining critical media literacy with climate change. She began by showing students a hoax made by the BBC (Jones, 2008) of flying penguins that looks so real by employing the documentary genre, that most students did not question its authenticity and became convinced that penguins could fly. However, once they saw the backstory about how the BBC faked the images of flying penguins and created the hoax (BBC, 2008), they returned to their previous beliefs that penguins cannot fly. One student exclaimed, "in 1 minute we believe something as fact, then with one video we changed our minds." This activity captivated the students' interest about the manipulative potential of media and the desire to not be fooled again.

Schooler taught her students about critical media literacy and had them practice using the key questions that support the conceptual understandings. Students watched the movie *Wall-E* (Morris & Stanton, 2008) and analyzed the film from multiple perspectives applying critical questions. Schooler explains, "when you are using these questions you need to frontload them with multiple opportunities to practice using them with different media." She also gave students a homework assignment to use the questions while watching commercials or any type of media.

To learn the scientific facts about climate change, students read informational texts and watched videos such as: Leonardo DeCaprio's 2016 Oscar acceptance speech, Balog's (2009) TED Talk on *Time Lapse Photography of Extreme Ice Loss*, Bill Nye the Science Guy, and a BrainPop animation. They also annotated an informational text about climate change from their school science textbook, then re-read it to create Cornell notes. To organize the information they used Thinking Maps: multi-flow maps (for cause and effects), tree maps (for categorizing), and a bubble map (for describing). After learning about the science, Schooler had her students create environmental-justice-wanted posters that conveyed information about climate change on one sheet of paper with an image and brief text. In order to make appropriate decisions about their choice of words, images, and design of their poster, students referred to the critical media literacy questions throughout the creation process.

Encouraging students to collaborate and discuss their ideas, Schooler separated her class into teams to read different picture books and view various media that address environmental issues. She had a heterogeneous group of mixed reading levels in which some struggling readers were unable to decode and/or comprehend grade-level texts. By using high-quality picture books (see Chapter 4 for a list of picture books) and multimedia texts such as: spoken word videos, TV commercials, online art exhibits, and animated cartoons, all the students had access to the content to be able to reflect critically and participate fully in the discussions. After critiquing the messages and the mediums of their various texts, students dressed up in costumes and made oral advertising pitches for their books and movies using language arts techniques of persuasion.

Schooler integrated this unit with poetry by having her students read Robert Frost's (1916/2001) *The Road Less Traveled*. They discussed the elements of poetry and considered how the poem relates to their discussions about climate change. Students made personal connections, such as, "right now we are at the part of the road where we have to make a decision. Should we help stop climate change or should we continue burning fossil fuels and cutting down trees until we destroy the entire environment?"

For their final project, student groups chose different environmental issues that they were most drawn to and worked collaboratively to create some type of media that combined images and words in order to present their information to their peers. The class generated a large list of possible media projects based on all the different items they could think of in which images and words are used together, such as: food packaging, posters, movies, animation, T-shirts, menus, etc. One group repurposed the food package of Nutella as a way to address the issue of deforestation as companies exploit palm oil to make Nutella. They created a new packaging label with information about the environmental impact that corporate farming of palm oil is having on the forests in Indonesia. One group made a T-shirt and another made a poster to address problems of global warming and the role of fossil fuels to accelerate climate change. A comic strip was created by one team that investigated lead contamination of the water in Flint, Michigan and problems of ammonia in the water in Los Angeles. Schooler reflects:

> During this unit my students became aware of the possibility of manipulation by the media and how to better recognize and analyze the media's influence in their lives. Through studying climate change, they learned that their actions have impact on the world, and that media can be used to positively spur change.

THE SOUNDS SPEAK VOLUMES

To help students understand the influence and potential of sounds, music, dialogue, and narration, they can analyze audio engineering by exploring the way sounds, words, and even sentences convey different meanings depending on the context in which they are created, voiced, and heard. There are codes and conventions for dialogue and narration that shape what and how we hear people speaking, rapping, and singing in media.

These are important elements for students to analyze in audio texts, as well as valuable production skills students should learn for public speaking and creating their own audio recordings (Shamburg, 2009). Students can learn about *tone painting*—the ways musical sounds conjure up ideas, feelings, and images. After listening to short clips of musical scores, they can discuss the role that music plays to tell stories, create atmosphere, and sometimes perpetuate stereotypes.

A common, yet invisible element in most multimedia productions, is the use of sound effects. Few video games, television shows, cartoons, or movies are created without a Foley artist adding sounds. When students create their own sound effects while reading books or telling stories, they creatively engage with texts on multiple levels that can access their intellectual, social, and emotional intelligences.

Students can also listen to podcasts such as the Commonwealth Club Climate One podcasts http://tinyw.in/y9V1 that feature guests addressing various issues associated with climate change. Working together, students can create podcasts that allow their voices to be heard and provide counter-stories to challenge dominant narratives of race, class, gender, sexuality, or any topic they feel is being misrepresented or underrepresented (Bell, 2010). They can also submit their own "climate change stories" http://tinyw.in/lmmA for potential airing on the Climate Connect radio program http://tinyw.in/WNsu produced by the Yale Climate Communications project.

There are also songs, like *Love Song to the Earth* (Gad et al., 2015), featuring a collection of famous singers, that directly address climate change and can be a meaningful way for more musically-inclined students to connect with environmental issues. For music created by youth, see the video of 13-year-old indigenous rights activist Xiuhtezcatl Martinez performing hip-hop about climate change http://tinyw.in/qBbD. ELA students can discuss their responses and write analyses of songs http://tinyw.in/nKcG; (for examples http://tinyw.in/w91F) that are used or could be used in the climate change movement. Below is an example of how a music teacher integrated music into lessons on climate change and culminated with students creating their own environmental songs.

At the University of California, Los Angeles (UCLA) Lab School, music teacher Nick Kello taught a unit about climate change and music to all the students in grades 3–6 to help them understand the role music has played and continues to play in social movements, especially environmental issues. Kello organized the unit around the guiding question, "What can music tell us about the way in which different human societies have related to their natural environment?" Through focusing his students on this question, Kello used music as a lens to understand the relationships between humans and nature. He began by reading aloud the book, *Brother Eagle, Sister Sky,* in which Susan Jeffers (2002) provides an adaptation of the famous speech by Chief Seattle from the 1850s.

While there is controversy about the actual words that Seattle spoke, this literature provided an entry point for Kello's students to reflect on the relationships humans have had with nature and to question the current ideas students carry about their connections to the land, water, and sky. Kello had his students consider various Native American perspectives by listening to music from contemporary Chumash people living in Santa Barbara and Hopi snake dance rituals in Arizona. Students analyzed musical attributes, the meanings of the lyrics, and the ritualistic elements of the music. Often returning to the guiding question, Kello led his students to reflect on Native American relationships with nature, through art, music, and rituals.

The next genre Kello introduced was folk music, by having students listen to different versions of Woody Guthrie's classic song, *This Land is Your Land*. Students analyzed various lyrics, purposes, and uses of the song and explored the ways music has been used to tell stories and question humans' relationship with nature. In one verse, Guthrie sings, "the wheat fields waving and the dust clouds rolling," which created an opportunity to examine the historical context of the American Dust Bowl. Kello showed students clips from Ken Burns' (2012) documentary, *The Dust Bowl* (available on PBS). Students learned about one of the worst man-made disasters in US history and were able to make connections between the greed and drought of the 1930s with the causes and effects of climate change today. Kello used music by Woody Guthrie as well as the following songs to help students explore the effects of manifest destiny, the Industrial Revolution, and humans' relationship to nature: *Big Yellow Taxi* by Joni Mitchell, *Where Do the Children Play?* by Cat Stevens, and *Mercy, Mercy Me (The Ecology)* by Marvin Gaye.

Kello had previously worked with the students to learn various songs of protest. For this unit they focused on environmental songs and issues. Students watched news clips about climate change and the movie trailer for *The Island President* (http://theisland president.com) to see how issues of climate change are not affecting everyone equally. Students learned about the water crisis in Flint, Michigan and even problems with contaminated water in downtown Los Angeles. Students also discussed climate change denial and US attitudes about climate change, comparing the way some politicians in the United States still question the facts of climate change while most of the world has already accepted the scientific reality of it. After discussing science and politics, Kello showed students examples of how songs and music have been used in social movements to galvanize issues and bring people together. Kello explains that the very act of making music goes against, given that,

> music is inherently social, the idea that music is for entertainment is a social construction, music has historically been linked to social ritual, rite, or event, not in isolation. Music brings people together; it is inherently participatory; people dance, tap, and sing along. It allows people to share in a single experience together. It binds and unites people with ideas and feelings and actions together at the same time. Music can be an emotional experience for building community and solidarity.

In order to help students understand how various aspects of music work to position the audience to think and feel certain ways, Kello played his students the popular theme song, *Everything Is Awesome,* from *The Lego Movie* (2014). He began by having students listen to the song with questions on the board for them to consider: "What is the emotional quality of the song, what is the instrumentation, and what does this have to do with climate change?" Having no background knowledge about the song's relation- ship to climate change, the students were intrigued to discover the connection. Kello showed them a music video created by Greenpeace (www.youtube.com/watch?v=CM_HFLIsaKo) that uses the same song slowed down, with harmonic alterations, and played over images of a pristine Lego Arctic filling up with black oil to the point that only the Shell flag remains above the muck. The song and video were part of a political campaign to pressure the toy company to break its ties with the oil company, as the final tagline reads, "Shell is polluting our kids' imaginations. Tell Lego to end its partnership with Shell." Kello explains that when his students watched the Greenpeace video

> they were so blown away, they kept wanting to see it over and over again. It is just so powerful; we talked about how the tone painting totally changes, major chords are substituted for minor chords, the tempo is slowed down, but the words stayed the same. That created a total cognitive dissonance between the words, the imagery in the video, and the emotional tone painting of the music.

Since the goal of the Greenpeace video was to disrupt the decades-long relationship that Shell Oil has had with Lego toys, Kello showed his students a newspaper article about Arctic drilling and a Lego set from the 1970s with a Shell gas station. They discussed the implications of this partnership and the dangers of drilling for oil in the Arctic. The students were fascinated with the way Greenpeace had used a popular song to fight against climate change, so when Kello finally told them how the Greenpeace video was seen by thousands of people and actually caused Lego to end their partnership with Shell Oil (Petroff, 2014), the students in every class jumped up and cheered. It was a powerful lesson that led wonderfully into the students creating their own climate change songs. They were inspired because this gave them the proof that music really can have an impact.

In order to show his students an example of somebody their own age using music to challenge the problems of climate change, Kello played the eco rap hip hop video of *Melting Ice* by Lil Peppi http://tinyurl.com/hc4cbjx (Hopkins, 2009). After preparing his students to understand the power of music for social change and the problems of climate change, Kello had them become music makers and work together to create their own songs that challenge climate change. Kello reviewed everything they had discussed throughout the unit about climate change and listed the issues as a way to remind them of the things they could include in their song. They also talked about solutions by having them listen to Prince Ea's music videos, especially *Man vs Earth* http://tinyurl.com/za3c2og which concludes with suggestions for reforestation and strategies for combating climate change. The lessons that Kello taught during the students' music class integrated well with the lessons they were learning during their other classes, especially the poetry writing they were doing in language arts. When they started writing song lyrics, Kello pointed out that this was just like writing poetry.

To write their songs, students first worked in pairs to compose two lines of a verse that had to rhyme and meet a specific number of syllables. Then pairs joined together into groups of four and reviewed each other's lines to create one four-line verse. They were writing and writing verses after verses. One example from a group of third graders:

> Greenhouse gases are polluting the sky,
> Ocean levels are rising too high,
> People are cutting down too many trees,
> The birds are dying and so are the bees.

Kello typed up their words for each class to review and they democratically chose ten verses and one chorus. They ended with a set of lyrics and Kello downloaded several free rap beats from the Internet. He talked about using free beats that were open source, and had the students choose the beat that resonated most with them. They practiced rapping the lyrics with the beat and then recorded their final product. They also talked about what to do with the recordings. Time was tight at the end of the school year, so the students decided to continue with this next year. They were excited to go public with their songs and share their music with the mayor, the president, friends, and family.

ENGAGING EYES AND EARS TO CREATE MULTIMEDIA DIGITAL STORIES

Since television, movies, and video games have accustomed youth to stories told with sounds and images, the combination of modalities for storytelling can make the process more significant for students. When combining aural and visual texts to create multimedia stories, it can be helpful to start by storyboarding ideas with simple sketches to accompany the written text. The storyboard is intended to support the writing process and help students plan out the visual and aural elements along with the dialogue and narration. There are numerous tools and strategies for making digital stories which can be as simple as using PowerPoint to combine drawings with narration or as sophisticated as a movie-making program (like iMovie, MovieMaker, or Final Cut) that allows students to edit their video. It is necessary to find the appropriate tool for your situation, but the tool is just a means for the most important work of learning how to tell a story (Ohler, 2008).

INDIGENOUS PEDAGOGY

Indigenous pedagogy provides examples of the power of oral storytelling, the use of metaphor and analogy to convey ideas beyond the literal meanings of words, the social value of interviewing elders and people whose voices are often marginalized or ignored, and the importance of nature-based knowledge (Arrows, 2013). For tens of thousands of years, people around the world have been passing along their values and entire cultural identities through oral traditions. About 500 years ago, following the invention of the printing press, in many parts of the world, print literacy flourished as oral storytelling waned. "Thus, the richness of oral communication was lost, which includes, from all points of view, a significant dimension of musicality, proxemics, gestural communication, spatial relationship, specific closeness and sensorial perception between those speaking" explain Tornero and Varis (2010, p. 106). Fortunately, many indigenous societies have continued to practice and preserve the tradition of oral storytelling, a distinctly human social practice that remains a powerful space for teaching and learning. Many aspects of indigenous pedagogy can benefit educators and students, such as oral storytelling that aligns better with visual and aural modalities of audiovisual media than it does with print-based literacy. Four Arrows (2013) writes:

> Although the Indigenous approaches may seem strange at first to some teachers, they will likely resonate at some level. All of us have ancestors who once lived in one place long enough to understand how to exist in relative harmony with the rhythms of the natural world. This nature-based knowledge is in our DNA.
>
> Arrows (2013, p. 2)

The next chapter takes us into other modalities and genres for addressing climate change, such as drama, gaming, and role play.

For additional resources, activities, and readings related to this chapter, go to http://tinyw.in/1oIe on the book's website.

REFERENCES

Arrows, F. (2013). *Teaching truly: A curriculum to indigenize mainstream education.* New York: Peter Lang.

Balog, J. (2009). *Time-lapse proof of extreme ice loss* [Video file]. TEDGlobal 2009, retrieved from http://tinyurl.com/pqq5u64.

BBC. (2008, April 1). *Making penguins fly on April Fools' Day 2008* [Video file]. British Broadcasting Corporation. Retrieved from www.youtube.com/watch?v=lzhDsojoqk8.

Beach, R. (2009). Digital tools for collecting, connecting, constructing, responding to, creating. In D. Kellner & R. Hammer (Eds.), *Media/cultural studies: Critical approaches* (pp. 206–228). New York: Peter Lang.

Bell, L. A. (2010). *Storytelling for social justice: Connecting narrative and the arts in antiracist teaching.* New York: Routledge.

Berge, R., Cohen, B. (Producers), & Shenk, J. (Director) (2011). *The island president* [Motion Picture]. United States: Samuel Goldwyn Films.

boyd, d. (2014). *It's complicated: The social lives of networked teens.* New Haven, CT: Yale University Press.

Buckingham, D. (2003). *Media education: Literacy, learning and contemporary culture.* Cambridge: Polity Press.

Burns, K. (Director). (2012). *The dust bowl* [Motion picture]. New York: Public Broadcasting System.

Common Core State Standards (2015). *Common core state standards for English language arts & literacy in history/social studies, science, and technical subjects.* Common Core State Standards Initiative. Retrieved from http://tinyurl.com/kjgs8a5.

Cooper, C. B. (2011). Media literacy as a key strategy toward improving public acceptance of climate change science. *BioScience, 61*(3), 231–237.

Coyle, K. (2005). Environmental literacy in America: What ten years of NEETF/Roper Research studies say about environmental literacy in the U.S. *National Environmental Education and Training Foundation.* Retrieved from http://tinyurl.com/jk3jfkj.

Daly, M., Gifford, L., Luedecke, G., McAllister, L., Nacu-Schmidt, A., Andrews, K., & Boykoff, M. (2015). World newspaper coverage of climate change or global warming, 2004–2015. Center for Science and Technology Policy Research, Cooperative Institute for Research in Environmental Sciences, University of Colorado. Retrieved from http://sciencepolicy.colorado.edu/media_coverage.

Dunaway, F. (2015). *Seeing green: The use and abuse of American environmental images.* Chicago: The University of Chicago Press.

Freire, P., & Macedo, D. (1987). *Literacy: Reading the word and the world.* Westport, CT: Bergin & Garvey.

Frost, R. (1916/2001). The road not taken. In R. Frost, *The road not taken: A selection of Robert Frosts's poems* (p. 270). New York: Holt.

Funk, S., Kellner, D., & Share, J. (2016). Critical media literacy as transformative pedagogy. In M. N. Yildiz & J. Keengwe (Eds.), *Handbook of research on media literacy in the digital age.* Hershey, PA: IGI Global.

Gad, T., Shanks, J., Bedingfield, N., & Paul, S. (2015). *Love song to the Earth.* [Recorded by Paul McCartney, Jon Bon Jovi, Sheryl Crow, Fergie, Colbie Caillat, Natasha Bedingfield, Sean Paul, Leona Lewis, Johnny Rzeznik (Goo Goo Dolls), Krewella, Angelique Kidjo, Nicole Scherzinger, Kelsea Ballerini, Christina Grimmie, Victoria Justice, & Q'orianka Kilcher].

Goldberg, V. (1991). *The power of photography: How photographs changed our lives.* New York: Abbeville Press.

Gordon, E. (2013). Beyond participation: Designing for the civic web. *Journal of Digital and Media Literacy. 1*(1). Retrieved from http://tinyw.in/MFnj.

Hall, S. (2003). The whites of their eyes: Racist ideologies and the media. In G. Dines & J. M. Humez (Eds.), *Gender, race, and class in media: A text reader* (pp. 89–93). Los Angeles: SAGE Publication.

Hansen, J., Kharecha, P., Sato, M., Masson-Delmotte, V., Ackerman, F., Beerling, D. J., Hearty, P. J., Hoegh-Guldberg, O., Hsu, S-L., Parmesan, C., Rockstrom, J., Rohling, E. J., Sachs, J., Smith, P., Steffen, K., Van Susteren, L., von Schuckmann, K., Zachos, J. C. (2013). Assessing "dangerous climate change": Required reduction of carbon emissions to protect young people, future generations and nature. *Plos One*. Retrieved from http://tinyw.in/bjf2

Hodgin, E. (2016). Educating youth for online civic and political dialogue: A conceptual framework for the digital age. *Journal of Digital and Media Literacy*, 4(1–2). Retrieved from http://tinyw.in/iAr8.

Hopkins, C. A. (2009). *Lil Peppi—melting ice* [Video file]. Retrieved from www.youtube.com/watch?v=yjXuldy-Ilw.

Howe, J. (2014). *Behind the curve: Science and the politics of global warming*. Seattle, WA: University of Washington Press.

Jeffers, S. (2002). *Brother eagle, sister sky*. New York: Puffin Books.

Jenkins, H., Shresthova, S., Gamber-Thompson, C., Kligler-Vilenchi, N., & Zimmerman, A. M. (2016). *By any media necessary: The new youth activism*. New York: New York University Press.

Jones, T. (2008, March 31). *Penguins—BBC* [Video file]. UK: British Broadcasting Corporation. Retrieved from www.youtube.com/watch?v=9dfWzp7rYR4.

Joseph, S. (2016, October 15). Young people advocate use of social media tools to mitigate climate change. [Web log post]. Retrieved from http://tinyw.in/BzsO.

Kalhoefer, K. (2015). How broadcast networks covered climate change in 2014 [Web log post]. Retrieved from http://tinyw.in/yAiI.

Kalhoefer, K. (2016, April 25). Study: CNN viewers see far more fossil fuel advertising than climate change reporting [Web log post]. Retrieved from http://tinyw.in/SZcr.

Klein, N. (2014). *This changes everything: Capitalism vs. the climate*. New York: Simon & Schuster.

Lenhart, A. (2015). Teens, social media & technology overview 2015: Smartphones facilitate shifts in communication landscape for teens. Washington, DC: Pew Research Center. Retrieved from http://pewrsr.ch/1NaUOUU.

Leonard, A., Sachs, J., & Fox, L. (2013). *The story of solutions: Why making real change starts with changing the game* [Video file]. United States: Free Range Studios. Retrieved from http://storyofstuff.org/movies/the-story-of-solutions/.

Lewis, J., & Boyce, T. (2009). Climate change and the media: The scale of the challenge. In T. Boyce & J. Lewis (Eds.), *Climate change and the media* (pp. 1–16). New York: Peter Lang.

López, A. (2014). *Greening media education: Bridging media literacy with green cultural citizenship*. New York: Peter Lang.

Mayer, J. (2016). *Dark money: The hidden history of the billionaires behind the rise of the radical right*. New York: Doubleday.

Media Matters for America. (2016). How broadcast networks covered climate change in 2015. Washington, DC: Author. Retrieved from http://tinyw.in/EEAL.

Morris, J., & Stanton, A. (2008). *Wall-E* [Motion Picture]. United States: Disney Pixar.

Newman, N., Fletcher, R., Levy D. A. L., & Nielsen, R. K. (2016). *Reuters institute digital news report 2016*. New York: Reuters. Retrieved from http://tinyw.in/AaiB.

Nixon, R. (2011, June 26). Slow violence [Web log post]. Retrieved from http://tinyw.in/zEt5.

Nixon, R. (2013). *Slow violence and the environmentalism of the poor*. Cambridge, MA: Harvard University Press.

Ohler, J. (2008). *Digital storytelling in the classroom*. Thousand Oaks, CA: Corwin Press.

O'Neill, S. J., Boykoff, M., Niemeyer, S., & Day, S. A. (2013). On the use of imagery for climate change engagement. *Global Environmental Change*, 23, 413–421.

Oreskes, N., & Conway, E. (2010). *Merchants of doubt: How a handful of scientists obscured the truth on issues from tobacco smoke to global warming*. New York: Bloomsbury Press.

Orlowski, J. (Director). (2012). *Chasing ice* [Motion Picture]. United States: Submarine Deluxe.

Perera, F. (2016, June 21). The case for a child-centered energy and climate policy. *Environmental Health News*. Retrieved from www.environmentalhealthnews.org/ehs/news/2016/june/opinion-the-case-for-a-child-centered-energy-and-climate-policy.

Petroff, A. (2014, October 9). *Lego ditches Shell after Arctic oil protests*. CNN Money. Retrieved from http://tinyurl.com/jfzv27n.

Rideout, V., Lauricella, A., & Wartella, E. (2011). Children, media, and race: Media use among white, black, Hispanic, and Asian American children. *Center on Media and Human Development School of Communication*. Chicago: Northwestern University.

Shamburg, C. (2009). *Student-powered podcasting: Teaching for 21st-century literacy*. Washington, DC: International Society for Technology in Education.

Share, J. (2015). *Media literacy is elementary: Teaching youth to critically read and create media*, 2nd ed. New York: Peter Lang Publishers.

Tornero, J. M., & Varis, T. (2010). *Media literacy and new humanism*. Moscow, Russian Federation: UNESCO. Retrieved from http://tinyurl.com/j4nrtve.

Chapter 7
Using Drama and Gaming to Address Climate Change

> Games are natural tools for climate change education and engagement . . . In this way, games provide "designed experiences" where players can learn through doing and being, rather than absorbing information from readings and traditional lecture formats. . . . They allow for visioning—for example, being able to envision oneself in the future—and seeing consequences of actions at different points in time. . . . Finding new, more effective solutions often involves a trial and error process, and games can make it easier and less intimidating to identify new strategies.
>
> Jason S. Wu and Joey J. Lee (2015, p. 413)

In this chapter, we describe how engaging students in drama and gaming activities provides them with simulated experiences of the effects of climate change, and opportunities to creatively practice formulating arguments and taking action.

Drama activities allow students to interact with peers in improvisation, role play, or creating skits. Drama provides a *"living through* experience" (Pirie, 1997, p. 52, emphasis original), assuming roles, addressing problems or dilemmas, responding to others, and/or inventing imagined spaces in dialogic, open-ended ways. Drama offers a valuable way to involve students in the "social drama" of conflicts and social debates about climate change (Smith & Howe, 2015). As the interaction unfolds, students experience emotions and adopt perspectives on events, norms, or policies. Drama can take place using familiar formats, for example a radio or television talk-show, trial, legislative hearing, conference, community meeting, etc.

As with the drama activities, games allow players to go beyond simply learning about climate change to actively engage in missions or projects involving decision-making processes (Wu & Lee, 2015). Games can transport students into complex systems requiring an understanding of contingencies and factors shaping climate change (Pitfield, 2012).

An essential component of any drama or game activity is to have students debrief or reflect on their experience in the activity reflecting on their emotions and perceptions in roles and what they have learned from the activity (Boldt et al. 2015; Pitfield, 2012).

DEVELOPING AND PERFORMING SCENES AND PLAYS

Starting from any of the climate fiction literary works described in Chapter 4, or on testimony or information about real-world climate events, students, perhaps in groups, can design and perform their own scenes and short plays.

Drawing on their reading and research, students can begin by establishing the characters, events, and locations where the scenes will take place. A simple three-scene approach, which can easily be made more complex, involves: a first scene to introduce characters and "set the stage"; a second scene that introduces a problem, crisis, or event, and perhaps additional characters; and, a third scene which either resolves the problem or sets forward a dilemma to be contemplated by the audience. Students can then collaborate on writing dialogue and a script. Center Stage has a helpful pdf guide to *Teaching Playwriting in Schools* at http://tinyurl.com/zepmnd8.

A powerful approach to drama work around climate change can be found in the theater activities of Augusto Boal (1993), particularly what he called "forum theater" and "invisible theater." Forum theater attempts to overcome the separation between actors and spectators. As a performance is taking place, or at certain prearranged key moments, or when the drama is being replayed a second time, members of the audience can tell the actors to behave differently or they can step forward and involve themselves in creating a different conclusion. For example, students might perform a conversation between teenagers starting a climate change club at their school and adults, either school personnel, parents, or community members, who object. At certain key points the audience could give directions for replaying the action differently or become involved themselves. Students could perform a high-level meeting of business people and elected government officials to plan new power plants or transportation systems.

A forum theater performance could be built around protesting environmentalists, police, and bystanders. A forum theater could be as simple as a family Thanksgiving Dinner discussion about climate change. Forum theater performance can be pretty much spontaneously created and developed entirely in the classroom setting. Given a setting, students can brainstorm ideas for dialogue before getting up to perform. Forum theater events focus on moments when critical discussion or action is taking place during which spectators and actors improvise strategies and solutions. Forum theater is a great starting point for discussion and writing.

Invisible theater is a kind of street performance that can take the issue of climate change beyond the cocoon of the classroom. Invisible theater takes place in a public space and the performers attempt to disguise the fact that what is happening is a performance. People who happen to be present and, thus turned into observers and bystanders, may even choose to participate. Thus during the invisible theater event or "happening", spectators are given every encouragement to view it as real.

Secondary students could design performances to take place at school in the hallway, lunchroom, or on the school grounds that would raise questions about climate change. Students might stage a climate change protest outside the school disrupted by deniers. Or carbon police could arrive in the cafeteria to arrest students eating meat, or in the parking lot to take into custody people not carpooling. Or students could stage heatstroke collapse caused by rising temperatures. Or . . . ? The possibilities for educating about climate change through "invisible theater" are endless. Obviously it would be wise to plan carefully, alert administrators and, after the performance, provide spectators with a page of information about the issues. Alerting the local press in advance might disseminate knowledge to the community. Invisible theater can also provoke discussion and writing, and plans for taking more action.

Through Boalian techniques, students can in essence practice taking action in their world. Boal was determined to break down the "fourth wall" that separates performers from audience, in order to help spectators break out of passivity and have theater take responsibility for social justice. Students using these techniques would gain from learning more about Boal's philosophy, approaches, and experience.

Another way to develop drama activities is to have students learn about innovative, real world climate protest actions or performance events to inspire them to create their own productions/events that address climate change (Kershaw, 2009; Lavery & Finburgh, 2015; Arons & May, 2016). For example:

- The Otesha Project www.otesha.ca that lasted from 2002 to 2015 involved a group of young people riding their bikes around Canada to perform plays about consumer choices and climate change (O'Shea, 2016).
- The Climate Change Theater Action project http://tinyw.in/zx3M involved people from throughout the world staging short productions associated with supporting the 2015 Paris Climate Conference.

Students could also read, view, and/or produce plays based on climate change:

- *The Heretic* (Bean, 2012) http://tinyw.in/rSeT, a comedy about debates on the science of climate change.
- *This Clement World* http://tinyw.in/5HPW by Cynthia Hopkins combines documentary film about an Arctic expedition, a folk opera for solo voice and chorale, and portrayal of a ghost of a Native American woman, a neutral alien observer from outer space; and a child from the not-so-distant future who has traveled back in time.
- *Mr. Burns* (Washburn, 2014) based on *The Simpsons* portrays a group of young people attempting to escape massive fires in a time in the future.
- *The Great Immensity* http://thegreatimmensity.org/about is a musical about a young woman traveling from Panama to the Canadian Arctic who meets people, scientists, indigenous community leaders, and tour guides coping with climate change.

ROLE-PLAY ACTIVITIES

One approach to engaging students in a drama or simulation activity involves providing them with a context and scenario that include a specific dilemma or challenge for them to solve. To help her students adopt different cultural perspectives in her literature class, Amanda Hagood (2016) has them focus on alternative points of view in a text. For example, students read T. C. Boyle's (1996) novel, *The Tortilla Curtain*, which portrays the worlds of two different couples living in the Topanga Canyon area of Los Angeles—an upper-middle-class couple and two undocumented Mexican immigrants who are camped out in a ravine next to the other couple's home. Students respond to differences in how these two couples perceive daily challenges associated with the same locations where the upper-middle-class couple is concerned about fear of distant urban violence and coyotes preying on their pets and the immigrant couple is coping with heat exposure, prejudices, actual violent crime, and dangerous working conditions.

This leads her largely middle-class students to reflect on the perspectives of disenfranchised people coping with climate change effects. Hagood applies this activity to her students' own lives, having them write about an environmental justice issue in their home towns; bringing environmental justice activists into the classroom for face-to-face conversation; arranging a "toxic tour" with local experts who can demonstrate, firsthand, the impact of environmental burdens on nearby neighborhoods; or engaging students in a long-term service project that allows them to connect with an environmentally disenfranchised group.

Linda Christensen (2009) has her inner-city language arts students engage in role playing "tea parties" in order to explore and understand complex and conflictive problems and issues. Students studying climate change can hold a "tea party" where they take on the persona of different actors, perhaps including oil company executives, representatives from coal producing states, Greenpeace activists, farmers who lost their crops from a drought, South Sea islanders losing their home from sea-level rise, Africans living in the Sahel region fleeing the expanding Sahara, etc.

In the similar Climate Change Mixer game (Bigelow, 2014), each student in a class adopts a different role based on actual people representing a range of perspectives on the impact of climate change—lawyers, scientists, corporate CEOs, politicians, farmers, Native Americans, activists, etc. The goal of this role play is to help students understand that "climate change affects everyone, everywhere. But not equally" (p. 92). Students then interact with each other to discuss questions regarding:

- Who is hurt by or benefits from the impacts of climate change and in what ways?
- Who will experience similar effects to that of the student's own role?
- Which role has narratives similar to the role's narratives?
- Who will need to make major life changes due to climate change?
- Which role lives on a different continent and how is the impact for that role different or similar to the student's own role?
- Which roles have ideas for how to address climate change and what are those ideas?
- Which roles are taking actions and how would the student take the same action?

Bigelow (2014, p. 94)

Some role-play activities described in *A People's Curriculum for the Earth* (Bigelow & Swinehart, 2014) are Climate Change Mixer, The Thingamabob Game, the Indigenous Peoples' Summit ("Don't Take Our Voices Away"), and the Climate Change Trial ("Who's to Blame for the Climate Crisis"). The Indigenous Peoples' Climate Summit role play was designed to help students consider issues of eco-justice related to the adverse effects of climate change on indigenous peoples in places such as the Pacific Islands given that 20 percent of the world's population are responsible for 60 percent of climate change emissions (O'Neill & Swinehart, 2010) (see the PBS Documentary Paradise Lost about the effects of climate change on the South Pacific islands http://tinyw.in/QR09).

The role play was based on the actual Indigenous Peoples' Global Summit on Climate Change, held in Anchorage, Alaska, in April 2009, in which representatives from eighty different countries met to address climate change effects on their countries http://tinyw.in/DtAm. In the role play, students adopt the roles of representatives of six different groups: the Dine (Navajo); Alaska Native (including the Yup'ik and the Iñupiaq); the Bambara of sub-Saharan Africa; and indigenous groups from Kiribati (central Pacific islands), the Caribbean, and the Amazon (for specific descriptions of the role play: http://tinyw.in/oxon). Students adopt different roles within their groups as indigenous peoples to then formulate positions on how their regions were being impacted by climate change to inform other groups.

In the Hot: One World, One Planet http://tinyw.in/5pgk role-play, "Aubrey" uses Google Hangout to interact with five other adolescents from around the world: "Natasha" from Russia, "Luiz" from Brazil, "Will" from Bangladesh, "Albert" from Kenya, and "Jia" from China. Each of these adolescents is experiencing similar impacts of climate change on their region. When "Aubrey's" grandfather discovers her interactions, he decides to create the simulation which involves students adopting the roles of the six adolescents (for a description of the six roles: http://tinyw.in/knCY) each of whom has a different perspective on climate change.

Students playing the game engage in five quests:

- Developing Climate Crisis: Join the challenge.
- Push and Pull of Energy and Carbon in our Lives: Learn about your role.

- CO_2 Balancing Act: Reduce atmospheric carbon dioxide.
- Say Goodbye to Business as Usual: Cut fossil fuel use.
- Powering the World: Find energy solutions to mitigate climate change.

To prepare for participation in the game, students view videos http://tinyw.in/pa3V, including "The Big Climate Change Experiment: Calling All Climate Doctors" to acquire information for use in their quests. A key aspect of engaging in these quests is accessing and connecting with scientists, engineers, journalists, government officials, and citizens to gain their perspectives on developing solutions (Harris et al., 2016). Students then adopt their different roles to engage in panel discussions about issues in each quest and propose possible solutions from each of the six roles' different perspectives.

Based on a simulation of the UN Climate Change Conference, Zach Zeichner's (2015) students wrote speeches addressed to world leaders, for example, arguing that wealthy nations need to assume greater responsibility for addressing climate change while other students argued that all nations need to equally share responsibilities.

In another role-play activity that involved 2-day conferences in Barcelona and Berlin (http://barcelonaprotocol.blogspot.com, http://berlinprotocol.blogspot.com) students from two universities adopted roles as delegate representatives of various countries, as well as fossil fuel industry lobbyists or observers (Paschall & Wüstenhagen, 2012). Members of the different countries' delegations were each given 20 minutes to make their presentations about

1. Geography, including how the country/countries would be affected by climate change.
2. Economy, including key sectors that could help or hinder efforts to address climate change and the availability of funding for climate-related projects.
3. Politics, including past stances in climate negotiations and current opinion polls.

Paschall & Wüstenhagen (2012, p. 519)

The delegation teams then created "position papers" identifying goals for reducing greenhouse gas emissions by 2020 and 2050, recommending the use of alternative energy sources, and funding for developing countries that are being adversely impacted by climate change. Next, the delegates drafted resolutions to present to the conference. Some students also assumed the role of the media who interviewed delegates and reported on the deliberations through live news presentations and a blog. Delegates also gave interviews, submitted press releases, and, for the Greenpeace representative, staged protests. This led to final votes on their resolutions that required a three-fourth majority to pass. As in any effective role play, students engaged in verbal debriefing using mind-mapping about their experience. Students also wrote their own reflection papers.

In his high school IB geography classroom in central Ohio, John Jordan employed a role play to have his students address their skepticism about effective governmental action on climate change (Beach, 2015). The students assumed the roles of members of an advisory group who were asked to draft policies and proposals for a major piece of legislation to present to a Senator, as played by the teacher, for feedback. To draft their proposals, the students conducted research in teams to synthesize and critique information, taking into account physical, legal, economic, and political dimensions of climate change.

One student, Keegan Flaherty, noted that participating in this activity "caused me to think more about what the real threat of global climate change is, because it gave my ideas more importance—we were actually going to do something with it, so it had to be more than just my opinion" (Beach, 2015, p. 12). Another student, Hayden Shenefield, learned that "policies can be put in place that don't require everything to change but can still be effective at slowing global climate change" (p. 12). And another student, Jordan, "came to think of the issue as a problem to be solved rather than a political issue to take sides on" (p. 12).

Middle-school students in Greeley, Colorado engaged in a mock US Senate committee debate regarding the need for funding of alternative energy sources (Redmond, 2016). Students assumed the role of Senators supporting funding of tidal energy versus solar power; hydroelectric against wind power; and geothermal opposite biomass, while members of the Greeley community assumed roles as members of the US Senate Committee for Energy and Natural Resources and as judges. Students were asked to justify their alternative energy choice based on startup costs, long-term sustainability, public sentiment, reliability, and more, with the group proposing tidal energy making the most effective presentation.

Students can go beyond their own national point of view to adopt the perspective of a global citizen. In this way they can better recognize that even if they may not currently be adversely impacted by climate change, there is a moral responsibility to be concerned about how others in the world are affected, as well as future generations.

Drawing on the 2015 UN Paris Conference talks in which developing countries sought to have developed countries pay for damage from climate change, Eleanor Stein (2015) has students engage in a role-play activity in small groups, each representing a different country. For example, while the US group may oppose any legally binding emission reduction target, the Bolivian group proposes creation of a global Climate Justice Tribunal for prosecuting nations who fail to reduce their emissions, resulting in the groups having to negotiate their conflicting agendas. They also study the petition by the Inuit Circumpolar Conference, an indigenous alliance of communities in Alaska and Canada, to the Inter-American Human Rights Commission in 2005 regarding the negative effects of the warming of the Arctic on their communities.

One benefit of engaging in role play is that students learn to empathize with alternative perspectives. In a study of participants engaged in a role-play activity addressing whether to drain or preserve a virtual lake, those participants who engaged in the role-play activity were more likely to opt for preserving the lake and employed more empathy-related reasoning than participants who simply read about the lake dilemma (Schrier, 2015).

For more classroom activities related to eco-justice issues, see online resources on the website, Integrate Environmental Justice activities http://tinyw.in/uU1j, summary of methods for teaching environmental justice from an InTeGrate workshop http://tinyw.in/iZoG, as well as materials for use with the Martusewicz, Edmundson, and Lupinacci (2011) http://tinyw.in/XEGC and Turner (2015) http://tinyw.in/XrPa books on eco-justice education. Having students adopt roles or characters with various national, class, race, or gender differences on environmental challenges can lead them to reflect critically on what may be their own privileged perspective.

ONLINE ROLE PLAY

Students can participate in virtual, online role plays perhaps similar to those of games to be discussed later in this chapter using a class blog; or online discussion forums on a class-learning management system (Moodle, Canvas, Edmodo, Schoology, Collaborize Classroom, Ning, etc.), Twitter, or a social networking site such as Facebook. One advantage of using online role plays is that students can assume anonymous, avatar roles so that their peers may not necessarily know which students are performing certain roles (Beach & Doerr-Stevens, 2011).

Students can also participate in virtual role-play simulations involving strategies for coping with climate change effects. The HOT: One World, One Climate simulation (see page 102) includes a scenario http://tinyw.in/75N2 in which a hurricane hits Maryland's Chesapeake Bay and the Eastern Shore destroying homes, schools, communities, and businesses requiring the residents of the area to move elsewhere, including "Aubrey Vale" who moved with her family to New York. Her grandfather, "Jack Hanover", is a scientist who focuses on climate change.

GAMES RELATED TO CLIMATE CHANGE

Another option for engaging students involves use of the many simulations, card/board games, role-playing games, and computer games focusing on climate change (Eisenack & Reckien, 2013; Katsaliaki & Mustafee, 2015; LeBourdais, 2016; Meadows, Sweeney, & Mehers, 2016). While some critics may dismiss video games as not fostering learning, James Gee (2007) explains how video games offer considerable pedagogical potential. In his book *What Video Games Have to Teach Us about Learning and Literacy*, Gee describes thirty-six learning principles that are built into good video games; among them are the ideas that video games promote active learning, risk taking, experimentation, problem-solving, collaboration, embodied experiences, multimodal learning, and more. Students then learn to engage in problem-solving associated with these contingencies and factors to define alternative solutions to reducing emissions or developing clean energy options associated with sustainability and conservation (Sandbrook, Adams, & Monteferri, 2015).

Mendis Condis (2015) notes a number of advantages from playing games associated with climate change given that students:

- Adopt nonhuman perspectives as species, animals, systems, etc., to experience the impacts of climate change by humans on the nonhuman.
- Learn to operate according to rules or language in alternative systems coping with climate change to then formulate strategies and arguments for coping with challenges in those systems.
- Understand how the environment is constructed based on narrative or visual designs to guide their play in a game, leading to critical thinking about how their lived world experience is constituted through narratives or advertising.

She cites the example of *Reus* www.reusgame.com in which players assume the role of the Earth itself. As the Earth, they have no control over humans' intentions, a reversal from the humans attempting to control Earth, requiring players to adopt a nonhuman perspective. Players advance by creating complementary ecosystems which benefit both humans and the Earth.

Fourteen-to fifteen-year-old Swedish students engaged in playing the *SimCity 4 Deluxe Edition* game http://tinyw.in/I9b4 to create sustainable future cities. They had to make choices about different levels of emissions of different energy systems, for example, the pros and cons of selecting windmills as opposed to power plants (Nilsson & Jakobsson, 2011). Some students critiqued the game platform itself as favoring a capitalist model of development through power plants. The experience of playing games can therefore spark further discussions about the game framework or contingencies and thus about issues of climate change.

Two important organizations supporting development of games related to climate change are Games for Change www.gamesforchange.org (for their games on climate change: http://goo.gl/qouHho) and the PoLAR Climate Change Education Partnership http://thepolarhub.org at Columbia University.

Adopting roles in games positions students as active agents imagining that there are solutions to addressing climate change, offering hope instead of disillusionment. Because most games involve working collaboratively, students learn to engage in problem-solving and decision making with others, practices essential to fostering change.

As with drama activities, it is important for teachers to facilitate and assist students to play the game effectively, and to debrief with them about what they learned (Eisenack & Reckien, 2013). Some computer games can provide their own internal feedback based on students' success in playing the game. At the same time, teacher-led discussion can lead to richer evaluation of the learning.

The following are card and board games as well as computer simulation games designed primarily for middle- and high-school students organized according to the focus of these games on certain aspects of addressing climate change. Based on playing some of these games, Allen's students provided their reviews.

ENACTING STRATEGIES FOR COPING WITH CLIMATE CHANGE

The following games engage players in collaboratively devising strategies for coping with climate change effects through adopting different roles to devise adaptation and mitigation efforts, requiring them to imagine ways to address climate change in those roles.

- *Act to Adapt* http://climatecentre.org/resources-games/act-to-adapt involves students as either "community members" who are attempting to develop strategies to cope with the effects of climate change or the role of "climate change deniers" attempting to undermine the "community members," resulting in a conflict between the two groups, leading to discussions on how to address climate change.
- *The Incredible Carbon Journey* is a board game that can be created using an attached file http://tinyw.in/19vw in which players experience the world before and after the influence of fossil fuel use as they move through different historical changes in the Earth.
- *Climate Quest* https://earthgames.org/games/climatequest for Mac and PC. Players adopt one of four roles—the urban planner, the ecologist, the agricultural scientist, or the climate scientist to determine which one can most effectively and quickly cope with climate disasters that appear on a map of the United States, based on actual impacts selected from the US National Climate Assessment.
- *Imagine Earth* www.imagineearth.info/gameplay is a role-play simulation involving manipulation of the Earth's resources. Angelo Negrito noted that:

    The graphics of this game are quite astonishing. When you play in campaign mode, the story behind the game is explained. The game takes place in the future after all the resources have been depleted on our planet Earth. Mankind's goal is to find an alternative option and must expand civilization to space. Economy and civilization will stop thriving at a certain point so when you play this game, your goal is to explore and populate distant planets, build up successful colonies without destroying your planet. The vital stats of your Earth are available in the user interface.

Imagine Earth has great concepts. The player must be obliged to build things and consume energy and resources at the same time. You are able to build infrastructure like power plants to supply energy. But keep in mind you are depleting food, land, and money. So the outcomes of your planet could either lead to global chaos or success. Natural disasters can also occur randomly when you are constructing your planet.

It becomes a constant and deadly cycle of production and consumption. The creators of this game really capture the themes and concept behind consumerism and profit. Many big businesses today forget how they impact everyone on a global scale, as they focus on profit and expansion. Playing this game is an eye-opener because you get to visualize Earth in a zoomed-out perspective.

– *FutureCoast* http://futurecoast.org engages students in listening to audio voicemails of people recorded in 2014, particularly people living in coastal areas, talking about the effects of climate change, serving to model ways for students to create their own descriptive narratives as well as imagining how to cope with the problems identified in these voicemails (for more information, see Pyper, 2014).
– *The Adventures of Carbon Bond* http://trpetersonlab.tamu.edu/carbon-bond focuses on students assuming the roles of people employing carbon capture and sequestration (CCS) as a mitigation strategy for climate change (Feldpausch-Parker et al., 2013).
– *Climate Health Impact* http://playgen.com/play/climate-health-impact http://tinyw.in/ IW72 involving players making decisions on how to cope with health effects of climate change through engaging in research on strategies for preventing the spread of certain diseases resulting from climate change.
– *Precipice* http://tinyw.in/0NYt is a 3D simulation game in which students are living in the world of the present and 2032 in which they interact with other characters coping with effects of climate change, requiring them to convince these characters of ways to address climate change. Clara Peeters, describes playing this game:

Initially you start out in the year 2030, when the world has been ravaged by floods and other various climate disasters. The game lets you go back in time to 2010 and interact with three people, George, Paula, and Marcus. Marcus and Paula are married, and Paula has all these great ideas about climate change and what society has to do as a whole to better the situation. You have three goals in the game, and each one is linked to a character and how your actions and conversation can get them to realize their potential when it comes to climate change and creating a better future not only for themselves but also for future generations. Entering into conversations with these characters, you are given several options for what to say, and your job is to prompt George and Marcus into realizing that their preconceived notions about climate change and how it is not going to affect them in their home is grossly wrong, or trying to get Paula to share her ideas with the general public. Then the game transports you back to 2030 to see how your initial actions changed or did not change the future. I enjoyed this game because it shows that even starting a conversation can change someone's point of view, their life, and the future.

ADOPTING AND NEGOTIATING POLICIES ON CLIMATE CHANGE

In these games, consistent with the goals of argumentative writing in Chapter 5, students learn to formulate arguments for adopting policies designed to reduce emissions or create clean energy options.

- *Keep Cool* is a board game www.spiel-keep-cool.de that involves three to six players in negotiations as representatives of different countries attempting to address climate change (Eisenack, 2013). Players select whether they want to employ "black" (fossil fuel) or "green" growth options. During the game, they must determine how to adapt the impacts of climate change such as droughts or floods. Players can also build high versus low carbon emission factories, which then results in changes in the global mean temperatures.
- *Cool It!* http://tinyw.in/VSBN (teachers' guide http://tinyw.in/cCfh) for middle-school students is a card game in which students collect enough "solution" versus "problem" cards in the categories of energy, transportation, and forests, to win the game.
- *World Climate* http://tinyw.in/haRZ (facilitator resources http://tinyw.in/0nNK) (Sterman et al., 2015) is an online game where students represent different countries and stakeholders to reduce greenhouse gas emissions. Working in teams, students formulate their policy positions based on mitigation strategies to gain support from other UN delegates. One advantage of the game is that through use of the C-ROADS (Climate Rapid Overview and Decision Support) computer simulation http://tinyw.in/Tjaa, students receive immediate feedback on the effects of their choices related to reductions in greenhouse gases, increased temperatures, sea-level rise, and other impacts, providing them with empirical data for supporting or challenging their claims. Analysis of students' participation in the game found increased willingness to take action on climate change (Sterman et al., 2015).
- *BBC Climate Challenge* http://tinyw.in/49Ae involves students adopting the role of President of the European Nations who must formulate policies to reduce emissions by 2100. Players choose policy cards from five different categories: National, Trade, Industry, Local, and Household. Each player begins in one of seven regions throughout the world to build cities based on use of alternative energies, recycling centers, and organic farms. Emma Garber noted that:

> This game starts with the player assuming the role of the President of the European Nations, and the task at hand is to stop climate change by the year 2100. The game is set up like an online card game where there are multiple options of what policies to enforce. The cards have rankings based on the supplies they use, the popularity the public has towards them, and the CO_2 emissions they release.
>
> The game is played in segments of 10 years per turn, and five cards (or five policies) can be picked to enforce every turn. The results of each turn are explained in a newspaper like form which are quite fun to read and pleasant to look at. The game was set up in a very interactive form, allowing for the player to click on objects to take them to different zones or subjects.
>
> Sadly, I was unable to win or beat the game, due to the fact that I am clearly a terrible leader when it comes to politics. I was constantly voted out of office, because I would tend to lean toward the climate change side of things, which most people were not very happy with. Trying to find a balance between what the people want and what the Earth needs was so difficult that I would only make it past a few turns. This game shows the reality of climate change and how politics and the

majority of our population affect it greatly. I would recommend this game to anyone who thinks climate change is an easy fix, or anyone who does not fully understand how our actions are increasing climate change and damaging our Earth.

– *Fate of the World* http://store.steampowered.com/app/80200 (also with an online version http://tinyw.in/tcvQ) involves students in establishing policies related to climate change and issues of economic production and population growth. Jacob Colegio described the game as based on:

> playing cards in certain regions of the globe. Each card does something different, such as implementing emissions taxes, starting vegetarian revolutions, committing to renewable energy sources, establishing research centers, etc. To play these cards, you have to first recruit agents for each region (North America, China, South Asia, Southern Africa, Europe, etc.). Recruiting agents and playing cards cost money, which you have a limited amount of during each turn. You have to manage your resources and prioritize; at the same time, you have to choose which particular cards you should play in each region in order to achieve your goals.
>
> At the end of each turn, you skip ahead 5 years and get to see some statistics about increases in CO_2 levels during that time, number of climate change-related deaths, whether each region's expected emissions rate is above or below average, etc. You are also shown news about recent developments in each nation, such as civil unrest, drilling breakthroughs, major milestones in global warming, etc. When you start the next turn, you have more funding and are able to recruit more agents and play more cards.
>
> The actual interface of *Fate of the World* looks kind of like Google Earth, except there is a lot of different buttons and menus to look through. You can read news about what is developing in each particular region or see statistics about various things (annual emissions, agriculture GDP, number of climate refugees, etc.). You can also see each region's "technology tree" and see what technologies that region has been developing, and what it will develop in the future (if you play certain cards). You also can see global statistics such as population change, temperature change, changes in the Earth's geography (such as melting ice caps), etc. (for more details http://tinyw.in/kk0G).

– *Eco Online Ecosystem Simulation Game* www.ucsusa.org/node/4577 involves students in creating policies and laws to support a sensitive ecosystem for their civilization using simulation data as evidence to generate support for their proposals.

– *ecoKoin* (formerly Greenify; iOS app: in beta for 2016) (Lee et al., 2013) includes use for older students of social networking to communicate with others based on specific missions for collective actions associated with choosing green products, making transportation choices, use of water and electricity, debating issues and sharing knowledge with others based on shared news feed and reports, leading to documenting these actions through shared photos or written descriptions to earn points.

REDESIGNING CITIES AND HOUSES

Students can also engage in games or simulations that require them to imagine alternative ways to redesign cities and houses in order to employ less energy and enhance density for use of mass transit.

- *EnerCities* www.enercities.eu involves students in building ecologically sustainable cities based on achieving a balance between energy sources, cash flow, economic growth, and environmental concerns.
- *Energy City* http://tinyw.in/4IKs requires students to research use of alternative solar and wind energy sources to provide energy for a city.
- *Future Delta 2.0* (FD2) http://futuredelta2.ca is a video game involving players in coping with climate change effects on the city of Delta in 2100 that includes flashbacks to 2015 when there were limited attempts to address climate change.
- *Electrocity* http://electrocity.co.nz involves making decisions about alternative energy sources (for Shane Stover's extended description: http://tinyw.in/SEp9):

> After you name your city, you are given a 5 x 5 grid with different geographical features. All starting maps will include some combination of rivers, mountains, hills, forests, bushes, ocean, and the town. From this point, it is up to you to decide how to spend your money. Some items like farming and campgrounds increase your population, while others like wind farms and gas plants increase your energy production.
>
> A player then advances through their turns, making purchases with the money they earn, as long as they produce more energy than they use and their environmental meter stays out of the red.
>
> What You Learn: Electrocity is a great tool for teachers to use in order to teach about renewable energy. Some purchases may seem appealing due to their cheap cost and high output, but their negative impacts on the environment certainly outweigh the benefits. Wind farms do not produce a lot of energy, but the cost of air is free and its effect on the environment is zero.
>
> On the contrary, coal and gas plants produce a much higher amount of energy, but they also use more to run and are terrible for the environment. Similarly, as your town grows, you could end up losing money each turn rather than making money. It is important to know whether your town can afford growth or if you need to start choosing your purchases more carefully. Almost all countries around the world can relate to this as we are all power hungry and push for more and more growth every day. Unfortunately, this comes with a big hit for the environment.

- *SimCity EDU* http://tinyw.in/z35E engages students in assuming the role of mayor who must balance the need to provide employment for citizens and also foster sustainability in the city.
- *Plan It Green* www.planitgreenlive.com/en involves students in planning a city through use of energy retrofits, clean energy jobs, and green building. Blaire LaCross explains how the game has players build and upgrade buildings while thinking about environmental impact.

> The game forces you, the city planner, to make tough decisions as you have to power your city while balancing emissions. The game is entertaining enough to play and certainly would be a useful learning tool for a teacher to use in the classroom:
> It is more geared toward students in elementary or middle school as it does not have complex moving parts. The game features informational videos about green technology being developed and gives players the chance to learn how such technology works on its most basic level.

- *Power Up!* http://sciencenetlinks.com/interactives/powerup.html provides students with choices of adding wind, trash, or solar plants to their city as sources of energy.
- *Mysusthouse* www.mysusthouse.org/game.html has younger students create a house or town based on sustainability criteria. Ali Coutts, a student in Allen's class, describes her experience playing this game:

> This game uses interactive prompts to guide you through building your own energy-efficient house, step-by-step, with you deciding what resources to use. Given a budget, you quickly realize how expensive certain resources can be so you must decide where to splurge and where to cut back to give yourself the most efficient home. The next series in this game takes you to a small town that is looking to expand; you must help them do so with sustainability and environmental awareness in mind. MySustHouse was an extremely educational game meant for middle- to high-school students to explore climate change, energy efficiency, and environmental consciousness.

COPING WITH ISSUES OF WATER, MELTING ARCTIC ICE, WARMING OCEANS, AND FARMING

- *Eyes on the Rise*. To experience the effect of sea rise, students can also employ the *Eyes on the Rise* app http://tinyw.in/uS9k or VirtualEYES http://tinyw.in/dY4J virtual reality tool to experience the impact of a 6-foot sea rise on South Florida by entering in certain addresses for specific Miami neighborhoods.
- *SMARTIC (Strategic Management of Resources in Times of Change)* www.camelclimate change.org/view/article/175297 involves addressing changes to the Arctic due to melting of ice and glaciers. Given the need to cope with these changes, students assume the roles of different stakeholders—countries, businesses, organizations, etc., to develop plans for how to address these challenges. Players use a copy of a map covered with clear acetate to then write on the map using grease pencils or dry eraser markers.
- *Earth Primer* www.earthprimer.com an iOS app game that engages students in visually altering geological landscapes to understand the effects of changes in glaciers/ice-melt, sea rise, drought, etc., on the Earth.
- *Water Flow* www.goodworldgames.com/water-flow. Students are assisting people in a village coping with lack of water by completing puzzles on how to capture and share water to different homes in their village, leading to awareness of the effects of drought on the village.
- *Losing the Lake* http://tinyw.in/R7e1 (facilitation guide http://tinyw.in/QFpw) is targeted for students in the Southwest United States, but could be played by any student related to addressing issues of drought and water conservation. Students learn about the loss of water in the Lake Mead reservoir that provides water for the Southwest United States region. They then engage in online computer simulation to acquire knowledge about the effects of droughts and melting ice in the Rocky Mountains related to the loss of water in the Colorado River.
- *EcoChains: Arctic Crisis* http://tinyw.in/O31O is a card game in which students learn about the impact of climate change on a range of different Arctic marine species (note, given the $25.00 cost, teachers can obtain the game at a discount).

- *Never Alone (Kisima Ingitchuna)* http://neveralonegame.com/game is based on the experiences of the Iñupiat, an Alaska Native people, coping with the effects of climate change on their Arctic region. Based on contributions by Iñupiat people, students adopt the role of a young female member of the community and a fox attempting to discover the source of a blizzard that threatens the community. One advantage of this game is that students experience the Iñupiat peoples' cultural perspective related to narratives and myths based on their association with nature.
- *Team WILD* www.arkive.org/education/team-wild (for education resources www.arkive.org/education) involves students assuming the role of scientists who are studying and attempting to conserve and protect coral reefs in Chagos threated by warming oceans, forest restoration in Brazil's Atlantic forests, and species in the African savannah.
- *WhyReef* http://reef.whyville.net is part of the part of the Whyville http://tinyw.in/lHaI platform (Educators Guide: http://tinyw.in/dzUb) in which students are studying and recommending changes to protect and preserve coral reefs by studying virtual reefs impacted by overfishing for food and aquariums, coral bleaching, too many nutrients, buried reef, and tourism, destruction impacting ocean quality and species. Conservation Connection www.hastac.org/node/8546 is an extension of the WhyReef game in which students share knowledge about how to preserve the Fiji coral reefs.

GAMES ABOUT LOCAL, SPECIFIC CONTEXTS OR REGIONS

- *The Carbon Cycle* http://goo.gl/m6Rxqz is an online interactive game for middle-school students who assume the role of carbon atoms and travel through the carbon cycle. They first read about the carbon cycle http://goo.gl/nD33Y to gain background knowledge. They then move along an online game board map of six different locations—atmosphere, plants, soils, shallow ocean, deep ocean, and marine life that can function as carbon reservoirs or pools for storing carbon leading to discussing their role in the carbon cycle.
- *Millennium Village* http://tinyw.in/eqTU requires students to inhabit a sub-Saharan African village in which they cope with the challenges of surviving with high temperatures, droughts, and diseases.
- *Fort McMoney* www.fortmcmoney.com/#/fortmcmoney; iOS App http://tinyw.in/7Kco uses documentary film to portray the world of Fort McMurray, Alberta, Canada and the Athabasca oil sands development to engage students in virtually exploring the site. Students interact with residents to determine a future direction for an oil-boom town based on an "addiction to oil" associated with extracting oil from sands related to the use of fracking practices throughout the United States and Canada, reflecting the larger issue of how to move away from oil as a means of economic support to alternative energy options. Because the documentary was made in 2013 at the peak of the oil boom, now that the demand for oil has diminished, students may bring that current perspective to bear on their experience with the game.

REFLECTING ON WHAT STUDENTS LEARN FROM PLAYING GAMES

As with drama activities, it is essential to have students reflect on what they learn about climate change from playing these games. In their reflections, students share what they perceive to be the problems or challenges they faced, the reasons that caused them, the strategies for coping with them, and the degree to which they were successful in addressing the problems or challenges. For example, in playing games involving roles for formulating, crafting, and voting on policies at the local, national, or global level for addressing climate change, students could reflect on what kinds of arguments were effective for achieving political support. In playing games assuming roles of city officials, students could reflect on some of the economic or political challenges they faced in attempting to make changes given lack of tax revenues or political support, as well as opposition from organizations such as the fossil fuel industry.

In reflecting on their experiences, students can also think critically about the larger systems constituting the game space (Meadows et al., 2016). Engaging in such "systems thinking" involves reflecting on how systems themselves are driven by particular goals or specific rules or norms. For example, in playing the *Oiligarchy* or *Fort McMoney* games based on oil production, students assuming the roles as oil company executives or workers are driven by the goal of maximizing profits through extracting as much oil as possible. Students reflecting on the game might consider how they were situated to adopt the perspective of a person who ignores the adverse effects of fracking.

Students can also reflect on the viability of the solutions they developed in playing these games. In playing the *Losing the Lake, 3rd World Farmer, The Watershed Game,* or *CityOne* games related to loss of water or water quality, students could reflect on the degree to which their water conservation and sustainability proposals may or may not have been successful in lived-world contexts. They could also consider real-world trade-offs, for example, that diverting water for use in cities may result in a lack of water for farms.

IS CLIMATE CHANGE A GAME?

Of course, climate change is not a game or a role play. As with literature, we view role plays and games as extending our students' power of imagination, and from the imagination, to better understand their world and how to behave in it. Amitav Ghosh puts it well,

> Climate change is first and foremost a cultural problem. Everybody thinks it is happening somewhere else. Everybody thinks it is happening on a screen and will not affect them . . . Everything has become spectacle and people think of themselves as spectators, yet we are not spectators.
>
> Ghosh (2016)

Augusto Boal (1993) uses theater to transform spectators into "spect-actors," people who critically understand what is happening in the world and join with others to take action.

As we have already seen in this book, climate change is a topic that is interdisciplinary. The next chapter helps us think more directly and fully about how English teachers can collaborate with colleagues in other disciplines to address climate change.

For additional resources, activities, and readings related to this chapter, go to http://tinyw. in/Z4s1 on the book's website.

REFERENCES

Arons, W., & May, T. J. (Eds.). (2016) *Readings in performance and ecology*. New York: Palgrave Macmillan.
Beach, R. (2015). Imagining a future for the planet through literature, writing, images, and drama. *Journal of Adolescent & Adult Literacy, 59*(1), 7–13.

Beach, R., & Doerr-Stevens, C. (2011). Using social networks for online role-play: Play that builds rhetorical capacity. *Journal of Educational Computing Research, 44*(1), 165–181.

Bean, R. (2012). *The heretic.* London: Oberon Books.

Bigelow, B. (2014). Climate change mixer. In B. Bigelow & T. Swinehart (Eds.), *A people's curriculum for the earth: Teaching climate change and the environmental crisis* (pp. 92–101). Milwaukee, WI: Rethinking Schools.

Bigelow, B., & Swinehart, T. (Eds.) (2014) *A people's curriculum for the earth: Teaching about the environmental crisis.* Milwaukee, WI: Rethinking Schools.

Boal, A. (1993). *Theater of the oppressed.* New York: Theater Communications Group.

Boldt, G., Lewis, C., & Leander, K. M. (2015). Moving, feeling, desiring, teaching. *Research in the Teaching of English, 49*(4), 430–441.

Boyle, T. C. (1996). *The tortilla curtain.* New York: Penguin.

Christensen, L. (2009). *Teaching for joy and justice.* Milwaukie: Rethinking Schools.

Condis, M. (2015). "Live in your world, play in ours": Video games, critical play, and the environmental humanities. *Resilience: A Journal of the Environmental Humanities, 2*(3), 87–104.

Eisenack, K. (2013). A climate change board game for interdisciplinary communication and education. *Simulation & Gaming, 44*(2–3), 328–348.

Eisenack, K., & Reckien, D. (2013). Climate change and simulation/gaming. *Simulation & Gaming, 44*(2–3), 245–252.

Feldpausch-Parker, A. M., O'Byrne, M., Endres, D., & Peterson, T. R. (2013). The adventures of carbon bond: Using a melodramatic game to explain CCS as a mitigation strategy for climate change. *Greenhouse Gases, 3*(1), 21–29.

Gee, J. P. (2007). *What video games have to teach us about learning and literacy.* New York: Palgrave Macmillan.

Ghosh, A. (2016). Television Interview on NDTV. Retrieved from http://tinyurl.com/hdmljbk.

Hagood, A. (2016). Close reading—and close writing—environmental justice. InTeGrate. Retrieved from http://tinyw.in/7e5X.

Harris, C. A., Kharecha, P., Goble, P., & Goble, R. (2016). The climate is a-changin': Teaching civic competence for a sustainable climate. *Social Studies and the Young Learner, 28*(3), 17–20.

Katsaliaki, K., & Mustafee, N. (2015). Edutainment for sustainable development: A survey of games in the field. *Simulation & Gaming, 46*(6), 647–672.

Kershaw, B. (2009). *Theatre ecology: Environments and performance events.* New York: Cambridge University Press.

Lavery, C., & Finburgh, C. (Eds.) (2015). *Rethinking the theatre of the absurd: Ecology, the environment and the greening of the modern stage.* New York: Bloomsbury Methuen.

LeBourdais, V. (2016). Let the games begin. *Green Teacher, 108.* Retrieved from http://greenteacher.com/let-the-games-begin/.

Lee, J. L., Matamoros, E., Kern, R., Marks, J., de Luna, C., & Jordan-Cooley, W. (2013). Greenify: Fostering sustainable communities via gamification. Retrieved from www.gameprof.com/wp-content/uploads/2013/03/Lee-et-al-2013-CHI-Greenify.pdf.

Martusewicz, R., Edmundson, J., & Lupinacci, J. (2011). *Ecojustice education: Toward diverse, democratic, and sustainable communities.* New York: Routledge.

Meadows, D., Sweeney, L. B., & Mehers, G. M. (2016). *The climate change playbook: 22 systems-thinking games for more effective communication about climate change.* White River Junction, VT: Chelsea Green Publishing.

Nilsson, E. M., & Jakobsson, A. (2011). Simulated sustainable societies: Students' reflections on creating future cities in computer games. *Journal of Science Educational Technology, 20*, 33–50.

O'Neill, J. T., & Swinehart, T. (2010). "Don't take our voices away"—A role play on the indigenous peoples' global summit on climate change. Zinn Educational Project. http://tinyw.in/Aij1.

O'Shea, M. (2016). Bikes, choices, action! Embodied performances of sustainability by a traveling theater group. In W. Arons & T. J. May (Eds.), *Readings in performance and ecology* (p. 137–145). New York: Palgrave Macmillan.

Paschall, M., & Wüstenhagen, R. (2012). More than a game: Learning about climate change through role-play. *Journal of Management Education, 36*(4), 510–543.

Pirie, B. (1997). *Reshaping high school English.* Urbana, IL: National Council of Teachers of English.

Pitfield, M. (2012). Transforming subject knowledge: Drama student teachers and the pursuit of pedagogical content knowledge. *Research in Drama Education: The Journal of Applied Theatre and Performance, 17*(3), 425–442.

Pyper, J. (2014, May 1). New climate-fiction (cli-fi) game sends players clues from the future [Web log post]. Retrieved from http://tinyw.in/vLQ3.

Redmond, J. (2016, January 16). Middle School students learn about alternative energy through mock U.S. Senate committee debate. *Greeley Tribune*. Retrieved from http://tinyw.in/OBDG.

Sandbrook, C., Adams, W. M., & Monteferri, B. (2015). Digital games and biodiversity conservation. *Conservation Letters, 8*(2), 118–124. Retrieved from http://tinyw.in/5eVc.

Schrier, K. (2015). Ethical thinking and sustainability in role-play participants: A preliminary study. *Simulation Gaming, 46*(6), 673–696.

Smith, P., & Howe, N. (2015). *Climate change as social drama: Global warming in the public sphere.* New York: Cambridge University Press.

Stein, E. (2015). Ignorance/denial-fear/paralysis/engagement/commitment: Reflections on a decade teaching climate change law. *Radical Teacher, 102*, 17–23.

Sterman, J., Franck, T., Fiddaman, T., Jones, A., McCauley, S., Rice, P., Sawin, E., Siegel, L., & Rooney-Varga, J. N. (2015). World Climate: A role-play simulation of climate negotiations. *Simulation & Gaming, 46*(3–4), 348–382.

Turner, R. (2015). *Teaching for ecojustice: Curriculum and lessons for secondary and college classrooms.* New York: Routledge.

Washburn, A. (2014). *Mr. Burns.* New York: Theatre Communications Group.

Wu, J. S., & Lee, J. J. (2015). Climate change games as tools for education and engagement. *Nature Climate Change, 5*, 413–418. Retrieved from www.nature.com/natureclimatechange.

Chapter 8
Interdisciplinary Teaching about Climate Change

Politicians think that if matters look difficult, compromise is a good approach. Unfortunately, nature and the laws of physics cannot compromise—they are what they are.

James Hansen (2009)

Climate is an ideal interdisciplinary theme for lifelong learning about the scientific process and the ways in which humans affect and are affected by the Earth's systems.

Mark McCaffrey (2015, p. 131)

Climate change is the most important issue facing life on Earth. It should concern all of us, including all teachers in all subjects. Climate change is an issue that can and should be studied in science, social science, English, math, languages, and other areas. As we have seen throughout this book, understanding climate change, why it happens, its impacts, and what to do about it raises questions relevant to English language arts and many other subjects. No one subject, discipline, or approach can take in all aspects of the issue. Simply knowing the science without understanding the human impact or cultural and political strategies necessary to address it lacks meaning. Simply knowing the social implications without understanding the science lacks depth and sophistication. Clearly, bringing multiple perspectives to bear on climate change is essential.

What does it mean to a middle-school or high-school language arts teacher to do inter-disciplinary teaching about climate change?

It can happen that a teacher of Earth Science can visit an English class and talk about the science of climate change, that is, if the Earth Science teacher happens to have an available prep hour at the same time she or he is needed. It can happen that an American Government teacher can do the same thing and talk about why the US Congress won't ratify international climate agreements. This kind of interdisciplinary teaching can add a lot to an English class. English students and teachers can learn more about science or politics relevant to literature they are reading.

Yet, in most high schools, this kind of interdisciplinary teaching is hard to make happen. It is challenging to find the right person and time to plan together, complicated to coordinate schedules, and tricky for teachers to leave their classrooms. Would it even be right to call teachers from different departments visiting each other's classroom "interdisciplinary" or would that be simply "cross-disciplinary?" Would the silos that keep ideas understood only narrowly be broken down?

In this book we argue that climate change is an appropriate topic for English language arts. Insofar as the topic is interdisciplinary, we ask English teachers not to wait to find another teacher in a different discipline that they can pair up with, but to right away to take on responsibility for addressing global warming in your language arts class. English is a subject that can encompass many topics, especially one with all of the social, cultural, and ethical dimensions of climate change.

We organize our discussion of interdisciplinary teaching in this chapter around a "cli-fi" short story and show English language arts teachers bringing information, ideas, and strategies from other disciplines into English. The strategies are fascinating and the results impressive. While doing that, we also provide interesting examples of English teachers and science and social studies teachers working together to create valuable interdisciplinary curriculum. We recognize that teachers from different disciplines working together is typically easier in middle schools where students are separated into groups and teachers are organized in teams, rather than in high schools separated by content-based departments. Middle-school teachers will find examples in this chapter that they can draw on, and teachers at other levels can look to outstanding middle-school teachers as models. Engaging students in interdisciplinary work can provide them with broader perspectives on climate change by engaging multiple ways of knowing, thinking, and believing found in different disciplines (Draper et al., 2010; Langone, 1992; McCaffrey, 2015).

A survey of members of the Association for the Study of Literature and Environment (ASLE), who largely identify as literature teachers, found that interdisciplinary instruction was perceived as enhancing teaching environmental literature courses as well as the use of outdoor experiences (Junker & Jacquemin, 2016). The same survey of members of the Association for Environmental Studies and Sciences (AESS), who largely identify with biological and environmental sciences, found similar results related to the value of interdisciplinary teaching and use of outdoor activities.

By interdisciplinary instruction, of course, we also mean instruction where you are working with your social studies, science, and math colleagues across the school to develop curriculum that provides students with knowledge about climate change from social studies, science, and math perspective. For example, in their social studies courses, students gain an understanding of how capitalist economic systems referred to in Chapter 3 shape consumption adversely impacting climate. In their Earth Science courses, students acquire an understanding of the ecosystems associated with the relationships between CO_2 emissions and effects on climate. In their math classes, students learn to analyze data presented in graphs and charts to understand information on shifts in temperatures and emissions.

Interacting with teachers in your building, you can identify when and how your colleagues are addressing these and other topics to then link your own instruction to these topics, knowing that your students are bringing background knowledge to your classrooms. These colleagues will then have some understanding of what is happening in your room—for example, your students are reading a certain cli-fi novel or engaging in a drama or game related to climate change and they can then connect their instruction to your instruction. It may be the case that you can only work with one or two other social studies, science, or math teachers who happen to have the same students who are in your courses. Through your interactions with your colleagues, you yourself are acquiring knowledge of these other disciplines that will enhance your understanding of climate change. If students perceive that you and some of their other teachers have a strong commitment to address climate change, this perception itself will enhance their own interest.

To foster this curriculum planning, you and your colleagues could employ an online site such as Google Docs or Forms to identify when and where certain topics related to climate change are being addressed in particular courses. In sharing your curriculum with your colleagues, you can indicate literacy practices you are focusing on so that they can build on those practices in crafting their activities. You may be focusing on persuasive writing practices described in Chapter 5, for example, providing evidence for certain claims, something that your social studies or science teachers may build into writing assignments in their classes. Or, you might use informal writing as a tool to formulate ideas and enhance discussion or small group student interactions with peers to foster collaborative learning (Liu, Varma, & Roehrig, 2014). Your colleagues may then employ writing- or discussion-to-learn activities in their classrooms.

In the Stanford Climate Change Education professional development project, science teachers in fourteen high schools and middle schools learned to focus on supporting their students' active use of discussion based on formulating claims and supporting evidence in the classroom (Holthuis et al., 2014). As part of that interaction, teachers helped students employ meta-talk, reflecting on their use of language, for example, their use of concepts such as "weather" and "climate." Classroom analysis indicated that the more interactions between students and/or with the teacher as facilitator, the more students learned, leading to gains in their understanding of and beliefs about climate change.

THE BENEFITS OF INTERDISCIPLINARY CLIMATE CHANGE INSTRUCTION

Combining ELA and social studies with science, students may frame climate change issues by going beyond a scientific "what-is" perspective to adopt an ethical stance as to the "what-should" people do given certain scientific findings. For example, given findings of adverse climate change effects on poor people in vulnerable countries, students can address the moral question as to issues of justice associated with the people generating the least emissions being impacted more than the people generating the most emissions (Turner, 2015).

Busch (2015) contrasts "Science Discourse" from a "Social Discourse" framing of climate change with the former focusing on the physical aspects of ecosystems and the latter focusing on the social aspects of climate change. She notes that applying only a science inquiry perspective without including some focus on the social and ethical aspects will make it less likely for students to perceive the relevance of addressing climate change. At the same time, students need knowledge of the "Science Discourse," suggesting the importance of students acquiring both of these frames through interdisciplinary instruction.

Randall Seltz, an English teacher at Jordan High School, in Sandy, Utah, whom we heard from in Chapter 5, describes how he would work collaboratively with teachers in different disciplines in sharing reading of informational texts:

If I were working with a biology teacher, I might have them collaborate with me and teach the students the formula to calculate how much the oceans will rise in a given set of years (e.g., how much will it differ in 1, 5, 10, 15 years). If I were a geography/world civilization teacher I might help students locate cities that are most at risk of being submerged based on the data they calculated in biology class. As a geography or world civilization teacher, I might point out cities or islands that are now underwater or under volcanic ash, or otherwise leveled by natural disasters to show that there is historical precedence for these kinds of disasters. Does climate change disproportionately affect low SES or high SES populations? How does climate change affect economic opportunity? How does a scarcity in necessary resources affect morality (e.g., is it okay to hurt others to obtain provisions for your family during a natural disaster?)? Maybe the connection in ELA class could be reading firsthand accounts of the places lost to the ocean or disaster.

THE COMMON CORE STATE STANDARDS AND THE NEXT GENERATION SCIENCE STANDARDS

Language arts and science standards have important connections. The authors of Language Arts Common Core State Standards (2010) believe that literacy skills are critical to science education, and the document includes a section on *Literacy in History/Social Studies, Science, and Technical Subjects*. The acronym "STEM" (Science, Technology, Engineering, and Mathematics) is now frequently replaced by "STEAM"—adding the "A" refers to the Arts—including literary and visual arts, also considered important to science education.

As an ELA teacher, you may be wondering whether the science teachers in your building will be focusing on climate change. The Next Generation Science Standards (NGSS) (Achieve, 2014) www.nextgenscience.org based on the National Research Council report, *A Framework for K-12 Science Education* (National Research Council, 2012) include a major focus on teaching about climate change. These standards also emphasize literacy instruction, for example, the ability to analyze the use of evidence to support one's argument as described in Chapter 5. The analysis of systems we describe in Chapter 3 to help organize language arts curriculum coincide with the Next Gen Science Standards. Science teachers are to focus on the fact that the:

> earth consists of a set of systems—atmosphere, hydrosphere, geosphere, and biosphere —that are intricately interconnected. These systems have differing sources of energy, and matter cycles within and among them in multiple ways and on various time scales.
>
> National Research Council (2012, p. 170) & Finley (2014)

There are also states that have developed their own curriculum frameworks associated with sustainability, for example, the Washington State Environmental and Sustainability Literacy Plan http://tinyw.in/fikS and the Wisconsin's Plan to Advance Education for Environmental Literacy and Sustainability http://tinyw.in/eHXb. You can access speakers using the Climate Voices Science Speakers Network http://climatevoices.org with expertise in science and climate change to present face-to-face or virtually to your school or class, or have teachers from other disciplines in your school who have an interest in climate change present to your class.

DISCIPLINARY PERSPECTIVES FOR INTERDISCIPLINARY INSTRUCTION

For engaging in interdisciplinary curriculum planning with other teachers in your school, you can draw on the following disciplinary perspectives—biological, historical, geographic/economic, sociological, and mathematical as critical perspectives (McClune & Alexander, 2015) for focusing on specific aspects of texts.

To illustrate this interdisciplinary "lens" approach in this chapter we will focus on a rich set of learning activities built around a single cli-fi short story "The Tamarisk Hunter" by Paolo Bacigalupi (2011). The story is twenty pages long and appropriate for juniors or seniors in high school. The methodology we describe can be used with other literary works that you would select, depending on the grade level you teach. The activity was developed by the InTeGrate project (Hanselman et al., 2016) described here: http://tinyw.in/FE5i. The story is found online here: http://tinyw.in/AY2T. More resources: background information for the story: http://tinyw.in/50xL; a teaching unit for the story: http://tinyw.in/Y9IX; and, an interview with the author: see pages 207–214 in the *Everything Change* short story anthology (Milkoreit, Martinez & Eschrich, 2016).

The story is set in a believable yet frightening future where there is a terrible drought in the Southwestern states, and cities along the Colorado River have been abandoned because they can no longer use water from the river. Instead there is a giant "straw" that takes the water over the mountains to California. The main character, Lolo, is paid a bounty by the government to cut down tamarisk cedar trees along the river bank in Utah, trees that are perceived to require much needed water from the river. At the same time, he is also secretly planting these trees, an illegal act, to make sure that he will continue to have employment. He also pays for the right to take small amounts of water for his own use. When law enforcement shows up, he fears they have found him out, instead he learns he will also no longer receive water, requiring him to also abandon the area. It is a dark and engaging climate change story rich with potential for interdisciplinary teaching.

BIOLOGICAL PERSPECTIVES

Understanding the setting for "The Tamarisk Hunter" includes understanding the relationships between the forest systems and droughts that today, and in the future, impact, and will impact, not only the Colorado River ecosystem, but also river and lake systems throughout the world. Reductions in river and lake water adversely impacts plants and animals. Droughts lead to forest fires that burn trees, which releases their stored CO_2. When trees die from droughts or fires they can no longer be absorbing CO_2. Students could look at the story through a biological lens and examine conflicting scientific analyses of the adverse effects of the invasive tamarisk salt cedar tree on water and native vegetation (Bishara, 2015).

Students could identify from the story examples of ecosystems threatened by climate change. In his book, *Half-Earth: Our Planet's Fight for Life*, biologist E. O. Wilson (2016) argues that we need to protect, preserve, and restore threatened ecosystems that make up half the world's surface, including the California Redwood Forest; Amazon River Basin; longleaf pine savannas of the American South; flatlands of northwest Europe; and grasslands of the Serengeti Gorongosa National Park in Mozambique, Congo Basin, Western Ghats of India, McMurdo Dry Valleys in Antarctica, and Borneo.

PHENOLOGY STUDY

Phenology is the study of plant and animal life cycles and how they are influenced by the different seasons, elevation, and climate changes. Phenology is reading of the "pulse of life" (Bradley, Leopold, Ross, & Huffaker, 1999). This study of phenology is obviously important to climate change. English teachers connected it with environmental literature described in Chapter 3 and local observation and place-based writing, discussed in Chapter 5. As students develop phenological knowledge, they can research and imagine how plants and animals in their area, or even in literary works, might be impacted by climate change.

Michele Koomen has her students engage in phenology study to address the question: How do plants and animals respond to seasonal changes? In other words, studying the environment to figure out how animals know when it is time to hibernate, and what "calendar" or "clock" plants use to begin flowering, leafing, or reproducing (Project Budburst, http://budburst.org).

Advance organizer writing or discussion prompt: Address aspects of phenology in the work of Aldo Leopold.

Over a period of 61 years, first Aldo Leopold and later his daughter, Nina Leopold Bradley, monitored 55 different species, starting in 1936. This included the return of migratory birds and blooming of many plants on his Wisconsin farm. Nina Bradley collected data between 1976 and 1982 on the same farm. Analysis found that more than one-third of the species' arrival (migrating birds) or phenophases (flowering plants) occurred earlier in the season (Bradley, Leopold, Ross, & Huffaker, 1999).

Writing or discussion prompt: What are implications of species' earlier arrival?

Possible responses: Most plants and animals have co-evolved, meaning that birds and insects depend on each other for food, reproduction, and habitat.

Students can participate as citizen scientist biologists collecting data to share with others documenting the effects of climate change. One key project is the National Phenology Network http://tinyw.in/e6lU based on the concept of phenology as the study of seasonal changes in the life cycle of plants and animals, for example, changes in bird, butterfly, or bee migration, flowering of plants, emergence of certain insects, pollination, food availability, increased diseases due to mosquitoes or ticks, etc., shifts that reflect changes in the seasons due to temperature increases. In recording this data, students learn that

> Every plant and animal is part of a story that affects us all, in ways we may not always appreciate in terms of the well-being of the environment. By tracking changes in the natural world we learn more about that story, how it's impacting us and what we can do to sustain the environment that sustains us.
>
> Backyard Phenology (2016, p. 3)

For example, documenting the death of trees in certain regions due to droughts and increased heat resulting in loss of trees that absorb CO_2, provides data to make the case to address the impact of climate change on droughts and increased heat.

Students can sign up on the Phenology Network http://tinyw.in/e6lU to serve as a participant sharing data using the online tool called Nature's Notebook http://tinyw.in/G4Yh to record (for the iOS app http://tinyw.in/GF2m and Android app http://tinyw.in/buep) observations of changes in plants, trees, and species over time, for example, recording when certain flowers or trees begin to bloom or certain crops do not grow. They can also perceive where others are recording data through the United States using the Phenology Visualization Tool http://tinyw.in/JhKy.

Michele Koomen asks students to respond to questions in a phenology journal to record the response of various living organisms as the seasons change by selecting one deciduous tree and one wildflower to document: In your notebook, record detailed observations of your plants with an illustration. How are your two observed plants responding to emerging winter or spring? Record minimum and maximum temperatures on the days of your strolls. What critters did you notice when you were out on your stroll (including birds and insects)? What were they doing? Finally, access weather records for your city from 30 years ago www.wunderground.com/history. Answer this question: What evidence do you have that the "amazing punctuality" is different today?

Geographic/economic perspectives. As noted in Chapter 3, geographic and economic perspectives afford insights into the varied adverse effects of climate change on different regions of the world (Morgan, 2013). Adopting the perspective of necessary economic growth based on fossil fuel consumption can have negative impacts on certain regions, leading to the need for development of clean energy options for those regions. Rather than rely on wood fires for cooking in developing countries, residents can employ solar-powered stoves.

Students could apply a geographic/economic perspective to "The Tamarisk Hunter" by studying the geographical features of the Colorado River in terms of how loss of water along the river in the Southwest has and will impact cities receiving water from that river. The loss of water from the Colorado River, coupled with droughts impacting the entire Southwest United States, has and will continue to adversely impact cities in that region. In the story, the big cities in California play political hardball and are able to dominate the region, making it impossible for locals to survive.

In the story, given that once Lolo loses his job and water for his farm, he now needs to move north, "where watersheds sometimes still run deep and where even if there are no more lush ferns or deep cold fish runs, at least there is still water for people" (Bacigalupi, 2011, p. 171), raising the question as to whether doing so would result in any improvements in terms of droughts. Students could also examine issues of the growth of the tamarisk trees along the river basin related to the impact of the trees on the basin's ecosystem, along with also examining how 60 percent of water use goes to agriculture and 30 percent for industrial use, raising questions as to whether reductions in those areas could be achieved, for example, by reducing excessive water consumption for cattle.

To examine local effects of climate change in their own geographical region in the United States on droughts, wildfires, sea-level rise, heat, extreme weather, and snow, students can consult the interactive map: Mapping the Stories of US Global Change: The 5 Key Problems http://tinyw.in/A8XH. They can then identify certain economic forces operating in their region impacting climate change effects, for example, dependency on cars or use of fracking or nitrogen fertilizers related to release of emissions in their regions.

Rogelio Rigor, a teacher at the Ida B. Wells High School for Social Justice (1997–2015) located in Seattle, Washington describes how in his science course, students critically analyze how climate change is interconnected with an economics perspective on the history of capital accumulation. Students focus on the concepts of *historical dialectic materialism*; the scientific approach in studying the concept of property; the continuing shifts and dynamics of human development based on historical socio-political forces; the *paradox of wealth*; the difference between *use value* and *exchange value* while extracting limited planetary resources; the importance of *sustainability* set against the *modes of production*; and the *role of the state* in structuring laws and regulations.

Emphasizing this interdependence, taken from Fritjof Capra's concept of *deep ecology,* allows students to examine the motivation and the eventual exploitation of the planet in a *modern capitalist global society*. Students are given extensive readings that critically discuss this, including work from Rachel Carson's (2002) *Silent Spring*, William Cronon's (2003) *Changes in the Land: Indians, Colonists, and the Ecology of New England*, Neil Postman's (1993) *Technopoly,* Jerry Mander's (2012) *Capitalism Papers: Fatal Flaws of an Obsolete System*, and Naomi Klein's (2015) book, *This Changes Everything: Capitalism vs. The Climate* (see also the documentary, *This Changes Everything,* http://thefilm.this changeseverything.org).

Science activities form the foundation of this analysis: learning *greenhouse qualities* of particular gases like CO_2, methane, and water vapor; how increases in such gases blanket the planet with *infra-red radiation,* providing a *positive feedback loop* upon the *albedo effect,* and thus, an *anthropogenic impact* on average planetary temperature given the expansion of capitalism in today's unrelenting quest for profit.

Students then read Manfred Max-Neef's (1992) *From the Outside Looking In: Experiences in Barefoot Economics,* which takes a hard look at the question of economic *growth* versus *development* based on capitalist exploitation of nature and production, distribution, and other societal relations. He shows how resource extraction, production, and distribution should be based on human need and development in order to avert nature's future devastation and its consequence for all life.

Films that supplement student discussions, among many others, include *Tambien La Lluvia* (*Even the Rain*) (Bollaín, 2010) establishing the parallel in Magellan's exploits in the past as connected with the current socio-political ramifications of water exploitation in Bolivia during the Cochabamba protests of 2000; as well as the compelling images in *Chasing Ice* (Orlowski, 2012), presenting in non-abstract terms the reality behind global warming. Finally, students read and discuss a chapter from Paulo Freire's (2013) *Education for Critical Consciousness,* as they grapple with the idea of either being *active* or *passive* participants in the struggle to make this a better world; this idea of being either a *subject* or *an object* in their consciousness and reality toward the global struggle for change.

ANALYZING SUBURBAN SPRAWL

As we noted in Chapter 3 in our discussion of the housing/community system, one aspect of dependency on private cars is low-density, suburban sprawl (Morgan, 2013). During the 1950s to 1990s in the United States, suburban sprawl was fueled by the appeal of owning a relatively inexpensive home with a lawn as well as "white flight" (when Whites left the increasingly racially diversified urban centers).

In the future world of "The Tamarisk Hunter" the towns and suburban neighborhoods of the Southwest that were developed without consideration for demands on water are portrayed as abandoned wastelands. The story can also be viewed through a lens of "development" that considers the long-term use of resources.

Sprawl has also led to a reduction of forests, wetlands, and grasslands for housing developments that include large lawns and golf courses proving social status (Ignatieva et al., 2015). In the United States, from 1982 to 1997, 1.4 million acres were converted into developed land each year for building larger suburban homes (Hanlon, Short, & Vicino, 2010). Densely populated urban spaces with ample mass transit options can reduce emissions (for an activity on energy use and population: Energy Use in the Americas, http://tinyw.in/8B4s). Future ecological development of urban centers requires a "resource revolution" (Heck, Rogers, & Carroll, 2014) involving shared transportation, cleaner energy alternatives, and denser housing development that should spur economic development (McGowan, 2013).

Students could study their own communities to identify projects associated with reduction of dependency on cars through increased mass transit, cycling, and walking options. Students might look at the Atlanta Beltline project http://beltline.org designed to increase use of parks, trails, and mass transit as well as considering long-term environmental consequences of development in their area.

Historical perspectives. Adopting a historical lens might involve contrasting the Holocene with the Anthropocene period as affected by the steam engine (Fleming, 2014). While people in the Holocene period experienced extreme hot and cold weather events resulting in droughts and disease leading to death or migration, the causes of these events were not due to increased human activity associated with the Anthropocene period. These shifts lead historians to pose these questions:

> What have people experienced, learned, feared about climate change in the past? How have they intervened? By what path have we reached the current state of climate apprehension? Can we possibly claim to have a complete understanding of climate change and other environmental problems if we ignore their intellectual, social, and cultural history.
>
> Fleming (2014, p. 584)

In adopting a historical perspective in response to "The Tamarisk Hunter," students could study historical changes in population development in the Southwest related to uses of water from the Colorado River. While Native Americans had access to plentiful water from the river in the past, with the development of dams for diversion of water for agriculture and water supply for cities, Native Americans lost access. As a result, 38 percent of Native American in Arizona, New Mexico, and Utah on reservations do not have water in their homes, and must truck in water from elsewhere (Gies, 2016). Students could study how the introduction of beetles thought to eradicate the tamarisk trees resulted in the beetles also eating other trees, resulting in loss of soaking up CO_2.

Applying a historical perspective on changes in ecosystems over time helps students understand the importance of maintaining a healthy balance in these systems, and an appreciation of:

> wildness as a valuable asset in human history. Water slipping through a riverbank or evaporating from the broad surfaces of leaves isn't a wasted resource. It's exactly what ecosystems need to continue their quiet, everyday services, purifying the air, strengthening the soil, and providing the water we drink. A healthy ecosystem, given the chance, will heal itself from damaging invasions, or accept new species as belonging within its web of interactions.
>
> Lamberton (2011)

Given the centrality of energy production for understanding climate change, it is important for students to have some historical understanding of the development of different kinds of energy use over time, as summarized, for example, by the US Department of Energy http://tinyw.in/M8St. When coal replaced wood as the primary source of energy in the mid 1700s, there was an increased demand for energy due to population growth. In the late 1800s and early 1900s, oil and natural gas began to supplement the use of coal, without realization that eventually these natural resources would be depleted.

Students could draw on these historical changes portraying changes in uses of energy in literary texts during different historical periods (Farca, 2015). For example, Charles Dickens portrayed the adverse impact of burning coal on London:

> Smoke lowering down from chimney pots, making a soft black drizzle, with flakes of soot in it as big as full-grown snowflakes—gone into mourning, one might imagine, for the death of the sun . . . Fog everywhere . . . fog down the river, where it rolls defiled among the tiers of shipping, and the waterside pollutions of a great (and dirty) city (Qtd. Langone 28).
>
> Reid (2010)

Matthew P. Bachand (2010) created an interdisciplinary unit that combines science and history with the study of literary texts to study the history of coal mining in the United States. In this unit students learn that while use of coal remains a major source for generation of electricity given that coal produces four times as many British Thermal Units (BTUs) as does oil, coal emits more CO_2 per kilogram of fuel than any other fossil fuel. He describes the process of how coal is used to create electricity in coal-fired power plants:

> Coal-fired power plants are basically very efficient steam engines. The coal is delivered to the power plant and dumped into a hopper. It is pulverized into coal dust—the same dust so dangerous to the miners—and mixed with air and blown into the boiler for combustion. The coal then combusts, generating extreme heat that superheats pipes lining the perimeter of the boiler. The water flowing through these pipes converts to highly pressurized steam, which shoots through the blades of a turbine, generating the rotation necessary to turn a generator.

To have students study this process, students work in groups to create presentations to answers one of the following questions:

- How is coal created?
- How is coal mined from the Earth?
- How is coal turned into electricity?
- How has coal burning become more efficient over time?
- How does coal mining affect the environment?
- What aspect of the process you are describing is the most difficult on the people involved?
- How has the process you described changed over time? What motivated the change?
- What challenges do those who must perform this task face at the present time (political, economic, scarcity concerns)?

In the unit, students study examples of the dangerous working conditions associated with coal mining, including explosions and lung disease from breathing in coal dust. They read examples of literary texts portraying characters living and working in communities based on coal mining:

D. H. Lawrence (1913/2009) *Sons and Lovers*: Portrays the life of a coal miner's wife (suitable for older students).

A. J. Cronin (1937/1983) *The Citadel*: Portrays the efforts of a doctor coping with the cultural traditions of a mining community.

Susan Campbell Bartoletti (1996) *A Coal Miner's Bride*, a young adult novel, portrays the experience of 13-year-old, who, as an arranged bride living in a coal town, experiences the challenge of living alone in the town after her husband dies in a mining accident. Students can also read Bartoletti's (1996) autobiographical account of life in a coal town, *Growing Up in Coal Country*.

Ellen Marie Wiseman (2015) *Coal River*, portrays the challenges of life in a coal town.

SOCIOLOGICAL PERSPECTIVES

To apply sociological perspectives to "The Tamarisk Hunter," students could examine how it is that an existing future government as portrayed in the story has the power to not only divert much of the water from the river basin to California, but also to stop water going to other sites. An example of this occurred at the "Phoenix Metro when the Central Arizona Project got turned off and then had its aqueducts blown to smithereens when Arizona wouldn't stop pumping out of Lake Mead" (Bacigalupi, 2011, p. 180). The government also flexed its power when it decided to no longer support Lolo's work and his farm's water supply, suggesting that the government is now semi-totalitarian based on support from higher-income people living in California to divert water for their own use.

Students could apply sociological perspectives to examine how differences in class status relate to beliefs and attitudes about consumption and emissions production (Dunlap & Brulle, 2015) (see the American Sociological Association's report, Climate Change and Society, http://tinyw in/ePV9). Given class disparities and economic inequality, higher income people are more likely to consume luxury products—expensive cars, large houses, boats, etc., requiring higher levels of energy than the amount of energy consumed by people with lower incomes (Zehr, 2015). It is also the case that people with higher incomes will be more likely to afford adaptation alternatives based on housing, food, or transportation than people with lower incomes. Given the sea rise in Miami, Florida that threatens housing near the ocean, wealthy investors are buying land for future housing development in some of the poorer neighborhoods that are at higher elevations, resulting in the displacement and gentrification of those neighborhoods (Vasilogambro, 2016).

Perceptions of climate change are related to class-based dispositions (McKibbon, 2001). An analysis of Boston residents found that while lower-income participants acknowledged the severity of climate change, they were more likely to perceive it as an issue of concern for higher-income people given that higher-income people engage in higher levels of consumption than lower-income people (Laidley, 2013). While lower-income people therefore perceived the need for a systemic transformation of the economic system of consumption, higher-income participants framed solutions to climate change in more individualistic terms based on market-based or technological solutions as opposed to reduction in consumption (Hoffman, 2015). To address issues of environmental justice (Reese, 2016; Stein, 2015), students could discuss how low-income people of color are often the most adversely impacted by environmental factors, for example, experiencing higher levels of health issues due to living near highways or congested urban roads.

PSYCHOLOGICAL PERSPECTIVES

In applying psychological perspectives to "The Tamarisk Hunter," students could discuss reasons for Lolo's determination to continue to live in areas near the Colorado River as well as his willingness to risk being caught and continue his work of cutting down the tamarisk. Students might consider their own connection to their home regions and their willingness to take risks to change their behaviors relative to addressing climate change.

It is also the case that students' perceptions of climate change and place are shaped by their psychological perspectives related to their beliefs, attitudes, and willingness to act (Weintrobe, 2013; Marshall, 2015; Stoknes, 2015). The American Psychological Association (APA) issued a report, Psychology and Global Climate Change: Addressing a Multi-faceted Phenomenon and Set of Challenges http://tinyw.in/kCDm that describes the psychological aspects of responding to risks by discounting or denying future and remote events, how perceptions of climate change relate to mental health issues of stress and anxiety, the social and community impacts of climate change, and the barriers impeding taking action on climate change.

A key factor shaping students' psychological perspectives has to do with how their relationship with the natural world is undermined by consumerism (Rust & Totton, 2012). Based on questions listed on page 40 by George Marshall (2015), students could discuss their psychological perceptions associated with climate change as related to:

- Victims of flooding, drought, and severe storms being less willing to talk about climate change or even accept that it is real.
- People being uncertain about climate change while at the same time being more easily convinced of the imminent dangers of terrorist attacks, meteorite strikes, or an alien invasion.
- Scientists being perceived normally as trusted professionals in our society being questioned, distrusted, hated, and even targets for violent abuse.

MATHEMATICAL PERSPECTIVES

Another important perspective involves the use of mathematics associated with calculations of quantitative data related to analysis of climate change. Students need to have some knowledge of mathematics to be able to interpret charts, graphs, or tables in reports about climate change. NASA's Earth Math http://tinyw.in/dfmI includes problems related to climate change requiring use of mathematics to solve those problems.

For engaging with "The Tamarisk Hunter," students could respond to the following quote from the story:

It took a little while before the bureaucrats realized what was going on, but finally someone with a sharp pencil did the math and realized that taking in people along with their water didn't solve a water shortage. So the immigration fences went up.

Bacigalupi (2011, p. 186)

Given this reference to mathematical calculations, students could study the different population regions of the Southwest to determine the number of people who may have wanted to migrate from cities such as Phoenix to move to the river basin. They could then calculate the populations of cities or communities in their own area, for example, populations of coastal cities who may be influenced by sea rise.

Students taking calculus, ecology, data structures, and physics courses at Ithaca College shared reports on climate change generated in their classes across the different courses, reports they drew on for work in these courses (Hamilton et al., 2010). Students in the calculus class used Excel to plot future changes in global temperatures, data that was shared in the other three courses, leading to questions about what factors are most likely to cause these temperature increases.

Students can calculate the amount of their carbon footprint in use of energy in their home based on data from utility bills, for transportation based on amount of gas employed for driving cars, and waste using the EPA's What Is Your Carbon Footprint activity http://tinyw.in/j9dp. They can also download the Bio-Agriculture calculator http://tinyw.in/MWlQ for calculating changes in emissions reductions influencing agriculture for the next 50 years associated with water and food shortages as well as the rate of land degradation.

In an interdisciplinary unit focusing on the speed with which the polar ice caps are melting, from a math perspective, based on viewing the video Earth Underwater portraying the melting of the Arctic http://tinyw.in/z8y6, students asked the questions: "What type of function is best to predict the rate of melting of the polar ice caps? When will the polar ice caps be gone, and what effect will this have on the Earth and humanity" (Schimizzi et al., 2016)? From a science perspective, based on watching the BBC's *The Great Melt* http://tinyw.in/ijvG, students ask the questions, "Why is the Arctic sea ice melting at an exponential rate? What are the potential outcomes for the biosphere if the polar sea ice continues to melt?"

From an English perspective, based on watching a debate between Marc Morano and Bill Nye on climate change http://tinyw.in/DAE4, students ask these questions: "What are the existing perspectives on climate change and global warming? What is some specific evidence to support these perspectives? What is your perspective on the issue, and how can you support it using relevant evidence?"

USE OF APPS FOR STUDYING CLIMATE CHANGE IN DIFFERENT DISCIPLINES

There are a large number of different iOS and Android apps students can employ for studying climate change across different disciplines. Students can use the iOS Adventure Learning http://tinyurl.com/q9gunaa app that includes descriptions of trips to the Arctic to study the influence of climate change on that region. And, they can access information about climate change on iOS http://tinyurl.com/p9qrzqp or Android http://tinyurl.com/aylzjrj NASA Earth Now, the iOS World Bank Climate Change DataFinder http://tinyurl.com/mm5ujl5, the Android Climate Change Challenge http://tinyurl.com/ohwaymz, or the iOS Painting with Time: Climate Change http://tinyurl.com/oqop8e3 that involves users viewing the impact of climate change through changing images of glaciers, land areas, or weather events.

- For Science iOS apps: http://tinyurl.com/mvjad3a.
- For iOS middle school science apps: http://tinyurl.com/n6hdtos.
- For iOS high school science apps: http://tinyurl.com/lh9zetx.
- APPitic: science iOS apps: http://tinyurl.com/kntrawv.
- Google Play Store: science Android apps: http://tinyurl.com/m9zcrjy.

In this chapter, we describe different disciplinary perspectives as ways of knowing and thinking that you, or teachers in other disciplines, can adopt related to interdisciplinary curriculum instruction. In doing so, you provide students with a range of different perspectives for addressing climate change, perspectives that they can draw on for formulating changes in status quo systems, based on the use of these perspectives.

SYNERGY

Interdisciplinary teaching, reaching across disciplines, in one class, between teachers or across a school lets students put ideas together. Given the importance of climate change, it makes sense for a cluster of teachers or a whole school to focus on the topic, and certainly it is most effective when they collaborate. Interdisciplinary teaching creates its own synergistic energy. A science fair invites presentations from students in English and social studies classes. School-wide assemblies have speakers who talk about climate change from different perspectives. School clubs form focused on climate change. School newspapers have articles about climate change. Documentary films are shown after school. Speech or debate teams address global warming. Student councils organize fundraising events for victims of climate change disasters. Students organize community climate change discussions in the school library. Students attend or organize climate change events outside school, and report back (MacLeod, 2010).

The activating synergy of teaching about climate change is further explored in the next chapter on how to foster students' civic engagement as climate activists making change to foster sustainable practices in their lives and their communities.

For additional resources, activities, and readings related to this chapter, go to http://tinyw.in/vIG1 on the book's website.

REFERENCES

Achieve (2014). *Next Generation Science Standards*. Washington, DC: National Academies Press.

Bachand, M. P. (2010). Energy generating a culture: Early American coal miners and coal mining culture. Retrieved from http://tinyw.in/kxBN.

Bacigalupi, P. (2011). The tamarisk hunter. In M. Martin (Ed.), *I'm with the bears* (pp. 171–189). New York: Verso.

Backyard Phenology. (2016). *Guidebook to Backyard Phenology*. Minneapolis, MN: University of Minnesota.

Bartoletti, S. C. (1996). *Growing up in coal country*. Boston: Houghton Mifflin.

Bartoletti, S. C. (2000). *A coal miner's bride*. New York: Scholastic.

Bishara, Y. (2015). *Q&A: The story behind an invasive plant in the southwest*. Associated Press.

Bollaín, I. (Director). (2010). *Tambien la lluvia (even the rain)* [Motion picture]. Spain: Morena Films.

Bradley, N. L., Leopold, A. C., Ross, J., & Huffaker, W. (1999). Phenological changes reflect climate change in Wisconsin. *Proceedings of the National Academy of Science, 96*(17), 9701–9704.

Busch, K. C. (2015). Talking climate science: How teachers frame climate change in the classroom & why it matters. Presentation at the NARST Conference.

Carson, R. (2002). *Silent spring*. New York: Houghton Mifflin.

Common Core State Standards (2010). *English language arts Common Core State Standards*. Washington, DC: National Governors Association and Council of Chief State School Officers. Retrieved from www.corestandards.org.

Cronin, A. J. (1937/1983). *The citadel*. Boston: Back Bay Books.

Cronon, W. (2003). *Changes in the land: Indians, colonists, and the ecology of New England*. New York: Hill & Wang.

Draper, R. J., Broomhead, P., Jensen, A. P., Nokes, J. D., & Siebert, D. (Eds.) (2010). *(Re)Imagining content-area literacy instruction*. New York: Teachers College Press.

Dunlap, R. E., & Brulle, R. J. (2015). *Climate change and society: Sociological perspectives*. New York: Oxford University Press.

Farca, P. A. (2015). *Energy in literature: Essays on energy and its social and environmental implications in twentieth and twenty-first century literary texts*. Oxford, UK: TrueHeart Academic Press.

Finley, F. N. (2014). The Anthropocene and the framework for K-12 science education. In D. Dalbotten, G. Roehrig, & P. Hamilton (Eds.), *Future Earth: Advancing civic understanding of the Anthropocene* (pp. 9–18). Washington, DC: American Geophysical Union.

Fleming, J. R. (2014). Climate, change, history. *Environment and History, 20*, 577–586.

Freire, P. (2013). *Education for critical consciousness*. New York: Bloomsbury.

Gies, E. (2016, April 22). The Navajo are fighting to get their water back [Web log post]. Retrieved from http://tinyw.in/Nd2s.

Hamilton, J. G., Rogers, M., Pfaff, T. J., & Erkan, A. (2010). Multidimensional education research: Managing multiple data streams. *Transformations: The Journal of Inclusive Scholarship & Pedagogy, 21*(1), 89–98.

Hanlon, B., Short, J. R., & Vicino, T. J. (2010). *Cities and suburbs: New metropolitan realities in the US*. New York: Routledge.

Hanselman, J., Oches, R., Sliko, J., & Wright, L. (2016). Cli-fi: Climate science in literary texts. InTeGrate. Retrieved from http://tinyw.in/FE5i.

Hansen, J. (2009). Compromise won't fix global warming. *Newsweek*. 12/3/09. Retrieved from: http://tinyurl.com/zodxf6f.

Heck, S., Rogers, M., & Carroll, P. (2014). *Resource revolution: How to capture the biggest business opportunity in a century*. Boston, MA: New Harvest Press/Houghton Mifflin Harcourt.

Hoffman, A. J. (2015). *How culture shapes the climate change debate*. Palo Alto, CA: Stanford University Press.

Holthuis, N., Lotan, R., Saltzman, J., Mastrandrea, M., & Wild. A. (2014). Supporting and understanding students' epistemological discourse about climate change. *Journal of Geoscience Education, 62*, 374–387.

Ignatieva, M., Ahrné, K., Wissman, J., Eriksson, T., Tidåker, P., Hedblom, M., Bengtsson, J. (2015). Lawn as a cultural and ecological phenomenon: A conceptual framework for transdisciplinary research. *Urban Forestry & Urban Greening, 14*(2), 383–387.

Junker, C. R., & Jacquemin, S. J. (2016). Bridging the gap: Surveying interdisciplinarity in the environmental literature classroom. *ISLE: Interdisciplinary Studies in Literature and Environment, 23*(2), 395–411.

Klein, N. (2015). *This changes everything: Capitalism vs. the climate.* New York: Simon & Schuster.

Laidley, T. (2013). Climate, class and culture: Political issues as cultural signifiers in the US. *The Sociological Review, 61*(1), 153–171.

Lamberton, M. L. (2011). The thirsty three: Confronting invasive saltcedar in the American southwest. *Terrain.org, 27.* Retrieved from http://tinyw.in/gn2O.

Langone, J. (1992). *Our endangered Earth.* Boston: Little, Brown and Company.

Lawrence, D. H. (1913/2009). *Sons and lovers.* New York: Digireads.

Liu, S., Varma, K., & Roehrig, G. (2014). Climate literacy and scientific reasoning. In D. Dalbotten, G. Roehrig, & P. Hamilton (Eds.), *Future Earth: Advancing civic understanding of the Anthropocene* (pp. 31–40). Washington, DC: American Geophysical Union.

MacLeod, C. (2010). Fun facts about green schools! Green School Initiative. Retrieved from http://tinyw.in/43K4.

Mander, J. (2012). *Capitalism papers: Fatal flaws of an obsolete system.* Berkeley, CA: Counterpoint Press.

Marshall, G. (2015). *Don't even think about it: Why our brains are wired to ignore climate change.* New York: Bloomsbury.

Max-Neef, M. (1992). *From the outside looking in: Experiences in barefoot economics.* London: Zed Books.

McCaffrey, M. S. (2015). *Climate smart & energy wise: Advancing science literacy, knowledge, and know-how.* Los Angeles: SAGE Publications.

McClune, B., & Alexander, J. (2015). Learning to read with a critical eye: Cultivating discerning readers of media reports with a science component. *SSR, 97*(359), 21–29.

McGowan, A. H. (2013). Renewable energy: An interdisciplinary problem solving course. *Systemics, Cybernetics and Informatics, 11*(1), 51–54.

McKibben, B. (2001). The comforting whirlwind: God and the environmental crisis. Sermon. Retrieved from http://tinyurl.com/j5d52b4.

Milkoreit, M., Martinez, M., & Eschrich. J. (Eds.). (2016). *Everything change: An anthology of climate change fiction.* Tempe, AZ: Arizona State University Press.

Morgan, J. (2013). *Teaching secondary geography as if the planet matters.* New York: Routledge.

National Research Council. (2012). *A framework for k-12 science education: Practices, crosscutting concepts, and core ideas.* Dulles, VA: The National Academy Press.

Orlowski, J. (Director). (2012). *Chasing ice* [Motion picture]. United States: Chasing Ice, LLC.

Postman, N. (1993). *Technopoly.* New York: Vintage.

Reese, G. (2016). Common human identity and the path to global climate justice. *Climatic Change, 134,* 521–531.

Reid, S. (2010). Pollution from our automobiles and what must be done [Web log post]. Retrieved from http://tinyw.in/CBbW.

Rust, M-J., & Totton, N. (Eds.) (2012). *Vital signs: Psychological responses to ecological crisis.* London: Karnac Books.

Schimizzi, J., Sheffler, C., Leichner, R., Mueller, T., & Yoruk, Y. (2016). Climate change: Cross-curricular math, English, science lesson. *OER Commons.* Retrieved from http://tinyw.in/19VB.

Stein, E. (2015). Ignorance/denial-fear/paralysis/engagement/commitment: Reflections on a decade teaching climate change law. *Radical Teacher, 102,* 17–22. Retrieved from http://radicalteacher.library.pitt.edu.

Stoknes, P. E. (2015). *What we think about when we try not to think about global warming.* White River Junction, VT: Chelsea Green Publishing.

Turner, R. J. (2015). *Teaching for ecojustice: Curriculum and lessons for secondary and college classrooms.* New York: Routledge.

Vasilogambro, M. (2016). Taking the high ground—and developing it. *The Atlantic.* Retrieved from http://tinyw.in/rY5k.

Weintrobe, S. (Ed.). (2013). *Engaging with climate change: Psychoanalytic and interdisciplinary perspectives.* New York: Routledge.

Wilson, E. O. (2016). *Half-Earth: Our planet's fight for life.* New York: W. W. Norton.

Wiseman, E. M. (2015). *Coal river.* New York: Penguin Andesite Press.

Zehr, S. (2015). The sociology of global climate change. *Wiley Interdisciplinary Research: Climate Change, 6,* 129–150.

Chapter 9
Acting in the Present: Changing the Future

If we ask the children to critique the world but then fail to encourage them to act, our classrooms can degenerate into factories of cynicism. While it's not a teacher's role to direct students to particular organizations, it is a teacher's role to suggest that ideas need to be acted upon and to offer students opportunities to do just that.

Bill Bigelow et al. (1994, p. 5)

Unfortunately for us, we're still not very good at controlling the future. What we're good at is telling ourselves the stories we want to hear, the stories that help us cope with existence in a wild, unpredictable world.

Roy Scranton (2016, p. 7)

"It's not climate change—it's everything change."

Margaret Atwood (2015)

When addressing climate change with young people, we need to stress the severity of the crisis and also draw on their imaginations, their hopes for their future and the world, and their willingness to share ideas, take stands, and become involved. Throughout this book we have given many examples of students taking action to inform others and address global warming. In this chapter, we deepen this focus to explore options for students to become involved in mitigating the consequences and adapting to the realities of climate change. The approach we have set forward is based on inquiry and democratic student-centered pedagogy. Instead of telling students what climate change means or what to do about it, we want to empower them to investigate, collaborate, develop their own conclusions, and devise ways to make a difference, drawing on their knowledge, their concerns, and their emerging literacies.

We think of change taking place on two levels: (1) students' own *personal* knowledge, understanding, and beliefs about climate change and related lifestyle changes necessary to reduce their carbon footprints; and (2) making changes in larger energy, economic, political, transportation, agriculture, and housing/community *systems,* referred to in Chapter 3 as part of the great social transition necessary to preserve the planet.

As secondary students make change in individual actions and social systems, they will draw not only on their understanding of the narratives of climate change causes but also on ideas about morality and justice. Students will come to understand that climate change is not just about their own family, community, or group but impacts all of nature and humanity. Young people may see it as an issue impacting the world in which they will be living—and the adults as failing to care for that world (Gardiner, 2011). Addressing climate change may include redefining basic values about happiness and success, from wealth and consumption to relationships and community (Martin, 2016). These moral understandings create positions from which to speak and act. Taking action is the best way to inspire hope.

> After Rebecca Young of North Davidson High School in Lexington, North Carolina, taught an environmental food-based unit that included Margaret Atwood's *Oryx and Crake* (Atwood, 2004), *The Year of the Flood* (Atwood, 2009), *The Windup Girl* (Bacigalupi, 2009), and *The Road* (McCarthy, 2007), one of her students asked, "So, what do we *do* with all this information now that we know it? Have any of us actually changed how we eat and where we shop?" Rebecca noted that
>
> > Now they were ready to make real change in their lives and were waiting for me to tell them how to do it. It was gratifying and terrifying at once: literature and life had come together in a most transformative potential but education had not prepared them to make the transformation.
>
> When Rebecca told them that she had "no easy answers," and asked them what they would do: Gradually, a few raised their hands to explain steps they had taken to change their eating habits and how their families shop for food. They got excited sharing stories of finding their local farmers and about how they had scolded their parents about what was off limits at the grocery store. It was serious fun. The practical and locally available steps they described demonstrated for the class how they might extend the empathy they felt for the characters and situations they had studied into immediate changes in their consumer actions.

GETTING INVOLVED IN ADDRESSING CLIMATE CHANGE

Interviews with twelve young adults ages 25 to 35 who were concerned about climate change, but had little willingness to become engaged in addressing it, showed that they lacked defined strategies and thus had a sense of powerlessness (Kenis & Mathijs, 2012). As one participant noted, "What can we really do? Taking to the street has no effect. Taking legal steps against companies has no effect. Politics doesn't work. Lobbying politicians . . . has no effect, or too little" (p. 50).

On the other side, analysis of seventeen narratives of young people from fourteen countries who became climate activists found that directly perceiving the effects of climate change was an important first step (Fisher, 2016). When a Nepalese 18-year-old observed that mountains in his country no longer had snow caps, "I was just deeply depressed by this." Others reported that experience of impacts of hurricanes, droughts, and flooding as well as poverty, water shortages, deforestation, and animal welfare led them to climate activism. Another participant was affected by the dead jellyfish on a local beach, and she became involved in climate activities in her middle and high school.

So what can teachers do to motivate their students? We believe there are three key steps.

1   First, students need to learn about the impacts of climate change in personally meaningful ways. It is important for students to understand how climate change is and will impact their own area and country. They also need to learn about warming's impact on others around the world, in ways that make people far away seem up close. Teachers could draw on the various strategies we have described in this book, using literature, film, testimony, research, writing, digital communication, and drama/games to make climate change meaningful at a personal level.

2   Second, as we have also illustrated in this book, knowledge of effective personal and community actions is important and inspiring. That is what the young people in the first study lacked. Rather than being overwhelmed by the enormity of the issue, students need to learn how to take one step at a time. Urban high-school students were more willing to become engaged in addressing climate change when they understood how their choices resulted in sustainable outcomes (McNeill & Vaughn, 2012). Teachers can help students research effective actions to take local and meaningful actions as well as supporting change at national and international levels.

3   Third, students are more likely to be motivated to make change when they are working collaboratively with others through collective action. Finding committed peers made a difference for the young people from fourteen countries who became climate activists. They were supported by participation in organized international youth movements. As one participant, Allison, noted:

> Something that is encouraging, is that the youth climate movement seems to be led by a body of very strong women and to be more racial/ethnic/gender/sexual orientation diverse especially on an international scale and that is exciting . . . for a lot of young people its [sic] about the community aspect, working in a movement with empowered dynamic people.
>
> Fisher (2016, p. 241)

The people students collaborate with can be other students, teachers, and community members, or, using new communication tools, they can be people in far-off places, climate victims, activists, or concerned global citizens. "More active" people in one study were then more likely to report that family members or friends were also engaged in climate change action, suggesting that a key factor is other people socially and geographically close to them (Doherty & Webler, 2016). As climate activist, Bill McKibben (2016) asserts:

> A good thing about movements is that you really do have brothers and sisters, and they do have your back. The fossil-fuel industry may threaten us as a planet, as a nation, and as individuals, but when we rise up together we've got a fighting chance against the powers that be. And perhaps that realization is just a little bit scary for them.
>
> McKibben (2016, p. 5)

Climate change will not be solved by a superhero using magical powers to round up criminals or disintegrate coal plants with krypton rays. Power to make a difference comes from joining organizations and building solidarity—that is how you work collaboratively with others to take collective action. Climate change and environmental organizations welcome young people—in fact some, such as 350.org, were started by young people. Learning about these organizations and what they do, joining or creating local chapters is essential. Below is a list of groups addressing climate change that students can learn about and become involved with:

350.org Go Local http://tinyw.in/hq6X
Alliance for Climate Education https://acespace.org
Citizens Climate Lobby Monthly Meetings http://tinyw.in/b2eW
Climate Action Network (CAN) http://tinyw.in/FAeP
Environmental Defense Fund Take Action http://tinyw.in/G0ix
Friends of the Earth Action Center http://tinyw.in/YyYO
Greenpeace Take Action http://tinyw.in/jMaR
iMatterYouth www.imatteryouth.org/imatternow
Our Children's Trust http://tinyw.in/ElNg or http://tinyw.in/JGWF
Sierra Student Coalition http://tinyw.in/cYAr
The Climate Reality Project Initiatives http://tinyw.in/TqT1
Union of Concerned Scientists Action Center http://tinyw.in/fy3g
Youth Climate Action Now (YouCAN) http://tinyw.in/JGWF

Allen's students research climate change organizations, choose one, and then undertake a climate action project where they develop a movement and/or messaging project. He suggests students focus on a particular climate change action group and analyze their strategy or messaging; then develop a climate change media project concept(s) and/or materials, and/or organize a local climate change event, funding, or membership drive.

Having students research and connect to environmental and climate change organizations is helpful to all of the change ideas that we put forward.

The rest of this chapter is divided into four main sections: (1) imagining sustainable futures; (2) taking action at the local level; (3) changing the way we eat; and, (4) civic and democratic projects.

In her classes, Diana Liverman (2014) encourages students to assume activist roles:

> I tell students that they can reduce their own environmental footprint through conservation, recycling, and changing consumption patterns; but I also empower them to maximize their "handprint" by spreading ideas, helping others or choosing a career that protects the environment. I give examples of how individuals change laws, campaign for low carbon public transportation and organize to elect officials who protect the environment. And I have students who lead campus "green" organizations—such as the "Compost Cats" that recycle campus, community and even zoo waste into compost.

IMAGINING SUSTAINABLE FUTURES

Using the imagination to think about the future can be helpful to taking action in the present. Based on their study of future projections of climate change effects and/or their reading of cli-fi literature, students can discuss or write projections of a future life in their geographical locations and think about adaptation and mitigation to address these effects. For example, if they live near oceans or rivers, they can imagine how their community might cope with flooding by building dikes and removing neighborhoods in potential flood zones. If they live near farmlands or forests impacted by droughts and/or forest fires, they can imagine alternative modes of food production or ways to reduce forest fires. If they live in urban areas, they can imagine developing alternative mass transit to reduce dependency on cars. Students can also experience these future worlds through use of the Scenarios of a State of Change http://tinyw.in/bQMs. Though designed to depict Wisconsin in 2050, what it depicts is relevant to any state. Students might also be stimulated to imagine the future by playing the *Lifestyle 2050* game http://life2050.jp/en/introduction.

Rita Turner's students imagine positive rather than negative future worlds (Turner, 2015). They begin by brainstorming possible futures by drawing and writing notes. Then they use Google image search to locate images consistent with their own vision. Students share their ideas and images, identify challenges for living in those worlds, and sustainable solutions. Students in one class listed some of the following solutions:

- Subsidies only for maintaining environmental standards, not oil or corn;
- Subsidies for local farming;
- Urban gardening;
- Pollution tax;
- Government support of research into green energy;
- Expand public transportation;
- Support for polyculture farming and plant-based cultures;
- Financial disincentives away from purchasing products made unsustainably or at a distance;
- Price of goods based on full cost of production and disposal (p. 180).

Turner asked students to identify initial steps needed to achieve these solutions, with many students noting the need for more education on or about these solutions.

TAKING ACTION AT THE LOCAL LEVEL

Engaging students with local examples of the effects of climate change and ways to take action has repeatedly been shown to impact student attitudes and engagement. To begin, students can research what other students have done in other areas. The Young Voices for the Planet http://tinyw.in/8ka7 documentary series is one starting point:

- *Dreaming in Green* http://tinyw.in/8Y7z (Cherry, 2011) portrays four Coral Gables, Florida middle-school students addressing the challenge of sea-level rise in the Miami area.
- *Kids Versus Global Warming* http://tinyw.in/iMdU portrays a 12-year-old, Alec Loorz, who created the iMatterNow project www.imatteryouth.org for organizing young people to petition for policy changes.
- *Team Marine* http://tinyw.in/9w2U portrays students in Santa Monica, California demonstrating the negative effects of plastic bags on ocean species and CO_2 emissions.
- *Green Ambassadors* http://tinyw.in/WbXX portrays students in South Los Angeles http://ecsonline.org engaged in projects involving recycling, composting, planting trees, reducing energy use, and educating elementary school students.

It is also inspiring for students to learn about what young people have done in other parts of the world. To celebrate Earth Day in India, students throughout India engaged in projects in their schools to foster sustainability, as reported in twenty-two case studies (Earth Day Network India, 2016). For example, one group of students went door-to-door to survey people regarding reduction of their carbon footprint. When they discovered through a follow-up survey that few people actually did reduce their carbon footprint, the students decided to interact with each of the 142 households six times, resulting in a 40 percent reduction in energy consumption. Students in another school created a radio station, School Radio www.schoolradio.in, to broadcast students' podcast productions about specific environmental issues (Gali, 2016). In recording these podcasts about sustainable development, solar energy, and water conservation, students developed skills communicating to a broader public.

Students can also create their own digital storytelling videos about strategies for coping with climate change. Linda Buturian's free downloadable book on creating digital stories, *The Changing Story* http://tinyw.in/cD90, includes examples of students' videos about climate change:

- Sara Aziz Hayat's graphic novel, *Remembering an Old Friend*, about her grandfather coping with the impact of drought in Pakistan http://tinyw.in/Nhf4. The NGO of the Leadership for Environment and Development Pakistan asked her to share her story on their site to educate Pakistanis about their water crisis/climate change.
- Spencer Peck's video, *Selica Sand Mining in the Midwest* http://tinyw.in/yDmE, portrays the negative impact of fracking in the Midwest.
- Phoebe Ward's video *Climate Change and the Mississippi River* http://tinyw.in/47Kkuh9a8, shows how extreme weather events cause flooding of the Mississippi River and damage to residents along the river.
- Austin Hermann's video *Water Wars* http://tinyw.in/nWRX, portrays people coping with drought.

Students in the Climate Education in an Age of Media (CAM) project http://tinyw.in/wGTA created public service announcement videos http://tinyw.in/Jdb0 to raise audience awareness about climate change (Rooney-Varga et al., 2014). Sixty-eight percent of the students surveyed indicated that creating and sharing their videos had a positive influence on taking action to address climate change.

Students can portray examples of local, place-based climate change projects. For example in the Walk In Your World project http://walkmy.world, users share online their experiences in a particular place or region. In the Connect to the World We Live In project http://tinyw.in/TjIz, University of Michigan students use local examples http://tinyw.in/KfCC and Environmental Case Studies http://tinyw.in/zChg to address eco-justice; see Great Lakes Environmental Justice http://tinyw.in/7ZSW.

Students can also contribute to sites collecting data from their local area to monitor climate change effects. For example, students can submit data on precipitation levels to the Community Collaborative Rain, Hail and Snow Network (CoCoRaHS) www.cocorahs.org.

For studying environmental justice issues in their own neighborhoods or communities, students can use mapping tools to generate data about the relationships between locations of power plants and the socio-economic status of certain neighborhoods or communities. Students can use the EPA's mapping tool, EJScreen www.epa.gov/ejscreen, to identify specific environmental data such as "traffic proximity" about emissions and demographic data such as poverty and race for particular neighborhoods or regions. Based on the Mapping Your Neighborhood http://tinyw.in/ZANY project, students can also use the National Institute of Health TOXMAP http://toxmap.nlm.nih.gov/toxmap to identify power plants in their community and determine emissions levels from those plants. It would be interesting to learn if many of these plants are located in or near low-income neighborhoods.

Local case-study projects might involve students identifying issues related to climate change in their own school, neighborhood, community, transportation systems, energy power plants, river/lakes, farms, etc. Students can then learn about this issue, study websites, have speakers visit class, interview people as a homework assignment, or even arrange to visit specific sites or locations to observe and interview people. Students might study:

- Instances of high levels of emissions from local power plants and explore alternative wind, solar, biomass, and even nuclear energy sources;
- Methane emissions from local waste incinerators to learn about implementing recycling and composting to divert food from waste as well as use of more environmentally sustainable incinerators;
- Local companies involved in industrial production to determine ways to reduce uses of energy and/or water in their production processes;
- Local farmers' animal agriculture practices to find ways to reduce meat consumption;
- Use of private cars to learn about shared ridership and public mass transit (students can calculate the level of emissions for their family cars by going to the CarbonCounter site http://carboncounter.com and entering in the name of their car(s). One study found that cleaner energy cars costs less to operate than higher emissions cars [Bichell, 2016].);
- Land use planning to find out about denser housing located near mass transit.

Given the impact of trash on incinerator waste, in her Arizona State University college course, Trash, Freaks, and SCUM, http://tinyw.in/sglW, Breanne Fahs (2015) had students collect trash that they created over a 2-day period that they must then carry around in a bag. Students then wrote a paper describing the kinds of trash they collected, changes in their lifestyle and consumption associated with producing less trash, and potential impacts on climate change through reduced consumption. This writing led to discussion of the relationship between consumption and climate change, including how consumption requires increased fossil fuel production.

CHANGING THE WAY WE EAT

As previously noted, one major contributor to greenhouse gas emissions is the food production and distribution system. Food is a great area for students to take action. There are many recent documentaries about the food system, *Food, Inc.*, (Kenner, 2008), *King Corn* (2007), *Farmageddon* (Canty, 2011), *The Garden* (Kennedy, 2014), and *Cowspiracy* (Anderson & Kuhn, 2014) as well as books on food production (Kingsolver, 2007; Pollan, 2007; Hauter, 2012; Ackerman-Leist, 2013).

An important way to take action to address climate change is for students to examine their own food choices, especially reducing meat consumption. Ninth grade students at Darrow School in upstate New York engaged in a year-long interdisciplinary study of the problems with fast food, including impacts of industrialized beef production on climate change (Werberger, 2015).

Students can also learn about issues of local food, and access to healthy and organic options, particularly in low-income urban neighborhood "food deserts" which lack grocery stores (Morgan, 2013). The video *Longing for a Local Lunch* http://tinyw.in/SFZ3 portrays students who pressured their school cafeteria to change their food offerings to provide more locally produced food. Food sovereignty is the right of peoples to healthy and culturally appropriate food produced through ecologically sound and sustainable methods, and their right to define their own food and agriculture systems (US Food, 2016). The existence of food deserts in low-income communities points to food sovereignty as an element of climate justice (Pope-Weidemann, 2015). Ron Finley, a "guerilla gardener" in south central Los Angeles discusses his work creating community gardens and planting in the heart of the city: https://goo.gl/H1EN3t.

Another important issue is food waste. One analysis of food waste indicates that as much as half of all food is wasted or lost before it is consumed (Parfitt et al., 2010). Challenges in the drying, storage, and transport of grain result in a loss of 40 percent of grains while more dairy products in Swedish homes are discarded than are consumed (MacDonald, 2016). This wasted food ends up in landfills, where, when it is burned, generates methane gas. Thus, composting food can be a way to address climate change and reduce the amount of methane gas produced from landfills (Brown, 2016). This is another area where students can promote new policies for homes, schools, and communities.

Allen's class about food and literature also visited the People's Food Co-Op (PFC) in Kalamazoo, founded in 1970 "to create access to food that is healthy for people, land, and the economy." The mission of the PFC involves use of the practices of:

- Striving to provide fresh, organic, and whole foods, offering our community healthy choices for a variety of dietary needs;
- Purchasing locally grown and produced goods, helping to keep local funds cycling back into our economy;
- Participating in and supporting our local farmers' markets, including the 100 Mile Market, the Kalamazoo Farmers' Market (on Bank St), and the Kalamazoo Foods Market;
- Providing access to food assistance programs (Supplemental Nutrition Assistance Program benefits) both at the store and at several local farmers' markets;
- Providing educational opportunities for our community related to food and food systems (such as cooking classes, tabling, speaking engagements, hosting events at the store and in the community).

At the Co-Op, Allen's students learned a lot about environmentally sound eating. Since the PFC provides a lot of healthy, non-meat options, it serves an important role in weaning people off meat consumption (meat produced in factory farms generates CO_2 and methane that contributes to 18–51 percent of all total annual greenhouse emissions [McKnight, 2014]). Their class projects included comparing prices and availability of foods in economically and ethnically different neighborhoods, working with the school cafeteria to develop more healthy choices, creating a healthy-food cookbook for young people that educated about food choices and consequences, and volunteering at a local food bank (syllabus: http://tinyurl.com/hjz3cwm).

CIVIC AND DEMOCRATIC PROJECTS

Perhaps the most important function of the public schools is preparing citizens for democratic participation. One of the more effective ways to address climate change is to influence social and political change at local and national levels. For English language arts students, it's only natural to develop writing, social media, and/or presentations to the school, media, or local community groups arguing for the need for change. According to the Common Core State Standards (Common Core State Standards, 2010), English language arts teachers are expected to prepare students to make presentations that support logical arguments appropriate for specific audiences and purposes.

- *Social media.* Given the ubiquity of social media in adolescents' lives, you can encourage students to employ social media tools such as Snapchat, Instagram, YouTube, Twitter, Facebook, Pinterest, Tumblr, or Google+ to share their perceptions and memes, images, and videos associated with climate change to not only influence their audience's beliefs and attitudes, but to also create communities associated with organized civic engagement. Jenkins et al. (2016) suggest that students are developing skills and dispositions of collaboration and participation through their use of social media "where political change is promoted through social and cultural mechanisms rather than through established political institutions, and where citizens see themselves as capable of expressing their political concerns—often through the production and circulation of media" (p. 2).

  In a program sponsored by the Climate Tracker initiative http://climatetracker.org, people, largely under age 30, employed social media and blog posts to communicate to the public and policy makers about climate change issues. In spring of 2016, they issued a challenge for members of the public to publish essays on the topic of "Breakfree from fossil fuels!" http://tinyw.in/tPhc. In using social media or blog posts, students can take advantage of the power of digital video and images as important rhetorical tools to engage a wider reach of audiences.

  Another advantage of students' use of social media is that, in contrast to classroom discussions, where students may defer to teachers and grading, social media may offer more freedom. Analysis of Swedish adolescents interacting on a social media forum about the topic, "global warming is a hoax," found that users engaged in passionate interactions to formulate positions and counter-arguments (Andersson & Öhman, 2016). Also, teachers can include students' experiences and ideas from their social media interactions to enhance engagement in classroom discussions.

  John Tinnell (2011) writes about the potential of the Internet to support "new forms of collectivity that situate these texts at the forefront of democratic endeavors in the public sphere" (p. 234). He encourages his college writing students to learn eco-blogging as a way for them to create online media that supports environmental justice and pushes green listing to the next level. Tinnell has his freshmen work in groups to choose an environmental injustice and/or environmental disaster and research it online, then write about their emotional connections to the mediated representations they encounter about the event (for examples: http://jtinnell.wix.com/ecoblogging).

- *Report cards.* Students in the Roots and Shoots Club at St. Louis Park High School in a Minneapolis suburb (part of Jane Goodall's Roots and Shoots global project, www.roots andshoots.org) drew on the Youth Climate Report Card developed by the iMatterYouth organization www.imatteryouth.org/imatternow, to create a climate change report card grading the St. Louis Park City Council on its efforts to address climate change. They gave the Council a D-minus for its zero emissions plan, a C for its carbon removal, an A on recycling and composting, and an A on renewable energy, leading to an overall B-minus grade (Raghavendran, 2016).

  Students also presented a resolution requesting reduction of "greenhouse gas emissions to levels that would protect our community's children and grandchildren from the risk of climate destruction." The Council had recently created an Environment and Sustainability Commission; members of the Council praised the students' efforts and indicated to them that, as one member noted, "We need to be pushed. We are trying to be very forward-thinking but we can do more. Help us do that."

– *Petitions.* Based on training from YouCAN, students in Eugene, Oregon petitioned their City Council to adopt mandatory emission reduction targets as well as a carbon reduction plan. With support from Our Children's Trust, students in Oregon filed a lawsuit in federal court requiring the government to enact a science-based plan to address climate change (McPherson, 2016) (for a video of students describing their lawsuit, http://tinyw.in/YDz5). Given the potential legal effects of such suits, fossil fuel industry groups have petitioned to join the government as defendants. Julia Olson, executive director of Our Children's Trust, noted that:

> This is the part of democracy that people don't see, but when you watch government lawyers, side by side with industry lawyers, stand up in front of a judge and say these kids don't have a right to be protected against catastrophic climate change, and the United States Constitution doesn't protect that right, that's powerful.

– *Position statements.* Students in schools can formulate position statements related to climate change, as did students at the Carolina Friends School in issuing their Climate Change Declaration:

> As students at Carolina Friends School, we recognize (1) that addressing climate change is an embodiment of our commitment to stewardship; (2) that the United States produces at least 20 percent of the world's CO_2 emissions, and therefore as US citizens we have a heightened responsibility to be vigilant in local, state, and national governments; and (3) that as students at a Quaker school, we must draw upon our history as organizers and our fortune of institutional support to be leaders on climate change.

Students, teachers, and parents in the Portland, Oregon public schools issued a statement asserting "WHEREAS, climate change is already having an enormous negative impact on nature and people around the world—which will only become worse—including present and future Portland Public Schools students, that the district support shared curriculum and professional development, activities promoting changes in their communities, and transformation of school buildings." The School Board approved this statement leading parents, community members, and educators applauding Portland's commitment to offer a climate curriculum that is "participatory, imaginative, and respectful of students' and teachers' creativity and eagerness to be part of addressing global problems . . ." (For a kit on the Portland efforts from *Rethinking Schools*, http://tinyw.in/osEO).

– *White papers.* Students in Alberta, Canada created a white paper that they presented to the Alberta government calling for more focus on climate change in the school curriculum as well as enhancing sustainability in school buildings (Dodge & Thompson, 2016). One of the leaders of this initiative, eleventh-grade student, Stephanie Zuwaduk, said, "We understand that climate change can be intimidating and overwhelming. But we believe that the antidote to despair is action. We must not stand idle and wait for someone else to initiate change. We must initiate change as the youth and as Albertans so that we have a brighter future in the wake of climate change." As a result of the students' work, the Alberta government passed "The Climate Change Leadership Implementation Act" that provides support for what the students were requesting.

- *Community discussions.* Pairs of students in Allen's class led eighty adult citizens from Kalamazoo divided into ten small groups in discussions at a local library in response to the book, *Don't Even Think About It: Why Our Brains Are Wired to Ignore Climate Change* (Marshall, 2015) http://tinyw.in/Qr1i. Based on her experience leading a discussion, Cece Watry commented:

  > Climate change is such a new topic and to see people who didn't grow up with the issue so passionate and interested was inspiring and made me very happy. They are also a group of people who know the topic—students, working citizens, parents, and some even grandparents and to get their wisdom and insight on all that is going on and what they've seen and been through was valuable.

  Students also organized viewing on the Western Michigan campus of the documentary *Racing Extinction* http://racingextinction.com portraying how some scientists, journalists, and activists are documenting the impact of climate change on the mass extinction of major species. You can have your students organize a presentation in your school featuring a local speaker or viewing of a documentary leading to discussions on ways to engage in efforts to foster change.

- *Online videos.* Students can create online messaging about addressing climate change. Having completed a Stanford University course on energy conservation https://sites.stanford.edu/glee, a group of Girl Scouts created a newscast about energy conservation in the home as well as energy reduction in their homes, leading to as much as a 49 percent saving, which is significant given that US homes account for 21 percent of the world's energy use (Kaplan, 2016).

- *Culture jamming.* Using humor, parody, and satire to respond to problematic media portrayals can prove to be an engaging pedagogical approach for students and provide powerful final products to disseminate and educate others. Students enjoy learning about and practicing culture jamming, subvertising, and adbusting (see *Adbusters* magazine: http://adbusters.org). Humor and irony can be revealing tools to de-naturalize media texts and expose their false claims and deceptions. A model students might emulate: during the 2016 Summer Olympics in Rio de Janeiro, ExxonMobile aired deceptive television commercials http://tinyurl.com/j5lmm2x that portrayed an environmentally conscious company, "powering the world responsibly." In response to this attempt at greenwashing Exxon's image, ClimateTruth.org created a parody video that exposes the hypocrisy of Exxon's claims by using the same music and style of the original commercial with additional text that challenges their assertions of environmental responsibility http://bit.ly/2b91CG2.

- *Divestment proposals.* Students on campuses have requested that colleges divest themselves of fossil fuel investments, protests organized under the umbrella of the Divest Fossil Fuel Student Network www.studentsdivest.org/nationalnetwork (DeWald, 2013). Todd Gitlin (2016) cites examples of the success of these student efforts resulting in changes in college policies:

  > Pitzer College divested from fossil fuels in 2014, and set up a Sustainability Fund to make environmentally responsible investments. Stanford University divested from coal, including mutual funds that include coal, in 2015. However, it continues to resist student demands for divestment beyond coal. Syracuse University and the University of Hawaii agreed to sell off their shares in all publicly traded companies

whose primary business is extraction of fossil fuels in 2015 . . . The University of California agreed in 2015 to sell some $200 million of its holdings in coal and oil sands.

- *Green Schools Initiative Projects.* Students can begin by studying their own schools and the degree to which their schools are employing practices associated with the Green Schools Initiative (Center for Green Schools: www.centerforgreenschools.org; Green Schools Initiative: www.greenschools.net; List of Schools: http://tinyw.in/UNnq; Green Schools Alliance: www.greenschoolsalliance.org; see the website for other Green School projects http://tinyw.in/BgjC.

  Students can study their school's lighting, computers, heating, cooling, use of alternative energy, transportation, etc., as well as food production/waste, and water use. To do so, they can employ the Green School Alliance's Eco-Action Team Environmental Audit Eco-Action Plan Monitor or the Evaluate link; Curriculum Involve the Community Creating Your Eco-Code http://tinyw.in/ixJ0 which provide a check list of different factors that can be addressed. They can also access suggested actions from the EPA's What You Can Do: At School http://tinyw.in/LRXr which includes the EPA's Climate Change Emission Calculator Kit http://tinyw.in/22Kh. Students can use this kit—as an Excel spreadsheet to determine their school's greenhouse gas emissions and how to reduce those emissions. To compare their own school's energy use with other schools, students can use the Energy Star Portfolio Manager http://tinyw.in/22Kh.

  Based on participation in action-oriented learning sponsored by the non-profit Spark-Y http://spark-y.org, students at Edison High School in Minneapolis worked on development of a community garden, greenhouse, tree trench, permeable pavement, stormwater storage tanks, and a rain garden designed to capture and treat about 1.5 million gallons of runoff that would have otherwise drained untreated into the Mississippi River (Peterson, 2016).

- *Political action.* Changing a country's policies influencing climate change, for example, billions of dollars in annual subsidies for the fossil fuel industry as opposed to subsidies for alternative energy, requires engaging in political action to exert pressure on politicians to change policies and adhere to agreements such as the 2015 Paris Climate Change emission reduction agreements. Students can engage in political action by becoming familiar with local, state, and national policies and laws to then contact their elected officials regarding needed changes in those policies and laws. As one of Allen's students, Shane Stover, noted,

  > Many environmental lawyers see the Clean Air Act http://tinyw.in/hplZ as a great way to use their legal power to reduce greenhouse gas emissions. This act "provides the authority and flexibility necessary to design a climate change program that maximizes efficacy and efficiency for state and federal regulators, regulated businesses, and, ultimately, the public at large" [citation deleted]. If we are able to get the right people in a position of power, thanks to legislators and the backing of lawyers, we should be able to create and enforce programs that could save our future.

  Students can learn about government policies relevant to addressing global warming and take action to support or revise those policies. At election time they can study the platforms of candidates and parties and participate in the democratic process by disseminating information relevant to their concern about climate change.

THE TEACHER'S ROLE IN FOSTERING CHANGE

We end this book by focusing on the importance of your role as a teacher committed to addressing climate change with your students. Rather than going at this alone, we recommend that you find ways to work with other teachers in language arts and in different related disciplines, in your school, community, and professional organizations (including the National Council of the Teachers of English, co-publisher of this book).

Why not form a group, sometimes called a professional learning community (PLC), around the topic of climate change to collaboratively plan curriculum and activities for your school and community? Such a group can provide much support and many ideas. The impact of your local group can be amplified by sharing ideas at teacher conferences and by using a website, blog, or wiki as an online repository for resources and curriculum you develop, similar to the wiki for this book http://climatechangela.pbworks.com/.

The Portland Public Schools' commitment to infusing climate change throughout their curriculum and supporting sustainability projects http://tinyw.in/osEO might inspire you and your colleagues to work with your school and district administrators to adopt similar approaches to focusing on climate change. A district-wide formal position statement provides support for those teachers who may be uncertain about teaching about global warming.

You can also participate in organizations working on climate change through education http://tinyw.in/k4cX as well as organizations working on the topic in general http://tinyw.in/qUpp. We will be donating our author royalty proceeds from this book to the Alliance for Climate Education https://acespace.org, which supports schools addressing climate change.

After reading this book, *you* are in a position to take leadership on climate change education in your building and community, and in state and national teacher conferences and organizations. By your efforts, you are preparing present and future generations to understand the most significant challenge facing life on Earth and to take part in creating a sustainable future for all of us.

For additional resources, activities, and readings related to this chapter, go to http://tinyw.in/NZ6I on the book's website.

REFERENCES

Ackerman-Leist, P. (2013). *Rebuilding the foodshed: How to create local, sustainable, and secure food systems.* White River Junction, VT: Chelsea Green Publishing.

Anderson, K., & Kuhn, K. (Directors). (2014). *Cowspiracy* [Motion picture]. USA: A.U.M. Films.

Andersson, E., & Öhman, J. (2016). Young people's conversations about environmental and sustainability issues in social media. *Environmental Education Research.* http://dx.doi.org/10.1080/13504622.2016.1149551.

Atwood, M. (2004). *Oryx and Crake.* New York: Anchor Press.

Atwood, M. (2009). *The year of the flood.* New York: Anchor Press.

Atwood, M. (2015, July 27). It's not climate change, it's everything change [Web log post]. Retrieved from http://tinyw.in/O4ty.

Bacigalupi, P. (2009). *Windup girl.* New York: Night Shade Books

Bichell, R. E. (2016, September 27). It may not cost you more to drive home in a climate-friendly car [Web log post]. Retrieved from http://tinyw.in/YF2p.

Bigelow, B., Christensen, L., Karp, S., Miner, B., & Peterson, B. (Eds.). (1994). *Rethinking our classrooms: teaching for equity and justice.* Milwaukee: Rethinking Schools.

Brown, S. (2016). Greenhouse gas accounting for landfill diversion of food scraps and yard waste. *Compost Science & Utilization, 24*(1), 11–19.

Canty, K. (Director). (2011). *Farmageddon* [Motion picture]. United States: Kristin Canty Productions.

Cherry, L (2011). Young voices on climate change: The Paul F-Brandwein 2010 NSTA Lecture *Journal of Science Educational Technology, 20,* 208–213.

Common Core State Standards (2010). *English language arts Common Core State Standards.* Washington, DC: National Governors Association and Council of Chief State School Officers.

DeWald, D. (2013). Students rise up to fight climate change with National Divestment Network. *Common Dreams.* Retrieved from http://tinyurl.com/jyx275p.

Dodge, D., & Thompson, D. (2016, June 27). 150. Student white paper calls for climate change and green energy in schools [Web log post]. Retrieved from http://tinyw.in/wNVq.

Doherty, K. L., & Webler, T. N. (2016). Social norms and efficacy beliefs drive the alarmed segment's public-sphere climate actions. *Nature Climate Change, 6,* 879–884.

Earth Day Network India (2016). *Pathways to green India: Innovative ideas from students.* New Delhi, India: Centre for Science and Environment). Retrieved from http://tinyw.in/nx7F.

Fahs, B. (2015). The weight of trash: Teaching sustainability and ecofeminism by asking undergraduates to carry around their own garbage. *Radical Teacher, 102,* 30.

Fisher, S. R. (2016). Life trajectories of youth committing to climate activism. *Environmental Education Research, 22*(2), 229–247.

Gali, A. (2016) For the students, by the students. In Earth Day Network India (Ed.), *Pathways to green India: Innovative ideas from students* (pp. 31–33). Kolkata, India: Earth Day Network.

Gardiner, S. M. (2011). *A perfect moral storm: The ethical tragedy of climate change.* New York: Oxford University Press.

Gitlin, T. (2016). Fossil fuels off campus. *Dissent Magazine.* Retrieved from http://tinyw.in/CR2f.

Hauter, W. (2012). *Foodopoly: The battle over the future of food and farming in America.* New York: New Press.

Jenkins, H., Shresthova, S., Gamber-Thompson, C., Kliger-Vilenchi, N., & Zimmerman, A. M. (2016). *By any media necessary: The new youth activism.* New York: New York University Press.

Kaplan, K. (2016, July 11). Science proves it: Girl Scouts really do make the world a better place. *Los Angeles Times.* Retrieved from http://tinyw.in/zaVI.

Kennedy, S. H. (Director). (2014). *The garden* [Motion picture]. United States: Black Valley Films.

Kenner, R. (Director). (2008). *Food, Inc.* [Motion picture]. United States: Magnolia Pictures.

Kenis, A., & Mathijs, E. (2012). Beyond individual behaviour change: The role of power, knowledge and strategy in tackling climate change. *Environmental Education Research, 18*(1), 45–65.

Kingsolver, B. (2007). *Animal, vegetable, miracle: A year of food life.* New York: HarperCollins

Liverman, D. (2014, August 20). How to teach about climate without making your students feel hopeless. *The Washington Post.* Retrieved from http://tinyw.in/qCk6.

MacDonald, J. (2016, February 4). We're wasting as much as half the food we produce. *JSTOR Daily.* Retrieved from http://tinyw.in/YeQl.

Marshall, G. (2015). *Don't even think about it: Why our brains are wired to ignore climate change.* New York: Bloomsbury.

Martin, C. E. (2016). *The new better off: Reinventing the American dream.* Berkeley, CA: Seal Press.

McCarthy, C. (2007). *The road.* New York: Vintage.

McKibben, B. (2016, August 7). Embarrassing photos of me, thanks to my right-wing stalkers. *The New York Times, 165*(57,317), 4–5.

McKnight, T. (2014, August 4). Want to have a real impact on climate change? Then become a vegetarian. *The Guardian.* Retrieved from http://tinyurl.com/zuyku4c.

McNeill, K. L., & Vaughn, M. H. (2012). Urban high school students' critical science agency: conceptual understandings and environmental actions around climate change. *Research in Science Education, 42,* 373–399.

McPherson, C. (2016). Why young Americans are suing Obama over climate change. *Rolling Stone.* Retrieved from http://tinyw.in/bpL8.

Morgan, J. (2013). *Teaching secondary geography as if the planet matters.* New York: Routledge.

Parfitt, J., Barthel, M., & Macnaughton, S. (2010). Food waste within food supply chains: Quantification and potential for change to 2050. *Philosophical Transactions of the Royal Society B, 365,* 3065–3081.

Peterson, Z. (2016, September, 20). Setting the standard for green schools [Web log post]. Retrieved from http://tinyw.in/v1Rj.

Pollan, M. (2007). *The omnivore's dilemma: A natural history of four meals.* New York: Penguin

Pope-Weidemann, M. (2015). Food sovereignty offers possible path toward climate justice. New Internationalist Blog. Retrieved from www.truth-out.org/opinion/item/34106-food-sovereignty-offers-possible-path-toward-climate-justice.

Raghavendran, B. (2016, March 22). St. Louis Park gets B- on students' climate report card. *Minneapolis Star Tribune*. Retrieved from http://tinyw.in/AZ8j-.

Rooney-Varga, J. N., Brisk, A. A., Adams, E., Shuldman, M., & Rath, K. (2014). Student media production to meet challenges in climate change science education. *Journal of Geosceience Education, 62,* 598–608.

Scranton, R. (2016, October 7). When the next hurricane hits Texas. *The New York Times, 166,* p. 7. Retrieved from http://tinyw.in/JFfx.

Tinnell, J. (2011). Scripting just sustainability: Through green listing towards eco-blogging. *Environmental Communication, 5*(2), 228–242.

Turner, R. J. (2015). *Teaching for ecojustice curriculum and lessons for secondary and college classrooms.* New York: Routledge.

US Food Sovereignty Alliance (2016). *Food sovereignty.* Retrieved from http://tinyurl.com/zlbz6c5.

Werberger, R. (2015). *From project-based learning to artistic thinking: Lessons learned from creating an unhappy meal.* Lanham, MD: Rowman & Littlefield Publishers.

Woolf, A. (Director). (2007). *King corn* [Motion picture]. United States: ITVS.

Index

media/digital analyses: civic engagement with digital media 89–90; create multimedia digital stories 95; indigenous pedagogy 95–96; infographics 88–89; photography 88–89; sounds speak volumes 92–95; students creating visual images 89; visual representations 90–91
Memory of Water (Itaranta) 61
methane, emissions of 1
Milkoreit, M. 52, 59, 64, 119
Moore 36
Moral Ground: Ethical Action for a Planet in Peril (Moore) 36
Morning Girl (Dorris) 35

Nature's Confession (Morin) 61
Nelson 36
Nixon, R. 51, 87

Odds Against Tomorrow (Rich) 62
Of Mice and Men (Steinbeck) 55
Oryx and Crake (Atwood) 62

Paschall, M. 103
People's History of the United States, A (Zinn) 35
Perera, F. 87
persuasive writing 74–79
place-based writing 68–72
Polar City Red (Laughter) 63
political action 142
Pope, R. 54
postcolonial perspectives 34–36
Postman, N. 122

Rapture, The (Jensen) 62
Reid, S. 124
report cards 139
Rich, N. 18
River Ran Wild, A (Cherry) 56
Robinson, K. S. 51, 53
Rolling Stone Magazine (McKibben) 24
Rose, J. 46

Sand County Almanac, A (Leopold) 38, 43, 53
Saxifrage, C. 63
Schuenemann, K. 78
Scranton, R. 131
Sea and the Summer, The (Turner) 63
Seitz, D. 69
Seuss, D. 56
Silent Spring (Carson) 53
Six Degrees: Our Future on a Hotter Planet (Lynas) 21–23

Sixty Days and Counting (Robinson) 62
Snyder, G. 58
social media 139
Somerville, M. 68, 69
Stein, E. 104
Steingraber, S. 69

teaching: capitalism and consumerism 39–40; English 8–9; environmental literature/ecocritical 40–43
Teaching Truly: A Curriculum to Indigenize Mainstream Education (Arrows) 34
Textual Intervention: Critical and Creative Strategies for Literary Studies (Pope) 54
This Changes Everything: Capitalism Vs. the Climate (Klein) 12, 39, 122
Thousand Acres, A: A Novel 43
Tinnell, J. 139
To Kill a Mockingbird (Lee) 55
Tornero, J. M. 95
Tyszczuk, R. 74

Ultimatum (Glass) 63
Under the Weather: Stories about Climate Change (Bradman) 59

Van Allsburg, C. 56
Varias, T. 95

Wagner, R. 78
Walden (Thoreau) 53
waterborne diseases 4
Water Knife, The (Bacigalupi) 62
water source contamination 4
Watry, C. 21
White Horse Trick (Thompson) 61
white papers 140
Wilson, E. O. 43, 44, 120
Winds of Change (Atcheson) 18
Winds of Change: Short Stories about Our Climate (Woodbury) 18–19, 59
Winter, J. 57
Word for World is Forest, The (LeGuin) 35
writing: creative writing 72–74; persuasive writing 74–79; place-based writing 68–72
Wu, J. S. 99
Wüstenhagen, R. 103

Zeichner, N. 43, 44
Zeichner, Z. 103
Zeitoun (novel) 63
Zinn, H. 35